A Course
of
Their Own

A Course
of
Their Own

A History of
African American
Golfers

JOHN H. KENNEDY

an Andrews McMeel
Publishing Imprint

**Andrews McMeel
Publishing**

Kansas City

00 01 02 03 04 QUF 10 9 8 7 6 5 4 3 2 1

Library of Congress Cataloging-in-Publication Data

Kennedy, John H.
   A course of their own : the life and times of black golf's
pioneers / John H. Kennedy.
      p. cm.
   ISBN 0-7407-0857-0 (hardcover)
      1. Afro-American golfers—Biography. 2. Discrimination
   in sports—United States—History. 3. Golf—
   Tournaments—United States—History. I. Title.

GV964.A1 .K46 2000
796.352'092'396073—dc21
[B] 00-028144

Book design and composition by
Kelly & Company, Lee's Summit, Missouri

To my parents

Contents

Foreword

My love for the game began in 1987, as my NBA playing career was winding down. Two friends, Philadelphia 76ers team physician Dr. Stanley Lorber and the late Philadelphia restaurateur Albert Taxin, urged me to take up the game. I've been hooked ever since.

Like millions of other golfers, I play the game for fun, competition, and the physical and mental challenge. It has given me many hours of pleasure and a few of pain. But I keep coming back.

As an African American, though, I can't ignore the game's treatment of those men who strove—as I did in basketball—to compete at the highest level. That history is replete with stories of courage and triumph, as well as of indignity and defeat. Unfortunately for all sports fans, they have gone largely untold.

In compelling fashion, this book brings those stories to life, and reconstructs an important chapter in American sports history. There's Bill Spiller, who took on the Professional Golfers' Association—on the golf course and inside a courtroom—and paid a terrible price. It tells of Howard Wheeler, the cross-handed wonder who may have been golf's first true African American star. You will learn about Pete Brown's physical courage, Charlie Sifford's persistence, and Lee Elder's breakthrough. And you will get to know Teddy Rhodes, who possessed the sweetest swing and gentlest personality but was too old by the time the color line was crossed in professional golf.

Sometimes it takes many years for history to speak its truth. This is one such case. So while we marvel at the incredible accomplishments of Tiger Woods, look back through this book as it pays homage to those who preceded him under the most trying and difficult of circumstances. His victories are their victories, too.

Julius "Dr. J" Erving
September 1999

Acknowledgments

Without the assistance of skilled and committed librarians, this book would not have been possible. At the top of the list is Stephen Breedlove, who among other things is the interlibrary loan librarian at La Salle University. For his persistence and patience, I shall always be grateful. Thanks also to librarians and researchers at Yale University, Temple University, Bryn Mawr College, Lincoln University, the University of Pennsylvania, Swarthmore College, St. Joseph's University, Villanova University, West Chester University, the University of California–Santa Cruz, Haverford College, and the Library of Congress. Thanks also to the *Philadelphia Inquirer,* which granted me access to its clip files; The Schomburg Collection and Billy Rose Collection at the New York Public Library; and the California African-American Museum. Thanks also to the people whose enthusiasm for preserving history lives at public libraries at Lower Merion Township, Philadelphia, Baltimore, Nashville, Atlanta, and Boca Grande. Jeanne Thivierge, a local history specialist in the Vollmayer Room at the Redwood City Public Library, is one of those people.

To Al Barkow, I owe a debt of gratitude for his insights, generosity, and trailblazing. He wrote about some of the golfers in this book, years before it became fashionable to do so. His interview with Bill Spiller, published in his book *Getting to the Dance Floor,* served as an invaluable framework to Spiller's story in these pages. He has graciously allowed me to use excerpts from that interview.

Special thanks to two very helpful people at Golf House, the headquarters of the United States Golf Association: Nancy E. Stulack, the museum registrar, and Rand Jerris, librarian/historian.

Thanks also to M. Christian Jones, whose labor and enthusiasm helped me document Spiller's years at Wiley College, along with a number of alums of the college who recalled Spiller's days in northeast Texas.

Thanks to the people who lived portions of this story or helped pass along the history, including Dottie May Campbell, Charles T. Bell, Tommy Bolt, John Myler, Margaret White, Tim Thomas, Joe Hampton, Rickey Hampton, Joe Roach, Bobby Mays, Jim Dent, Phyllis Meekins, Ruby Wheeler, Frank Snow, Maggie Hathaway, James Walker, Jr., Art Wall, Gordon Chavis, Sam Lacy, Walter Ferguson, Charles Dorton, George Johnson, Felton Mason, Bob Goalby, Rose Harper Elder, Gary Player, James Black, Harold Dunovant, Thomas "Smitty" Smith, Al Besselink, Jackie Burke, Jr., Joe Black, Jack Tuthill, Bill Dickey, Dick Lotz, Pamela Stewart, Bobby Stroble, Tom Place, Justice Stanley Mosk, Bill Wright, Bob Rickey, Robert Horton, Eural Clark, Willie Greer, Curtis Sifford, and Mason Funk of Fox Sports in Los Angeles. I feel lucky to have met Cliff Brown and enjoyed his company before he passed away early last year. There are many others.

Special thanks to Pete and Margaret Brown, who welcomed me to Dayton, Ohio, on more than one occasion. Also to Bill Spiller, Jr., for sharing memories of his father, and to Maggie Hathaway, who spent an afternoon with me at Chester Washington Golf Course and at a nine-hole course nearby that has been renamed for her. Thanks to Peggy White for her hospitality at the Teddy Rhodes charity tournament in Nashville.

My gratitude to Christine Schillig and Allan Stark at Andrews McMeel for devoting their energy to this project. Also at AMP, thanks to Kelly Gilbert and Annette Corkey.

Without the guidance and friendship of Randy Voorhees, at Mountain Lion, Inc., this book would be little more than an interesting idea. Thanks also to John Monteleone, who helped launch this project with his advice and encouragement.

Finally, my wife, Jane, and my daughter, Emily, have been unflagging sources of patience, wisdom, and love. The journey of this book begins and ends with them.

1

Into the Light

His challenges were similar to those that other African Americans faced when they tried to cross the color line in a sport—in his case, golf. His story is among scores of others about African American men who tried to become professional golfers but usually could not. He, like them, had days of triumph but more of failure; of exhilaration but mostly of despair. His competitive fire burned hot, as did theirs. But his passion—some said it was more like rage—for fairness, for respect, for equality, set him apart. It just may have consumed him.

Perhaps it began for Bill Spiller when, as a twelve-year-old boy growing up in Oklahoma, he tried to return an item he had bought at a department store. The clerk, a white man, first rejected the request and then, when the boy appeared to be speaking out of turn, slapped him.

Young Bill never told his father, for fear his old man would march to the store and get himself killed, but the kid told himself that no one would ever put his hands on him like that again. Not yet a teenager, he vowed to carry a gun, which, he claimed, he did for the next several years. "The next guy who puts his hands on me is going to look down this barrel" was how he described his feelings to an interviewer years later.

It would be easy to say that that incident defined him and stoked a lifelong hatred of whites, but it didn't, in part because of his mother. During the Depression, she patiently fed the hoboes who came to the Spiller house in Oklahoma, those legions of men cut adrift from jobs, family, and security. Many of the men were white.

It puzzled young Bill, because his mother was helping the same people who had kept his family down. "If the white man is so evil," he recalled asking his mother, "why do you give them food?" The mother looked at her boy and dispensed some simple wisdom: her mother had taught her never to turn away a hungry person, and she would do the same.

Spiller would remember his mother's words all his life, just as he would remember that store clerk's violent slap. Perhaps those influences—kindness and rage—could never be balanced in a man's life. Spiller, for one, chose confrontation as the path to fairness in golf.

That choice, heroic as it may have been, did not produce a fairy-tale life. But it was his way to affirmatively step out from the shadows and into the sunlight, rather than to wait patiently as the day—his day—passed by.

2

First a Job, Then a Game

Many of this country's finest African American golfers learned the game by caddying. Pete Brown started at age eleven, in Jackson, Mississippi. Charlie Sifford began around age ten, in Charlotte, North Carolina. Lee Elder and Teddy Rhodes started carrying golf bags before they hit their teens.

Many white kids found the game the same way, starting as caddies, but their opportunities for employment in the game didn't stop at caddie master, or locker-room attendant, or backroom worker in the pro shop. If they had the skills, and sometimes even if they didn't, whites could become club professionals and touring pros.

There were no country club memberships for blacks and, until the fifties, few places for them to play on a regular basis. Even public courses were segregated, particularly in the South. If you were lucky, you lived in a city like Baltimore, which at least paid lip service to the "separate but equal" standard of segregation, and you could find a hardscrabble golf course built especially for Negroes.

Like Walter "Chink" Stewart, they'd often play any way they could. Carrying bags for twenty-five cents a side at age nine, Stewart fell under the spell of the game and would walk seven miles each day after school to get to the golf course. Some kids made their own golf clubs, from twisted coat hangers or crudely fashioned tree branches. Rocks, acorns, you name it, served as balls.

Caddies were allowed to play only on days the courses were closed—usually Mondays—or when it rained, as the members fortified themselves in the clubhouse with a hot meal or a stiff drink. They'd sneak on the course to play at first light, before the club opened for play, or at twilight, racing the dark and the night watchman. More than once, said Stewart, some guys would drive by in a car and shoot at him and his friends. "Yeah. We'd get down on our stomachs and when they went away we'd get up and finish the hole," he said. "These guys were hired to shoot at us."

Might that explain the prototypical caddie swing—fast and short? "That's because we were always trying to hit the ball hard," said Stewart. "See, we didn't always have whole sets of clubs and many times just had to use a club that wasn't enough to get us to where we had to go and so we hit the hell out of it."

Bobby Mays was like most African American kids who learned to play golf. First, it was a job, which gave him exposure to the game. Before the civil rights struggle changed things, a Negro walking on a golf course usually meant he was working for a white man. Growing up in Greenville, South Carolina, Mays started playing golf at about nine, before he had even seen a golf course.

"I used to just walk the streets with my own stick, hitting stones and stuff. I didn't know nothing about golf, never heard of the game of golf. My uncle, he was like a street cleaner, sweeping the streets and so forth. And this white lady called him and say, 'Mister, you want some clubs?' She didn't know what they were. He brought 'em to the house. He said, 'Bob, I got something for you.' Just so happened my cousin was at the [Greenville] country club. And when he got home, I said, 'I got something here in a bag. I don't know what it is, could you tell me?' He said, 'They're golf clubs.' I said, 'Golf clubs? What do you do with 'em?' He said, 'Okay, one day I'll take you down to the club and I'll show you.'

"After school, I would catch the bus—it cost seven cents—so I go down to the country club. I was small. I couldn't carry the bags. So what happened, they would have me picking the balls up. They would put me out on the driving range. They had this Scotchman there, Mr. Ferguson, and he would show the lady how to take the club back. And I would be watching and I would be watching, every little move. I wanted to learn how to play this game. That's how I learned, from Mr. Ferguson. So for about, I guess, six months, that's all I did. They had me out there. Nobody else was going to pick up the balls. They wanted to go out and caddie. It was like fifty-five cents for eighteen holes. That was big money. You'd get a dime tip from some of 'em and some you'd get a quarter tip. After I didn't have anybody to run balls for, I would go back of the caddie house. I would go back there, and I'd just hit balls.

"Then the gambling started. All the caddies would play a nickel a hole. So I guess for about two months, I didn't take any money from 'em. They would just wait for me to make that little money, you know. My grandmother raised me. She'd say 'You went to the country club; where's the money at?' I'd say, 'Well, I didn't get no bag today; I didn't chase no balls.' But they were winning the money. But I'm gonna beat them. I would practice, every chance I got. And I said, 'These guys winning my money. I gotta find a way to beat 'em.' So I kept practicing, practicing. When I come home from the country club, I would go in the school yard. I had a hole at the top of the school yard and all the way down to the bottom and that's where I did my practicing.

"So I guess about a year after that, they had a caddie tournament on the regular golf course, on a Monday. I won. I shot seventy-four. I was going to be a good player real fast. I practiced at it."

From such modest beginnings, caddies actually dreamed of a future in golf, mimicking the games of better golfers in their towns. For those who chose to stay in the caddie shack, the prospects were bleak, the benefits few. Even in the latter part of the twentieth century, a caddie couldn't expect much more than twenty-five dollars for carrying a bag eighteen holes. Frequently they had fewer amenities than migrant workers. No job security, no overtime, no paid vacation, no health benefits.

For those who dreamed about playing against the best golfers, the odds were long, the opportunities scarce, the encouragement virtually nonexistent. Mays and other kids who grew up before World War II knew little about blacks' history in golf. They had never heard of Dr. George F. Grant, a Boston dentist who played golf around the turn of the century and gained the first patent for a golf tee, patent number 638,920. (He never sought to make money on the invention, and twenty-five years later, a white golfer from New Jersey registered his own patent, marketed the tee, and was widely credited as the inventor until recent years.)

Mays had never heard of any accomplished African American golfers, who could be role models for a young kid taking up the game. Sure, he looked up to the heavyweight boxing champion of the world, Joe Louis. But in golf, the only person he might consider as his idol was a young white amateur in Greenville, someone May caddied for.

But there were role models in golf, even for boys who grew up before World War II. Mays and other young blacks had never heard of him, but John Shippen had played with the best of his time.

3

"We Will Play with You or without You"

The Shinnecock Indian Reservation and the Shinnecock Hills Golf Club weren't far from each other, as the crow flies, but they were worlds apart. The club was the preserve of the monied who took the Long Island Rail Road out to Southampton, and then rode by carriage to the clubhouse, designed by famed architect Stanford White.

John Shippen was well known to club members. By age eighteen, he had caddied for many of them, had given lessons to a few of them, and could beat any of them in an honest game of golf. He was African American. Still, he could play better than anyone around.

In 1896, when the newly formed United States Golf Association (USGA) brought its second open championship to Shinnecock, the club's members, in what seems in retrospect as a bold move, entered Shippen and Oscar Bunn, a full-blooded Shinnecock, in the event. The betting was that either one had as good a chance to win the whole thing on the club's White Course.

Shippen was the son of an African American Presbyterian clergyman who came to the reservation to teach school and minister. Around that time, Willie Dunn, a Scottish golf pro, made the long trip out from New York to design the golf course. Dunn relied heavily on the Shinnecocks to help build the course and on their children to help caddie for New York's industrial giants who dabbled in this new game imported from across the Atlantic.

Shippen and Bunn both learned the game under Dunn's tutelage, and Shippen became so proficient that the Scotsman allowed him to give lessons. At age sixteen, Shippen was paid to teach members at another club, the exclusive Maidstone Club in East Hampton. And as Dunn's unofficial assistant pro, he was the members' ringer when the open championship came along.

There were a few things different about the open back then. It was only a thirty-six-hole tournament, played on a single day. There were no qualifying rounds. You entered; you played. And most of the entrants were either Scots or English, who comprised most of the professional ranks in an America recently smitten with the game and accustomed to importing its professionals and golf course designers for the clubs popping up around the East and Midwest.

That July weekend actually featured two tournaments. On Friday was the U.S. Amateur, considered the province of gentlemen who had skills around the golf course. In fact, many of the world's best golfers were amateurs. The next day, Saturday, was the U.S. Open, an event open to both amateurs and professionals.

The first open, held the previous year at Newport, Rhode Island, was won by a transplanted Englishman, Horace Rawlins, against a field of nine other pros and one amateur. But this year was different, with a much larger field expected and a stream of spectators arriving throughout the day in their carriages. "The gay costumes of the ladies and the scarlet-coated club members made a very pretty picture, scattered as they were, all over the hills," said one newspaper account.

The members at Shinnecock apparently saw nothing wrong in entering Shippen and Bunn in the tournament, because in the country club caste system, golf pros were viewed as hired help, anyway.

But the other golfers thought otherwise. On Friday night, they met and decided that if Shippen and Bunn played, the two men would play alone. The pros resolved to boycott the open.

What happened next was either an act of great conscience and integrity in the face of racism or shrewd arm-twisting—or perhaps some combination of the two.

Theodore A. Havemayer, then president of the USGA, met with the pros and heard their demands. To this day, it is unclear what Havemayer said. The most widely accepted version is that he simply and firmly informed the pros that his organization ran the tournament and, if need be, the open championship would be a two-man tournament. Shippen and Bunn would play, with or without the foreign-born pros.

A second version has Havemayer also downplaying Shippen's race, asserting that he was half Shinnecock and thus somehow more palatable to the rebellious pros. That account, however, has come under some attack in recent years by golf historians.

"The account's specious insinuation that the professionals found Indians acceptable, but not blacks, ignored the white players' objections to the presence of both a black [Shippen] and an Indian [Bunn]," wrote Peter Stevens in *Golf Journal.* Clara Johnson, one of Shippen's daughters, still fumed years later over that account, because it perpetuated a view that Shippen was half black, half Shinnecock. Mrs. Johnson said he was the son of black parents, a minister and his wife who had come to live on the reservation from Anacostia, Maryland, just outside Washington, D.C. The confusion may have come over the fact that Shippen himself took a full-blooded Shinnecock as his wife. "My father was a Negro," said

Johnson. "Every time I meet somebody, I have to correct that story."

Whichever version is accurate, the boycott dissolved in the face of the USGA's ultimate refusal to back down about Shippen and Bunn.

"We will play with you or without you," Havemayer was quoted as telling the pros.

His threat wasn't without risk. The fledgling USGA might not have been able to absorb a mass walkout in the tournament's second year, or endure an angry group of professionals refusing to play in future tournaments. But Havemeyer called their bluff, and the next day, July 18, three dozen golfers, in pairs, teed off.

Shippen, barely eighteen, and with a stiff breeze in his face, stepped up to tee off in the U.S. Open. He was paired with Charles Macdonald, who had won the U.S. Amateur the year before and was considered one of America's finest golfers. But Macdonald couldn't keep up with the local kid, who knew the winds that swept across the course and the nooks and crannies of each hole, including the Belfry, the Crater, the Plateau, the Small Hole, the Cloister, Longacre, and Sandy Mount. Shippen hit a long ball off the tee, with a three-quarters swing that relied on a strong and supple snap of the wrists.

He finished the morning round with a 78, tied for the lead with four other golfers. Macdonald, angered at his play that yielded an 83, withdrew and merely kept Shippen's score in the afternoon round. Bunn, known as a big hitter, had worse luck, finishing with an 89. Shippen teed off in the second round with no playing partner.

He stayed among the leaders throughout most of the round, in fact playing better than he had in the morning. Then he stepped to the tee at the par-4 13th, a hole he was accustomed to routinely parring.

"It was a little, easy par four. I'd played it many times and I knew I just had to stay on the right side of the fairway with my drive. Well, I played it too far to the right and the ball landed in a sand road. Bad trouble in those days before sand wedges. I kept hitting the ball along the road, unable to lift it out of the sand."

By the time he rolled in a ten-footer to finish the hole, Shippen had taken a disastrous 11. And his chance to win the open was dashed. He posted an 81 for a thirty-six-hole total of 159, in fifth place, seven strokes behind James Foulis, a Scottish pro from the Chicago Golf Club. Bunn finished twenty-first at 89-85—174. Shippen collected ten dollars, and became the first African American to win prize money in an American tournament.

What's more, Shippen had made a name for himself. The *Chicago Tribune* called him "the most remarkable player in the United States." The *New York Herald* gushed that he was "the Boy Wonder of Golf."

Shippen never fulfilled that promise nor did he match that finish, though he played in four more U.S. Opens—in 1899, 1900, 1902, and 1903. He seemed to bear no scars from the experience, however. He became a well-regarded golf instructor, tutoring Walter J. Travis, who won the 1904 British Amateur, and some of the country's wealthiest duffers, including steel magnate Henry Frick. After many years as a superintendent at golf clubs along the East Coast, Shippen came to Shady Rest Country Club in Scotch Plains, New Jersey, perhaps the first black golf club in the United

States. Known as Ship to many of its members, he had joined a club that was an important social and cultural institution in the New York area. But many were unaware of the kind, quiet man's playing record, until after he died in 1969.

He never stopped wondering how he might have played Shinnecock's 13th differently in 1896. "You know, I wished a hundred times I could have played that little par four again," he said. "It sure would have been something to win that day."

4

Creating a World

Education, not golf, was the way Bill Spiller planned to get ahead. Sure, he had tried golf as a kid. His father worked at the country club in Bartlesville, just outside Tulsa, and took young Bill there to shine shoes in the locker room and, on occasion, to bootleg some whiskey.

But, like other athletes, Bill thought the game looked easy, especially for a kid who played a lot of baseball and expected to hit the ball a country mile. When it took him eight swings to make contact with the golf ball, and then to dribble it only ten feet, Spiller had had enough of golf.

"This is not for me," Spiller told his father, and the pledge stuck, at least for a while.

As a teenager, he excelled in other sports, notably as a star on his high school track and basketball teams. And he had his sights set on becoming a teacher, a position of learning and respect.

So he headed to Wiley College, a small black college in the piney woods of northeast Texas. There, in the 1930s, Spiller found a refuge for blacks seeking entry into the middle class, although it was not insulated from the times, its politics and racial attitudes. Students from Wiley never mixed with students from the white college in town, East Baptist, or even the other black school, Bishop College. And if you wanted to see a movie at the Paramount in downtown Marshall, you had to heed the COLORED UPSTAIRS sign and sit in the balcony.

Wiley grads knew they were headed for decent jobs as teachers, lawyers, and even doctors. But those jobs would be in a segregated world.

"There were not many opportunities open to blacks in those years," said Dr. James Farmer, the civil rights leader, who attended Wiley with Spiller.

"If a black person wanted to enter the middle class, he had to be a doctor or a teacher. That was about it. There were a few black lawyers, but not many, and those few usually starved to death, because no one would hire them for an important case. They couldn't win it. So most of the grads of Wiley went into teaching, at least to start with, and some became entrepreneurs and started little businesses in the black community. What else could they do? There was no thought of running for president or for the Senate. So our hands were tied."

Wiley created its own world, of about 400 students and a faculty that attended not just to your studies but to your future. Ham Boswell, a Los Angeles kid, dressed to kill for his first day in English class, and hemmed and hawed when Professor M. B. Tolson called on him for an answer. Tolson then turned to a farm boy from Mississippi, who had spent far less time in a classroom because he had to tend the crops. But the boy had read the lesson.

As Boswell crossed campus the next day, out from behind a tree popped Tolson. "Hello, Boswell," said Tolson. "You're a smart man, but you're lazy. I've got my eye on you."

Boswell, who became an ordained Episcopal minister, never forgot that moment. "He was right," Boswell said. "I thought it wasn't what you knew but how you looked and what you had. The materials, the buildings, were not half as good as the materials, buildings, and supplies at the high school I went to. That's why I didn't take it seriously at first. But those people took an interest in me. Turned me around."

The college was the world of Dr. Matthew Dogan, president of the school. He made it his business to attract students to his little corner of Texas and make sure they fit in there. ("Young man," he told one football player, "I think you can help us in the choir more than out there on the football field.")

"If you called Wiley and said, 'I've got twenty-five dollars and I'd like to go to Wiley,' he'd say, 'C'mon, son, we'll work it out,'" said Boswell. "That was Dr. Dogan; he would find a way. You might end up his chauffeur or a dishwasher, but Dr. Dogan would find a way. And Bill Spiller, I'm certain, came in that way."

At Wiley, sports quickly became more important to Spiller. He studied education and sociology, but he also talked to friends about someday becoming a professional athlete. He played basketball for the Wiley Wildcats, and was a dominant distance runner who would have beaten the runners at the white schools had he been given the chance. It was here, too, that his competitiveness fully flowered.

"He was a strong personality," said Boswell. "He was more of a strong personality than someone with a loose temper. He would fight in a minute, but he wasn't a bully. If you took him on, you had something to deal with, no doubt about it."

Like any upperclassman, he tried to get away with as much as he could with younger students. James Farmer, who was four years younger and several pounds lighter, remembered putting on the gloves and boxing Spiller in the gymnasium. The match drew a crowd. In the first round, Farmer threw a punch, and Spiller countered with a jab that sent the tall but scrawny Farmer to the canvas.

"People who were watching it said I bounced. But I got up without a count and went after him. He ran backwards faster than I could run forwards, all over the ring. I was throwing lefts and rights in the air and could not catch him. The same thing happened in the second round: I went down; I chased him again and couldn't catch him," said Farmer, who was overmatched.

Classmates also remember him for his sense of humor—he was always ready with a joke. He joined a fraternity, the Kappas, and dated some women on campus, but he was also known by some as a bit of a loner, working several jobs to pay his way. He hung out with one group that was always hustling money, including a scheme to wash and iron shirts in half an hour. He also might have dropped out of Wiley for a year or so to earn enough money to finish his studies.

Boundless opportunity did not await Spiller when he graduated in 1938. "You were going to work in a system of your own color," said Dr. Fred E. Lewis, a Wiley graduate who became a school principal. "You weren't going to work in a system with whites." What Spiller found was a teaching job at a dirt-poor, rural school for sixty dollars a month, when his white counterparts would be making ninety dollars a month at their schools.

Even at the twilight of the Depression years, better money could be made elsewhere. "I could do better than that in a pool hall," Spiller told author Al Barkow years later. So he headed west, where his mother lived.

When he got to Los Angeles, it took him months to find a job. When he finally got one, it was hardly the career he had dreamed of. He became a redcap at the new train depot, Union Station, the kind of job that would chafe at him the rest of his working days, the kind of work that would inspire him to write a protest poem about hauling bags for ten-cent tips.

5

"Yep, It's All in How You Were Brought Up"

George S. May sure didn't look like golf's iconoclast.
If you bumped into him on the street, you came face-to-face with a middle-aged white man, of medium height, balding, with glasses and a build that showed a fair amount of settling around the middle.

On the golf course, however, he stood out. May might be dressed in lettuce-green slacks and a jade-and-yellow shirt in a floral pattern, with matching eyeglass frames. But he was so much more than flashy golf attire; he was a revolutionary in his sport.

May's All-American Tournaments in Chicago spanned two decades, and changed the way tournaments were run, players were paid, golf fans were regarded.

And not least, George S. May helped change the way Negroes were treated by the elitest of sports. He simply let them play.

The head of George S. May Enterprises, he was a businessman by training. His worldwide operations helped troubled companies run more efficiently. Applying the same principles to golf, May soon proved that golf could be a popular spectator sport. But it took work, money, and imagination.

May dived into golf in a big way during the Depression, when he bought up the shares of other members of the struggling Tam

O'Shanter Country Club, which straddled the Chicago River, until eventually he owned 98 percent.

Very quickly, with lots of cash, a flair for the dramatic, and an entrepreneurial style, he transformed tournament golf, after seeing firsthand why golf failed to appeal to broader audiences. Arriving in Cleveland for the U.S. Open in 1940, May spent $2.00 for a cab to the Canterbury Country Club and then paid another $3.30 for a ticket. Even for the country's premier golf tournament, that was too much money, he figured, and it helped explain the sparse attendance.

From the get-go, May put his tournament on the map, announcing that $11,000 in prizes would be awarded in its inaugural year, 1941. That was exactly $1,000 more than the total awarded at the tour's richest tournaments in Los Angeles and Miami. And he kept raising the purses so that no one had a bigger first prize. In fact, if you won his tournament, you'd probably end up the year as the top money winner on the professional tour. Sometimes a golfer could win more money through May's other awards than with a high finish in the tournament.

That was only the beginning.

Any description of a George May tournament always mentioned the "carnival atmosphere." The description wasn't far off. For one, May didn't conduct just one "All-American" tournament, he held four—sometimes simultaneously. Often the men's professional, men's amateur, women's professional, and women's amateur were scheduled for play at the same time on the Tam O'Shanter course. And he eventually added a second event, the World Championship, which featured the top finishers in the All-American, and for higher stakes.

May quickly became a fan favorite, and for good reason. He slashed ticket prices, and if that didn't sell out the tournament, he'd hire a plane and shower downtown Chicago with free tickets. He urged families to bring a picnic basket and a big blanket to spread on the lush grounds. He also opened the clubhouse to anyone who paid to get into the tournament. In effect, George S. May brought a George S. May Enterprises approach to golf. "He could do anything; he was a computer," said Dottie May Campbell, May's daughter. "He could track the important things, throw out the garbage."

But May saw that golf needed more. If the sport charged for admission, it was obligated to entertain the fans, and he didn't mind bringing change to a hidebound sport to achieve success.

During the tournament's first year, May decided to make the Tam easier rather than tougher, allowing the golfers to shoot from the front tees and shoot lower scores. As a result, Leonard Dodson shot a course record 65 on the first day. May took great delight in seeing 40,000 fans swarm into the Tam's gates during the four-day event. (First prize was $2,000, double the check for the winner of the U.S. Open or the PGA Championship.)

In 1942, May offered $500 to the golfer who broke Dodson's course record. The morning of the final round, he bumped the prize up to $750. That evening, as Byron Nelson measured a seven-footer on the 18th green to shoot a 64, May abruptly informed Nelson from the edge of the green that he'd bump the award to $1,000. Nelson's putt stopped a few inches short of the cup.

May asked the players to join in his adventure, to become part of the show, and some of them balked. For example, he asked them to wear numbers on their backs so that the fans could more readily identify them—a common practice in most team sports. He stopped short of requiring uniforms, although he could be spotted in a crowd with his own type of uniform—the most colorful silk shirt and matching eyeglass frames.

When the laconic Ben Hogan, who took himself far too seriously for May's tastes, protested about the numbers and suggested he wouldn't play the Tam anymore, May was reported to have turned to him and said: "Let the colored boys win it, then."

It stands as one of May's crowning achievements that he even wanted the "colored boys" to play in his tournament. Few others in his time did.

For decades, black players had been routinely denied entry to golf tournaments as a matter of social custom, but in the forties, the Professional Golfers' Association of America went a step further and codified the racism.

The organization was important to all professional golfers. It was the governing body for golf pros, both the glamorous men who played the tournament circuit and the club pros who ran golf operations at country clubs and municipal courses across the country.

If May's extravaganza gave hope to blacks that they could compete on equal footing, the PGA dampened their enthusiasm during its annual meeting in late 1943, and dealt with what it considered a routine matter of defining just who could become a member of the organization, and thus compete in professional golf tournaments across America. The issue apparently came up when the possibility of a woman becoming a sanctioned pro was raised.

The discussion turned to blacks and without much discussion, Section 1, Article III, of the PGA's constitution and bylaws was adopted to say:

"Professional golfers of the Caucasian race, over the age of eighteen years, residing in North or South America, and who have served at least five years in the profession (either in the employ of a golf club in the capacity of a professional or in the employ of a professional as his assistant) shall be eligible for membership."

Little has been written about the adoption of the language and, according to the PGA of America, no notes or minutes survive to reveal more details. But Herb Graffis, who wrote the PGA's authorized history in 1975, said the matter was proposed as an amendment by the Michigan section of the PGA. When it was adopted, an anonymous delegate was said to sum up a general view of those in attendance: "Show us some good golf clubs Negroes have established, and we can talk this over again."

Ironically, what began as a discussion entertaining the prospect of women as PGA members ended as an unequivocal slap at blacks. A woman could argue that the clause allowed for her membership; it left no room for blacks.

If the reason for excluding blacks was based on the establishment of a black-owned golf club, the group need only look to Shady Rest, a country club where John Shippen ended up in northern New Jersey. The PGA consensus view also ignored the accomplishments of a number of black golfers who had developed under the most difficult of circumstances.

It also ignored the United Golfers Association (UGA), which had established a circuit of tournaments for professionals and amateurs.

The UGA roots date back to the 1920s, when Dr. George Adams and Dr. Albert Harris, two Negro physicians from Washington, D.C., looked around and found there was no place for them to play golf. In the summer, they headed to New England to a place that allowed them to play every day, the Mapledale Country Club, in Stow, Massachusetts.

It was a 196-acre estate, complete with twenty-room mansion that a local black man named Robert Hawkins had purchased and turned into a club featuring golf, horseback riding, and tennis. An avid golfer himself, Hawkins had been a caddie growing up in Massachusetts and later in Vermont, after his family moved there in 1902. After high school, he went to work at several country clubs in Vermont before he became general manager of Sandy Burr Country Club, the first black to reach that position in New England. At Sandy Burr, he got the idea of owning his own country club for Negroes.

With Mapledale, Hawkins realized his dream. And starting in 1926, through the organizing skills of the two doctors from Washington, D.C., Mapledale's nine-hole golf course hosted the first national golf tournaments held for Negroes, and they were sponsored by a brand-new organization called the United Golfers Association.

The fledgling organization was an attempt to gather supporters of golf together, to play tournaments, to have a social center for their love for the game. Golf was predominately a game for whites—in large part because of segregation and economic demands—but it was no longer their exclusive preserve. Twenty-six clubs originally organized under the UGA banner, although these in no way resembled the golf clubs that many white golfers enjoyed. These were merely groups of black men and women who played at local public golf courses, when they were allowed.

"Well, like they say, if they won't let you join the party, have a party of your own," boxing champ and golfer Joe Louis once said about the UGA.

Despite the restrictions, the number of blacks playing golf had risen to about 50,000 by the thirties. (Although the Depression apparently claimed Mapledale from Hawkins, who organized another country club in 1938.)

The Negro National was the showcase event of the year. It was usually played on municipal courses in northern cities—Detroit, Cleveland, Pittsburgh, Philadelphia, Hartford, Chicago—and attracted black golfers from all over the country. It featured separate divisions for pros and amateurs, men and women. And for a black pro who was the best hustler on his home course, the Negro National was a different level, where thirty or forty golfers were his match or better. In its early days, a golfer named Walter Speedy was the dominant golfer. He also wasn't afraid to play at courses where he wasn't wanted, and was arrested several times because of it.

The tournament, usually conducted in late summer, always attracted a large contingent of reporters from the largest black newspapers of the day, and occasionally from mainstream publications. In 1938, *Time* magazine noted that the National, held near Chicago at Palos Park that year, attracted some entrants who carried their own bags and others who paid white caddies one dollar per round. The lone white contestant was a man who paid his entry so that he could keep up his daily regimen of play at Palos Park.

Playing in the tournament were some of the greats, foremost among them Robert "Pat" Ball, the hometown favorite who'd already won the Negro National title twice, and dapper John Dendy, who'd won three times. By the second day, however, all eyes were on Howard Wheeler, who won his first National in 1933 and would win his last twenty-five years later.

But the *Time* account was typical of coverage by the mainstream press, which at best, viewed the tournaments as curiosities and at worst, as down-home theater with racial caricatures for actors:

"After the first round, however, the greater part of the gallery of 300 trudged around after lanky, woolly-topped Howard Wheeler of Atlanta—watched him tee up on the edge of a match folder, shuffle along the fairways in a Stepin Fetchit gait, plop down on the greens while waiting his turn to putt. A onetime professional whose occupation has been 'just walkin' round' since he lost his job at Atlanta's Lincoln (Negro) Country Club in 1933, 29-year-old Howard Wheeler proved last week that he could still teach folks a few golfing tricks."

Wheeler, in fact, shot 284 on a tough, hilly course he'd never seen before, "results that would please many a top-flight white golfer," according to *Time*. In fact, his score was just three strokes higher than the U.S. Open record.

When the PGA adopted its Caucasians-only clause in 1943, it probably believed that it wasn't out of step with other major sports like baseball, which wouldn't see its first black big leaguer for another four years. But what major sport spelled out those segregationist attitudes in black and white, as the PGA did? The clause officially institutionalized the discrimination that had reigned over the PGA for decades. Dewey Brown, an accomplished club-maker, teacher, and golf professional, is a case in point.

Brown had been granted membership to the PGA in 1928, the first African American to do so. At age thirty, he had already established a reputation as a fine club-maker—President Warren G. Harding was one of his satisfied customers, as was Chick Evans, who won the 1916 U.S. Amateur with Brown's clubs—as well as an instructor at several clubs in New York, New Jersey, and Pennsylvania. Abruptly, and without explanation, the PGA rescinded his membership in 1934. While Brown never hid his ancestry, he was light-skinned. "To this day—even though they are unable to substantiate their suspicions with irrefutable evidence—Brown family members remain convinced that someone informed PGA officials of Dewey Brown's African ancestry, and that was the reason for his expulsion," wrote Calvin Sinnette in his history of black golf.

More than three decades later, after the Caucasians-only clause was expunged, Brown submitted his name and was formally reelected to PGA membership.

No blacks were invited to George S. May's first tournament in 1941. But the following July, May didn't blink when he was asked whether Negroes could compete. May had seen officials bumble the race issue at another Chicago tournament earlier that year, and he would not make the same mistake.

In May 1942, seven black golfers had tried to enter the Hale America National Open at Olympia Fields Country Club, a tournament affiliated with the USGA, but they were turned away by a club official who said Negroes were not allowed to use the golf course or clubhouse. Among the golfers was the redoubtable Pat Ball, the reigning UGA National champion from Chicago, and Clyde Martin, Joe Louis's golf tutor at the time. When they sought help at USGA headquarters in New York, their appeal fell on deaf ears. Joseph C. Dey, Jr., the executive secretary of the USGA, returned the players entry fees, writing that it was not the USGA's call, "but was made by the club over whose property and decision we were unable to exercise any control."

Benjamin Grant, a Chicago alderman and golf enthusiast who had accompanied Ball to Olympia Fields, quickly looked elsewhere for an organization or individual whose idea of fair play and competition was more open-minded. Grant wrote George May, asking that he allow blacks to compete on merit alone.

May barely hesitated, firing back a letter to Grant that said the All-American Tournaments would be true to their name.

"These tournaments are open to any American who is willing and able to qualify under the rules of competition which have been set up for all participants," wrote May.

"I am fully aware that Negroes are being called upon, together with the peoples of every race and color and creed, to do their full share in the national war effort and I know that many thousands of your people are presently serving with the country's armed forces. Private Joe Louis comes to mind in this connection as an outstanding example of all-around good citizenship. I can see no reason, therefore, why they should not contribute their services on an equal basis with everyone else in such patriotic sports events as the Tam O'Shanter tournaments which, as you know, are being staged for the benefit of the Army Emergency Relief. Their participation will not only be permitted at the Tam O'Shanter tournaments, it will be welcomed."

Dottie May Campbell was a young girl during the early days of her father's tournaments, and often stayed overnight in her dad's apartment in the clubhouse. She remembers her father calling someone in Washington to determine whether it would hurt or harm the cause of blacks if they were invited or encouraged to come to the tournament.

"I can remember him hanging up and saying, 'Washington said it was okay.' He probably would have done it anyway. . . . My dad was truly the most democratic person I've ever known. He did not see color. He was also that way with ethnicity and religion. Everybody was everybody."

But May saw what he was up against. Many white players, usually from southern states, wouldn't play with the Negro golfers. In 1942, for example, Calvin Searles, Howard Wheeler, and Zeke Hartsfield made the cut and played in the same group on Saturday and Sunday. When Leonard Dodson, a white pro from Oklahoma, volunteered to play with black golfers, the press got to calling him Booker T. Dodson.

Still, it was a momentous occasion for many of the Negro golfers. It was the first time some had played in a major tournament, since the U.S. Open and the Los Angeles Open were the only U.S. tournaments where they were allowed to compete against white golfers. Likewise, for fans, it was the first time they had seen a Negro swing a golf club, much less compete in a tournament at such a high level.

There were some nervous moments. Eural Clark, the promising young black amateur from Los Angeles, heard his name announced at the first tee, looked at the large gallery around him, and nervously took a swing. "I topped the ball right off that first tee, in front of all them people," Clark remembered, laughing. "I looked up; the ball was rolling down the fairway."

But from the beginning, blacks made an impression at the All-American. In 1942, Ball had a miserable day, shooting 80 during qualifying on Wednesday with three putts on seven greens. But he sent a roar through the gallery when he came to the 445-yard par-4 13th hole, and lofted his second shot onto the green and into the hole for an eagle 2.

A young golfer from New Orleans, twenty-three-year-old Calvin Searles, played the steadiest golf of the qualifying round, carding a

73. He shot 72, 74, and 74 on the first three days, before he blew up on Sunday with an 88.

But that year, the golfer who drew crowds was Howard "Butch" Wheeler, who piqued the galleries' curiosity with his unorthodox cross-handed grip—his left hand beneath his right hand, the opposite way of the Vardon grip that most golfers use to hold a club. "Everybody was fascinated about how he could hit cross-handed," said Dottie Campbell. And as the *Chicago Tribune* noted, Wheeler's "drives with a cross-handed grip already have caused considerable staring."

A rumor whipped across the golf course and into the clubhouse that Wheeler had driven the ball 365 yards. Many reported watching Wheeler hitting a 300-yard drive, then repeating the feat in case someone missed it. "Late coming newspapermen had missed the shot, so Wheeler obligingly trudged back, mounted his ball on the matchbox he was using for a tee, and did the shot over again, distance and all," according to one account.

"Jesus Christ, he could hit the ball," said Bob Rickey, an executive with MacGregor Equipment.

Wheeler may have been the first black golfer with star quality.

He was tall, about six feet two, and rail thin, and came out of Atlanta, Georgia, born into a family of six children on April 8, 1911. About the time he completed elementary school, he began caddying at local clubs, including the Brookhaven Country Club, where he was one of the legendary Bobby Jones's caddies. He won his first tournament in 1931 and by 1933, at age twenty-two, was already a rising star, having defeated John Dendy in the Southern Open and captured his first UGA National in Kankakee, Illinois.

Like most black golfers of his time, Wheeler could not make a living on the professional tour and had no access to club jobs as anything other than a caddie. But he found a benefactor, of sorts. Eddie Mallory, a bandleader who became the singer Ethel Waters's husband, loved the fast life, sharp clothes, and golf. He met Wheeler in the late thirties and put him on the payroll as his wife's chauffeur for a period of time.

Wheeler ultimately settled in Los Angeles and had begun playing in more tournaments by the early 1940s, including the All-American Open at the Tam O'Shanter.

And he could put on a show. Though photographs rarely caught him smiling, Wheeler was known on the Negro tour as the Clown Prince of Golf with a substantial bag of tricks. For one, he routinely teed up the ball, not with Dr. George F. Grant's invention, but with a matchbox or a Coca-Cola bottle. On some occasions, legend has it, he lit the matchbox and plucked the ball from the blaze with a short, quick swing, sending it down the fairway. He sometimes liked to tee off with his legs spread out, as though attempting a split. He was even known to hit a "skimmer," a shot that skipped across a lake or river.

Beyond the show, however, was a versatile player who could hit the long ball. Though his physical peak came and went before blacks routinely played on tour, many white pros speak with respect for Wheeler, having encountered him in some friendly game somewhere.

Bob Goalby went looking for a game at a course called Hubbard Heights in Stamford, Connecticut, and ended up in a foursome with Wheeler. "He whacked it out there," said Goalby, the 1968 Masters champion. "He drove it dead straight, eighteen holes. I was impressed."

He often left course records in his path. At Cobbs Creek in Philadelphia, he shot 63; at Taylor Park in Chicago, 62; and at

Manor Golf Club in Reading, Pennsylvania, 62. After he moved to Philadelphia, he held forth at Cobbs Creek, and for many years was the man to beat.

One young man who tried was a cocky seventeen-year-old kid, Charlie Sifford, who had come north to Philly from North Carolina. Sifford was working at the National Biscuit Company one day when he noticed a black man walking down the street carrying a set of golf clubs. The man was headed for Cobbs Creek, a place, Sifford was amazed to learn, that had no special rules or restrictions. Once there, the short, stocky Sifford spotted Wheeler on the driving range, walked up, and introduced himself. "I'm Charlie Sifford, and I'm gonna whip your ass on that golf course."

Sifford had twenty dollars in his pocket, and soon enough Wheeler was putting it in his. The more-experienced Wheeler taught the brash young golfer a lesson he wouldn't soon forget. Sifford bought a new set of golf clubs and worked feverishly on his game until he was good enough to beat Wheeler a few weeks later.

In Sifford's view, Wheeler never appeared to have a burning desire to play on the white tour. He seemed content to play black tournaments, the Tam, and individual money matches against anyone who challenged him. Nevertheless, he may have been the first black pro who was a gate attraction at white tournaments. Shippen nearly won the U.S. Open five decades earlier, but Wheeler had a more spectacular game and attracted crowds, both white and black. Wheeler was the first pro to win the UGA National three times in a row, and won it six times before he was through, matched by only one other golfer, Sifford. It was no small compliment when Dr. George Adams, one of the founders of the UGA, called Wheeler the "black Arnold Palmer of his time."

Like most other Negro golfers of that era, Wheeler encountered the indignities that were commonplace in his day. At the 1950 U.S Open at Merion, just a few miles from Cobbs Creek, Wheeler couldn't find anyone to play a practice round with him. He went off the first tee alone and as he did, a number of Merion members gathered on the clubhouse veranda to watch. "As Wheeler's drive whistled straight down the middle of the fairway like a projectile, the club members broke into a spontaneous volley of applause that compensated big Howard for all the rebuffs he had suffered," a sportswriter noted at the time.

When he tried to qualify for the U.S. Open the next year at Oakland Hills outside Detroit, Wheeler got little cooperation from open officials. He was never notified of his tee time, for example, nor was his name published in the newspaper along with those of all the other golfers trying to qualify. He showed up anyway, played two decent rounds, but failed to make the finals by one stroke. As he sat in the locker room one day, tying his shoes, Wheeler later recalled to a reporter, he heard a man ask him: "Well, how'd you do today, boy?"

Wheeler kept tying his shoes.

"I said, how'd you do today, boy?" the man asked again, tugging at Wheeler's sleeve.

Wheeler looked up, his face impassive. "Just fine, Mister."

The man smiled and turned to leave, but returned, and cleared his throat. "I didn't mean it that way."

"Mean what, what way?"

"Well, I asked, 'How'd you do today, boy,' and you said, 'Just fine, Mister.' I didn't mean 'boy' the way you thought."

"Oh, that's okay. I guess it just depends on how you were brought up. Now my folks told me when I was a boy that when you don't know a man's name, it's proper to call him 'Mister.' Yep, it's all in how you were brought up."

The next day, the same man greeted Wheeler as he was teeing off.

"How are you today, Mr. Wheeler?"

Wheeler laughed as he told the reporter: "He not only remembered to call me 'Mister,' but even found out what my last name was."

Wheeler didn't seem to feel he was unusual, an accomplished Negro professional golfer. "Tournaments weren't made for golfers of any particular race, just good golfers. And I know I'm not the only Negro who ever swung a golf club well."

At the Tam O'Shanter, George S. May recognized a good golfer when he saw one. He also knew a crowd pleaser when he saw one. In 1942, at the first Tam blacks were invited to enter, George May singled out Wheeler for something other than his twelve-over-par 300, the lowest score among the blacks who qualified.

With Byron Nelson's gallery still ringing the 18th green, May awarded Wheeler $200 as the tournament's "most glamorous" player.

It might have been the first time such a title had been bestowed at a golf tournament. It drew big headlines in the *Chicago Defender*, the town's leading black newspaper, for, after all, no Negro had won any money at a white tournament in a long, long time, perhaps not since Shippen took home ten dollars at the 1896 U.S. Open.

While some golf tournaments closed down during the war years, May was undeterred. The purses grew, as did the galleries, and the best golfers still came to the Tam, sometimes in their army uniforms. The tournament became a promotional event for the war effort; fans were entered in drawings and players could get their winnings in war bonds. Red Cross ambulances were on display, parked between holes.

In the 1944 tournament, Private Calvin Searles played well, and his short, mercurial career at the All-American would create some lore that persists today among black golfers.

Searles was stationed at Camp Breckinridge, Kentucky, and was among several Negro golfers who qualified to play in the tournament that year. First prize was $13,462.50 worth of war bonds, although no Negro had finished in the money yet.

Little is known of Searles, except that he learned the game as a caddie at a New Orleans country club, had the gumption to compete, and at twenty-five, was relatively young for a competitor in a major tournament. Searles barely qualified, shooting a 77, the cutoff point, and opened with a 74, with six other golfers, including Ray Mangrum. Johnny Bulla, an airline pilot, shot a torrid 65 to lead, with Byron Nelson three back at 68.

On Friday, Searles fired a 73, and fell nine shots behind Nelson, the soft-spoken and polite Texan who had become a favorite at the Tam, in no small part because he had won the tournament twice already. Along the way, Lord Byron, as the scribes liked to call him, had established himself as the game's dominant player.

Even for John Byron Nelson, though, 1944 was the beginning of a streak of golf that has rarely been matched. During the war years, Nelson, a hemophiliac and thus disqualified from military duty, turned around and found that some of his stiffest competition—the dour Ben Hogan and flashy Jimmy Demaret—were in uniform. The tour, however, had not been suspended, and Nelson, with his cool personality and near mechanical ability to score pars and birdies, went off on an historic run. In 1944, he won seven tournaments and was the leading money winner, with $35,000 in winnings, a superlative performance under any circumstance.

The next year has yet to be matched by any golfer. Nelson won nineteen tournaments, eleven of them in a row. By the time the streak was broken, when an amateur won in Memphis, Nelson was relieved. "Every tournament was getting tougher," he said in his soft drawl. "I couldn't keep a thing in my stomach."

So as the 1944 All-American began, Nelson was showing flashes of the brilliance that would surface during the next eighteen months.

But on Saturday, Searles made his move up through the pack. He carded three birdies to shoot a three-under 69 and pull within five strokes of Nelson, who was edging back to the pack with an ordinary 73. "Pvt. Searles was thus in a six-way tie for sixth place, much to the surprise of the followers of the open and of course to the white professionals," the *Chicago Defender* wrote.

Then the rains came late Saturday and into Sunday, and the final round was postponed until Monday.

Of course, George May had planned for every contingency, and rain was one of them. He had taken out rain insurance, and collected on it that Sunday. One year, he would collect on the insurance even though there was no rain-out. His policy with Lloyd's of London kicked in when it rained at the weather bureau in downtown Chicago, but the Tam was twenty miles from the center of Chicago, on the city's northwest fringe. "And one year it rained downtown, but the sun shone at the tournament, and he collected," his daughter said.

In 1944, it rained on the Tam, and rained some more. And by Monday morning, the tournament had resumed, but the greens were bumpy and soggy.

And the legend of Calvin Searles grew.

Searles, the story goes, was leading the tournament, outpacing the wondrous Byron Nelson, as he came to the 16th hole. With three holes to play, Searles was to be the first Negro to win a major professional tournament, and the world's richest.

The three-par 16th, however, was one of the toughest holes on the golf course. At 215 yards, it forced players to hit a long iron or fairway wood from a tee box set back in a grove of trees. The Chicago River cut across the hole just below the tee and then meandered along the left side of the hole and then behind the hole, ready to snatch an errant shot hit left. And the hole's large, irregularly shaped green sometimes required putts exceeding 80 feet. It was a test that many failed, carding 4s and even 5s.

For Searles, the test was too great.

He apparently wore the mantle heavily, a burden for any twenty-five-year-old, much less an obscure former caddie from New Orleans.

His first shot plunked into the river. He stepped up, and hit another into the drink. And he never recovered. When he was done with 16—or rather, it was done with him—he had a quadruple bogey 7 on his card, and had shot himself out of contention. Searles finished with a 79—exactly ten shots more than he took on his previous round.

That story, in its generalities, was well known and repeated in clubhouses for years afterward. Leonard Reed, Joe Louis's traveling secretary and a fair golfer himself, repeated the story with some authority. Eural Clark and Joe Roach, two of the finest amateurs of their time, and others have heard vague versions, but weren't there. And Searles's catastrophe that day may very well have been true. But the part about him winning the tournament, if not for his collapse at the end, appears to be a fable.

Searles was within five strokes of Nelson going into that last day, and would have needed a 64 to tie him. Nelson fired a final-round 69 to win. Even had Searles parred the 16th, he would have finished ten shots behind Nelson, who won his third All-American Open title.

There's no doubt Searles had talent, and the shame of his final-day round was that by finishing fifteen shots back, he slipped out of the money, into a tie for twenty-fifth place. Still, sportswriter F. A. "Fay" Young wrote then that Searles "holds a position higher than any other colored golfer has ever enjoyed in golf in the United States." The promise of Searles, sadly, would be unfulfilled; that soggy Monday round in August 1944 would be his last in George May's tournament. Private Calvin Searles was killed in action before the war ended the following year.

6

A Change in the Wind

T he world, suddenly, seemed a different place.

As the GIs streamed home in 1945, Negroes stood ready to take advantage of responsibilities they had been handed during World War II.

Still segregated, the military nonetheless was pushed to allow Negroes into such important positions as pilots, tank men, artillery-men, infantrymen, paratroopers, and more. By war's end, there were more than 7,000 Negro officers, where there had been only 5 in 1940. At home, Negro workers manned the production lines that built the U.S. war machine, with significant advances in access to more highly skilled positions. In government work, nearly 20 percent of all federal employees were Negroes by 1944, up from less than 9 percent in 1938.

These advances triggered heady expectations in postwar America. There was reason to believe change might seep into every corner of American life, as a long-delayed reward for blacks who once again had served their country and wondered when they would get a greater stake in their own country.

In sports, those expectations were intensified on April 15, 1947, a bitter cold Tuesday. That day, Jackie Robinson trotted onto Ebbets Field for the season opener against the Boston Braves, wearing No. 42 for the Brooklyn Dodgers. A Negro was now in the major leagues. Perhaps the world *was* a different place.

Black golfers, however, had to be content playing in just a few PGA events and showcasing their talents in their own national open—the UGA National.

By now, a loosely knit circuit of tournaments was available to the Negro golfer, if he had a car that could take a beating from all the mileage. In Washington, there was the Capital Cities; in Detroit, Joe Louis's invitational. The Lone Star was in Houston; the North-South, in Miami; the Skyview, in North Carolina. Prize money was also available in tournaments in Dayton, Chicago, Cleveland, Toledo, and Pittsburgh. If you wanted to go that far, Denver hosted a tournament also.

But the UGA National was far and away the most important black tournament of the year. It drew bigger galleries than any other black tournament, in part because it usually drew the best black golfers. It was a grand social event, too, since the black celebrities who loved golf also made an effort to appear there. Joe Louis, for example, played in the amateur division whenever he could, and so did Billy Eckstine, Jackie Robinson, and Sugar Ray Robinson, who had his own tournament for many years.

In 1947, the National came to Howard Wheeler's backyard— Cobbs Creek on Philadelphia's western edge. For a muni, Cobbs Creek was one of the more challenging courses in the country. *Golf World* rhapsodized about the event when it said, "Negro club winders from all sections, of all sizes, shapes and styles, of both sexes, hit many a brilliant golf shot over the twisting, rugged terrain of one of the toughest natural layouts in the country and, like their white friends, missed some, too."

But at Cobbs Creek that year, there was an ever-so-slight, almost imperceptible, shifting of the ground underneath black pros.

On the surface, conditions for blacks had not changed much. On the PGA Tour, there was little opportunity. They could try the Tam O'Shanter in Chicago and now the Los Angeles Open and even the U.S. Open, America's preeminent golf tournament, hosted by the USGA, but it required a commitment of three weeks and playing on several golf courses to eventually qualify for the tournament. It was an investment in time, energy, and money that few blacks had the resources to undertake.

Those willing to take a longer trip had a chance to play in the Canadian Open, which admitted a black competitor as early as the thirties. When the tournament was played in New Brunswick in 1939, an unidentified Negro arrived at the 1st tee with a valid letter of acceptance. Play was temporarily halted, but the man was allowed to play after officials found a pro, Harold McSpaden, willing to be paired with him. McSpaden shot a low score the first day, and wouldn't change partners for the second. McSpaden went on to win the tournament. In later years, Spiller and Rhodes made the trip north, reporting no problems at the tournament, in hotels, or at restaurants. "Hell, maybe it was too cold up there for the Mason-Dixon line to exist," Sifford quipped in his biography.

They were still barred from playing at virtually every country club in America—except on Mondays, caddie day—and at a large number of public courses, particularly in the South. No Negro professional was certified by the PGA or held a head pro's job at a half-decent golf course. Full-time jobs in the game were rare, except as caddie masters or pro shop assistants who often worked out back.

Their rite of passage from amateur status to the professional ranks still entailed little more than deciding to accept cash rather than a trophy when they won a tournament. "Most of us are pros by acclamation," said A. D. V. Crosby, the president of the UGA, a self-proclaimed professional golfer at the time but officially a schoolteacher from Columbus, Ohio.

But there was change in the wind, and in black golf, it found its expression in who would be the reigning standard-bearer, the man people looked to as the best of the Negro golfers.

The end of the war found Howard Wheeler as the presiding champion of black professional golf. He had won the first postwar UGA National, in Pittsburgh in 1946, and now was back at his old haunt, Cobbs Creek. He had taken all comers here so many times before, and usually had come out on top.

Here Wheeler faced his old traveling buddy Zeke Hartsfield, a contemporary in age and, like Wheeler, from Atlanta. Hartsfield had never won the UGA National title, but this skinny guy was a different player when money was on the line. Chatty and friendly, Hartsfield had friends in every town who would often put him up, and golfing buddies, too. Charlie Sifford recalled that Hartsfield couldn't hit the ball very far, but he was the man you wanted as your partner. "At a tournament, he could shoot nine birdies and nine bogies for a round, but when the betting started, he always found a way to win."

Wheeler's real worries at Cobbs were three other golfers, younger men who had dedicated themselves to the game and to getting on the white tour. "God, those guys were great," said Joe Louis, years later.

One of them was Bill Spiller. He had taken up the game five years earlier, at the age of twenty-nine. While he was working at the L.A. train station, the guys were always gambling on something—betting on sports, pool, dice, cards. It helped pass the time. And one day, one coworker challenged Spiller to a game of golf.

"You can beat me playing pool, but you can't beat me playing golf," the guy said to Spiller. Despite his reputation as a fierce competitor, Spiller didn't take the bait at first; he'd had a taste of the game years earlier and didn't see any point in chasing a little white ball around.

But the guy dragged him out to Sunset Fields, on Christmas Eve, yet, and gave him a stroke a hole. Soon he was giving him only two strokes a side. Finally, they played even up. Spiller was a quick study. He played his first tournament, the Southern California Open, in the five-to-seven-handicap division, and won in a playoff. He won a seventy-five-dollar war bond, and suddenly, he was a player. Or so he thought.

He put in his entry to qualify for the Los Angeles Open and played that year at the Wilshire Country Club. It was a good thing he didn't qualify, because when he stayed and watched the tournament, he knew he would have embarrassed himself. He was nowhere near ready to play on the same course with these pros.

"What would I be doing out there with my little old slice?" Spiller told Al Barkow years later. "I had never seen any players like that. I was carried away with Toney Penna's irons, the way he hit them. Johnny Bulla was one of my favorite drivers. And Byron Nelson."

Byron Nelson, the smooth-swinging Texan with the boyish face and the killer all-around game, became his model. Spiller was so taken, he bought a Nelson instructional book and read every word. He bought other golf books "and would get under a tree and read something, then go practice it, read some more, practice it."

He kept at it, and within a few years turned pro, in 1947. He came east to play in the UGA circuit, and in the UGA National at Cobbs, and lost a lot of money finding out how many good black golfers there were. But he got better all the time.

In addition to the slender, athletic Spiller, Wheeler had to worry about the shorter, stocky Charlie Sifford. Sifford was a wiser, more accomplished player than the kid who had brashly challenged Wheeler on the driving range at Cobbs Creek and who had learned a costly lesson because of it.

Sifford had come north from Charlotte, North Carolina, with his boyhood friend Walter Ferguson, to live in Philadelphia with his uncle. The third of six kids, Charlie grew up in a household governed by his mother, Eliza, and her Southern Baptist rules and rituals. Starting at age ten, he found a refuge at the golf course, a place where he found a way to make money as a caddie, and a lifelong vocation. He also began smoking his trademark cigars out at the golf course, at age twelve. He'd carry the bag for sixty cents, give his mother fifty cents, and keep the ten cents to buy stogies.

By age fifteen, he could shoot 70 or lower. "I started playing because I realized that I could hit the ball just as easy as I could hand the club to somebody else," he said.

Sifford soon impressed white pros at the Carolina Country Club with his commitment to golf—Clayton Heafner and Sutton Alexander among them. But his temper got him into trouble, and it precipitated a dramatic move that would set him on his lifelong path.

As Sifford tells it in his autobiography, he was seventeen when Alexander started getting pressure from the club's members about him and other black kids. The pro told him he hadn't done anything wrong but suggested he might be in danger if he continued to play there. Reading between the lines, Sifford concluded that he had become an embarrassment because he had become too good a player.

But his problems off the golf course were more serious. A confrontation with a white storekeeper had landed him in jail.

The owner, a large, nasty drunk, stopped Sifford one day when he entered the store to get groceries for his mother. "Hey, little nigger, go tell my wife to come here," the man told him.

"You know me, sir," Sifford responded, "and you know my daddy won't put up with you talking to me like that."

"Shut your mouth, nigger, and do like I told you," the storekeeper said.

"Call me that again, and I'm gonna go upside your head with a bottle!"

When the man got only more belligerent, Sifford was true to his word.

The man dropped to the floor, unconscious and with a split forehead. After he ran home and told his folks, Charlie was sent to live with his aunt across town until things cooled down. But he couldn't stay off the golf course for long. The police caught up with him on the 12th hole, where he was caddying, and arrested him. After he was bailed out, he knew there was no way to beat the rap—with the help of his parents and the golf pro, he bought a railroad ticket north.

Though the winters were longer in Philadelphia, Sifford found the playing conditions, particularly at Cobbs Creek, to his liking. The army would take him to Okinawa during the war, but Sifford returned to Philadelphia, where he rediscovered his golf game and met his future wife, Rose Crumbley.

After the war, Sifford turned to his friend Walter Ferguson, a good golfer himself, and said: "Man, we can make us a living playing golf."

It was a life that appealed to Ferguson, whether or not he could develop his game to compete on the tour. At six feet four, with a pencil-thin mustache, Ferguson was sometimes called "Dark Gable" for his resemblance to Clark Gable, the reigning movie idol. He had a natural, wristy swing and never had to practice much. But Ferguson also knew that if he was to compete, he had a fight ahead, and that there was a strong possibility that he'd end up in jail or dead. He wasn't the kind of person who backed away from a fight. "I can't take a lot of shit," he would recall years later. "Even at sixteen years old, in North Carolina, I wouldn't sit in the back of the bus." He was smart enough not to invite trouble; besides, Ferguson had found himself a good woman in Philadelphia, and that's where he decided to stay.

But it surprised him that Charlie would embark on the journey. Charlie was never an easy person to get along with. He would never win a popularity contest. He was a shy man, with little education, and seemed to carry a smoldering anger and a forbidding countenance.

But Charlie would surprise a lot of people. He would have the game, and he would have the patience, to keep grinding, to keep playing where he could, and to take advantage of opportunities when they presented themselves.

Sifford's game caught the attention of Joe Louis and Joe's pro, Teddy Rhodes, who recommended him to Billy Eckstine. It was an enormous boost for any golfer, particularly for a Negro pro with few prospects to win big purses. He became Eckstine's personal assistant, which meant "golf instructor."

With Eckstine, known as Mr. B, Charlie had hitched his wagon to a genuine, crossover pop star. Much as Joe Louis appealed to a mass audience with his prowess in the ring, Eckstine made his mark with a velvet-smooth baritone that could descend to deliver bass notes and climb into a tenor's range, using superior technique. By 1946, Eckstine had begun to steadily build his reputation, until in 1950, he appeared at the Paramount Theater in New York City and broke the six-year attendance record held by another well-known crooner, Frank Sinatra. Mr. B loved to play golf, and he paid Charlie $150 a week, plus road expenses. "While he would be in the theater," Charlie said about Eckstine, "I'd be out on the greens. He was my first real supporter."

A third man, however, was the most likely to succeed Wheeler as the crown prince of black golf. Even Spiller and Sifford would concede that.

Teddy Rhodes, originally from Nashville, appeared to be the true heir in several ways. He was a thirty-four-year-old soft-spoken gentleman whom Joe Louis had taken on as his personal pro a few years earlier. He already was known as one of golf's stylish dressers, but what set him apart was his swing. He was the most underrated swing stylist in the game, black or white. There were few who could swing a club like Teddy.

Born to Frank and Della Rhodes in 1913, Rhodes was the youngest of nine children, the second boy. Around the fifth grade, he lost interest in school and shortly thereafter started caddying.

After school and on weekends, Teddy would travel by streetcar from north Nashville out to Belle Meade Country Club, where he became one of the kids that club members would ask for. In his spare time around the caddie shack, he and his friends would twist coat hangers into reasonable facsimiles of golf clubs, and whittle corks into golf balls. Sometimes they would drag a lawn mower over to Hadley and Watkins Parks and fashion their own greens, dodging cowpats and embedding tree branches into the dirt to serve as flagsticks.

His horizons didn't stretch much further than the Cumberland River, at first. He became known as one of Nashville's best golfers, and as a pretty decent gambler on the golf course, even though there were no golf courses for blacks in those days. (Not until 1954 did the Cumberland Golf Course, a nine-hole layout for blacks, open.) Rhodes was forced to play very early or very late on other golf courses, except on days when caddies were allowed. The head pro at Belle Meade, George Livingstone, took notice of the skinny young kid.

"I remember when he decided to leave town and didn't have enough money to buy a set of clubs," said his old caddie master John Lee "Pap" Bates. "I told Mr. Livingstone about Teddy. I also told him I had a barrel full of clubs, which had been discarded by our members through the years. There must have been 300 in that barrel. 'You let him pick any he wants,' Mister Livingstone said, 'and if he doesn't find what he needs, tell me and I'll give him a set myself.'"

In 1943, Rhodes joined the navy, and set aside golf for a while. But before he joined up, Rhodes took time off work and hopped the train to Dayton, Ohio, to play in a Negro golf tournament, the Joe Louis Open. There he met Louis himself and started a lifelong friendship. Rhodes, then twenty-nine, visited Louis in New York, and before long, the champ invited him to travel with him and teach him what he knew about the game.

"I gladly accepted," Rhodes said, years later. "He bought me some golf clubs, as I didn't have any, and shoes and whatnot, and I started off as a golf pro from there."

Rhodes wasn't in the navy long, according to his Nashville friend Joe Hampton, because of a kidney problem. After his discharge, he picked back up with Louis in Chicago and remained his personal pro until the early fifties, traveling around the country and around the world, playing golf with the champ. It provided Rhodes with some financial security while he worked on his game. Louis, for example, sent Teddy to hone his skills with Ray Mangrum, one of the golfing Mangrum brothers, both of whom played on the PGA Tour.

"[Mangrum] put a bushel of balls down there, and [Teddy's] mouth was watering like a dog over a fox," said Hampton. But Mangrum would make Rhodes swing the club for a long time before he ever let him strike a ball. As the years went on, Rhodes refined a swing that has been described as one of the smoothest and most rhythmic in the game. "I've seen many of 'em play, and I've played smooth," said Robert Horton, a teaching pro in Chicago for six decades. "They used to tell me how smooth I was. But I wasn't near as smooth as Teddy."

At five feet eleven and about 150 pounds, Rhodes was not physically imposing. But he had a presence. George May's daughter, Dorothy Campbell, remembered Rhodes as one of the few golfers who stopped conversation when he walked into a room. The man had something special. "This guy without a doubt was the classiest, flashiest guy you've ever seen. He made Clark Gable look plain. He was a beautiful human being; he really was," she said.

As if anyone needed any more evidence, Rhodes had been

crowned "America's greatest Negro golfer" that January by the *Los Angeles Times* after he had shot an opening-round 71 in the L.A. Open.

He came to Cobbs Creek that summer as the brightest star in a new constellation of black golfers.

But that year, Howard Wheeler would hold them all off.

Sifford finished second, four shots back. Zeke and Spiller finished third, ten shots off, after Spiller fired a final-round 69. And Rhodes was fifth, eleven behind Wheeler. After a second-round 67, Wheeler had little trouble with the field, shooting 71 and 74 to take his second straight UGA National title.

He now had won four times, more than any other golfer—more than Pat Ball and John Dendy, who each had collected three UGA National crowns. Wheeler would repeat the following year, in Indianapolis. But his time at the top was running short. The next group of golfers was ready to inherit his title. Beyond that, they were prepared to stake a claim on the PGA Tour, where they belonged.

7

"Land of the Free and Home of the Brave"

Throughout the forties, as Spiller lugged bags at Union Station in Los Angeles and worked other jobs of no consequence, his drive to be something more burned in his gut. Something had made him think that his other dream, aside from becoming a teacher, might still be possible. He might make a living as an athlete, specifically a professional golfer.

Some black golfers were happy just to play and slip quietly off the golf course. Not Spiller. He demanded to be treated like any other man, white or black. He refused to fade into the background; he was a college-educated man and a professional golfer, someone to be respected. Woe be unto those who felt otherwise.

As Spiller came into his prime playing-years, in the late forties, there was little talk on America's sports pages of blacks crossing the color line in pro golf. Major-league baseball was the subject of those stories: who would become the first Negro to play for a big-league ball club. Baseball's Branch Rickey was looking for the right man to bring to the Brooklyn Dodgers—not just a superior player, but a man who would and could endure the enormous pressures, day in and day out, that would confront him at each ball field, in every city. But in golf, there was no such attention paid to Negroes and no powerful men calculating just how to get them on the nation's premier golf courses so that they could compete against the best. Golf had no Branch Rickey.

So Spiller and a handful of other Negro golfers were left to quietly push on their own to be recognized in their sport, and not just on the United Golfers Association circuit. They were up against some formidable social and institutional forces. For one, many of the tournaments were played in the South, and a black man on a southern golf course did one thing: caddie, period. In addition, the PGA's Caucasians-only clause effectively barred blacks from playing anywhere on tour, unless sponsors insisted on it. Only in Los Angeles and at the Tam O'Shanter did that happen. (The Canadian Open also was an exception, for golfers that were willing to travel that far north.)

By 1948, it was clear that the incremental approach wasn't for Spiller, and that year, he took a step to thrust the black golfer onto the sports pages of mainstream America's newspapers. That Teddy Rhodes joined with Spiller to confront the PGA was more surprising.

It was Rhodes's nature, his disposition, his outlook on life, that threw him into such dramatic contrast with Spiller. For all of Spiller's vinegar, Rhodes oozed honey. It was an attitude that helped him negotiate the difficult years before the Civil Rights Movement opened things up. "I've seen it both ways," he'd say later on. "But if I had my preference, I'd take the nice way, because when you get something that way, it's a lot sweeter to have."

In the complicated and sometimes ambiguous waters of race relations, Rhodes wanted only to play golf, and he wasn't about to give anyone a reason to kick him off the golf course. Any reason, that is, that he could control. Perhaps he had an easier time swallowing his true feelings, when Spiller felt compelled to voice his to anyone who would listen.

"Teddy was not a fighter," said Maggie Hathaway, an activist in Los Angeles who championed the cause of black golfers. "He was, let's say, a compassionate peacekeeper."

In Phoenix years later, Teddy and Joe Louis left the locker room and headed for the first tee, only to encounter a woman who stared at them with such unvarnished hatred that they stopped in their tracks. Before they could get off the first tee, the woman had gathered enough support from others to force them to move their belongings out of the locker room and into the caddies' quarters. They did so courteously, quietly, without complaint.

On rare occasions, Teddy's easygoing style skirted the edge of Jim Crow accommodation. Hathaway, who credited Rhodes with being a true pioneer for blacks in golf, remembered a ritual at the L.A. Open, when Teddy would bring a box of sand and spread it just outside the clubhouse and do a sand dance for the white pros inside. "It was embarrassing," said Hathaway, "but [the white pros] accepted it as comedy. Teddy would ask Charlie [Sifford] to join him. Charlie was very quiet, shy, conservative. He'd do a few steps, but Teddy did the whole dance." She shuddered at the thought.

Even when he was admitted to a locker room or a clubhouse dining room, he would turn a deaf ear to some of the slurs people would utter in a stage whisper loud enough to be heard. Time after time, he'd walk away or stay away from the clubhouse. In his view, he couldn't fight back, even if he wanted to, because it would only make it worse.

For Spiller, 1948 started in exhilarating fashion, with his name written alongside that of a golf icon, Ben Hogan. Spiller shot a 68 on the first round of the Los Angeles Open to tie Hogan for the first-round lead of the tournament, until a golfer in the final three-some posted a 67.

It was a dream, a day he would recall for the rest of his life. He had gotten a chance, and he had shown them what he could do. Spiller and Hogan, Hogan and Spiller. Tied for the lead. At the Riviera Country Club.

The dream wouldn't last. Spiller would blow up the next round and tumble down in the tournament standings. But he had gotten a chance and played well enough—an aggregate score of 296 for thirty-sixth place—to qualify for the next stop on the PGA Tour, the Richmond Open, across the bay from San Francisco. Teddy had made it, too, finishing twenty-first.

In the Bay Area, the big news was not that two black pros from L.A. would play, but that Hogan would not. He had notified the tournament at the last minute that he couldn't make it because of "business commitments" in Southern California. Hogan's pullout and the indecision of other pros had promoter Pat Markovich fuming and threatening to cancel future tournaments in Richmond.

"He can't do this to us," Markovich cried out when he heard of Hogan's decision. "Either Hogan plays or there'll be no more Richmond Opens—ever!"

At the last minute, Jimmy Demaret, the leading money winner on the Tour and one of its most popular golfers, committed to Richmond. Demaret brought color to any tournament—quite literally, he was the most stylish dresser on tour—and he had an engaging personality. With Bobby Locke, the enigmatic South African; Sam Snead; Cary Middlecoff; Lloyd Mangrum; and others filling out the tournament slate, the local sportswriters had plenty to write about.

Spiller and Rhodes generated not a single word in the pretournament coverage, until they stepped onto the golf course for a practice round Monday, three days before the tournament was to begin.

George Schneiter, a player on the Tour and the PGA's tournament director, approached the men after their round. And for the first time, an official with the PGA articulated the policy that had been in effect since the PGA began but had been put into writing only six years earlier.

Rules are rules, Schneiter told them.

"So I said," Spiller recounted years later, "'Mr. Schneiter, I'm a college graduate. I understand English. If you want to say something to me, say it. I'll understand you.' So he says something about having nothing against us fellows personally, but the PGA bylaws say so-and-so, and this was the first time I got to see the PGA bylaws. It said in there that membership was for Caucasians only." For his part, Schneiter said Spiller knew what to expect when he came north. "I heard Spiller say on the radio during the Los Angeles Open that he wasn't eligible to play in a PGA tournament," Schneiter told a reporter. "So he obviously knew about the situation."

The Richmond Golf Club was under contract with the PGA to put on the tournament and thereby had to abide by PGA rules. On the other hand, that contract stipulated that the top sixty finishers in Los Angeles would be automatically eligible to play, without qualifying. Spiller and Rhodes arrived at the course on Sunday and paid their ten-dollar entry fees to Richmond tournament director and head pro Pat Markovich.

"I do not have anything to do with recognition of entrants. If I did, you can bet that Ben Hogan wouldn't have pulled out of this tournament," said Markovich. "As far as I'm concerned, if a man can swing a golf stick well enough to compete in a major tournament, he is entitled to do so."

But already the PGA was getting heat in the local press. *Oakland Tribune* columnist Alan Ward said the Richmond club didn't deserve any blame. "The tournament is being run by the snooty PGA, which not only bars Negroes from participation in its events, but from membership in the organization.

"All this, you understand, took place in the U.S.A., land of the free and home of the brave, in the year 1948."

To no avail.

By Wednesday, Spiller and Rhodes had returned to Los Angeles, but before they did, Spiller contacted a friend of his in Berkeley, who contacted Ira Blue, a radio personality, who spoke out on the air about the Richmond Open. But they weren't done yet. They had hired a lawyer, Jonathan Rowell, and they began making noises about suing the PGA for discrimination.

"He said he would take the case, no charge," said Spiller.

Rowell had bona fide white-liberal credentials. The son of Chester Rowell, a longtime political columnist for the *Chronicle*, Rowell had occasionally represented the NAACP. He was president of a civic group in his hometown of Redwood City, south of San Francisco, that was formed after the house of John Walker, a Negro, was burned to the ground. Rowell had filed a lawsuit on Walker's behalf against those accused of the arson.

"He was a very liberal guy in an era when being that liberal wasn't popular," said Melvin Cohn, a retired judge who was active in Democratic politics in the Bay Area. "He was one of those guys who was always pursuing a cause. And he really believed in them; it wasn't a bunch of nonsense." And Rowell wasn't afraid of political battles; he would mount an unsuccessful bid that year for Congress.

On the third day of the tournament, played under brilliant blue skies, Rowell drove to the Richmond Golf Club and walked to the front gate, just like the thousands of other spectators. There he found Francis Watson, the chairman of the Richmond Open.

Rowell handed Watson a "show cause" order—a notification that a lawsuit had been filed—and then started through the gate.

"Where are you going?" Watson demanded.

"I'm going up to the clubhouse to serve George Schneiter," Rowell said.

"Well, that'll cost you $1.80," said Watson.

Rowell paid the admission and entered the tournament. The lawsuit, filed in Contra Costa Superior Court, asked for $315,000 damages for Spiller, Rhodes, and Madison Gunter, a Negro amateur who'd also been denied entry.

There was no last-minute reprieve. The tournament went on without Spiller, Rhodes, and Gunter. The main sports story that week was E. J. "Dutch" Harrison, a tall thirty-eight-year-old who had won pro tournaments in Reading, Reno, and Hawaii the previous year. At Richmond, on Thursday, he dropped a thirty-foot putt on the 18th for an eagle, a course-record 65, and a one-shot lead.

Harrison never looked back, leading at the end of each day. On Sunday, coming to the last hole of the tournament, Harrison needed a par to win. Instead, he chipped within two feet and sank the putt to win by two. Over four sun-kissed days, Harrison had shot eagle, birdie, birdie, birdie on the final hole. "I'm going to build me a bed right here on this here eighteenth green," said Harrison, a Will Rogers–type character from Little Rock, Arkansas. "I love it."

But the Negroes' lawsuit, while forgotten for a few days, resurfaced that final day to lend a comic note to the proceedings. As he was handed the winner's check by tournament chairman Watson, Harrison played it to the hilt, scratching his head when he noticed that the check was truly blank. It had no figures and no signature on it.

"This check looks a little blank to me, Francis," said Harrison. "I can't buy any hot dogs or hamburgers with this. Can't you scribble a little something on it?"

Watson could only shake his head. Reporters speculated that tournament officials, afraid the lawsuit would attach the funds—in effect, freeze the prize money—promised to pay the golfers soon, probably at the PGA's next winter stop in Phoenix. Officials denied it, saying they hadn't had time to fill in the winner's name on the check, but the effect was great copy for the next day's papers.

"Blankety Blank," said the *Examiner*, in a caption over a photo showing a bemused Harrison holding up the blank piece of paper. "Harrison Wins $2,000 I.O.U.," read a headline.

As the Tour moved on, the bad publicity didn't stop.

Less than a week later, George May visited the Bay Area on business. With little prompting, May lashed out at the PGA, the USGA, and the white golfers who failed to welcome blacks to the tournaments.

It was no surprise that May would tweak the PGA whenever possible; he'd had his beefs with them long before Richmond. But he didn't hesitate to wade in again. (The feeling was mutual, since some PGA officials couldn't abide the three-ring circuses May called tournaments. And some players were indignant that they would be treated like other athletes, wearing numbers on their backs so the uninitiated fans could identify them.)

But May cut to the quick. He had been successful in marketing golf and luring a whole new group of fans to his tournament, people who otherwise had little in common with the country club set. He told reporters in San Francisco that the golfing establishment was trying to keep the game full of people like them: wealthy and white. "They don't want the fellow from the wrong side of the tracks to get into golf," May said. "They want to restrict the game and keep it for the rich men."

May didn't stop there. He took a shot at one of the icons of the game, Ben Hogan, and other unnamed white pros from the South. (Hogan, of course had refused to wear a number on his back and stopped playing at the Tam.)

"It's just the case of some of those narrow-minded hot-shots from the South, refusing to play with the Negroes. I found that out in my All-American tournament in Chicago. Sure, Ben Hogan and a half-dozen other fellows didn't show up last year because they claimed they didn't want to wear those numbers on their backs. But don't kid yourself, the main reason behind it was the fact that I've always had Negroes play and they don't like it.

"Y'know what those groups are afraid of? They fear a Negro will come along and win one of the tournaments."

May said the "Caucasians-only clause" was wrong and told PGA president Ed Dudley when he saw him the week before. "If the PGA doesn't strike its Caucasian clause from the bylaws, somebody's going to get caught by the State's antidiscrimination laws. . . . I believe this suit against the PGA will do much to erase the Caucasian clause from the bylaws."

An outlaw like May sounding off was one thing, but the sponsors of the L.A. Open, which allowed Negroes to play, chimed in. "We will never countenance an event which bars the entrance of racial groups," said Don Freeman, president of the L.A. Chamber of Commerce.

In the Bay Area, the PGA continued to take a public relations beating. On its editorial page on January 21, 1948, the *Oakland Tribune* called the decision to bar the golfers "un-American and unsportsmanlike," bringing shame to California.

And a columnist for the *Chronicle* noted that the unseemly affair had brought that shame to its backyard. "The suits haven't been decided yet, and, in themselves, are not very important," said Darrell Wilson. "What counts is that the spotlight is now on golf's racial problem. The public has been informed, and with considerable emphasis, that colored players are actually deprived of a chance to make a living.

"This is not a new condition and naturally many knew of it. But for the first time, the point was forcibly brought home to the public that these men could not compete for prizes in an 'Open' tournament because their skin happened to be black. And it happened at Richmond."

The lawsuit seemed to reopen the debate about racial progress, gradualism versus confrontation. R. G. Lynch, the sports editor of the *Milwaukee Sentinel,* called the lawsuit a mistake. "Real progress is being made against racial discrimination and Negroes would be wise not to interrupt this progress by exerting pressure in the wrong places. We are not discussing the right and the wrong of the matter; merely the practical aspects."

In fact, Lynch raised the question that no others seemed to want to touch but must have been a topic of conversation at PGA headquarters. Should or could private clubs be told what to do? Even if the PGA insisted that Negroes play in all tournaments, including the southern one, would it find a large chunk of its tour fall apart, for lack of sponsors and clubs to host events? "And then who would be 'deprived of the opportunity to make a living?'" Lynch asked.

The South, as always, was the bogeyman under the bed. For the PGA to maintain the status quo—and to keep a lid on the racial issue that would disrupt the Tour's swing through the South— black golfers were excluded virtually everywhere. Only a few bold tournaments, George May's All-American and the Los Angeles Open, refused to abide by the PGA's restriction.

"The PGA operates open tournaments in practically every state, and it certainly cannot approach this subject in the South in a similar manner as in some of the Northern states, or California," *Golf World* magazine opined. "The ramifications of this problem are far reaching."

Dudley had already made noises about changing the situation, suggesting perhaps that the Caucasian clause be eliminated. From his Augusta, Georgia, home, he spoke by telephone with Harry Kingman, the secretary of the University of California YMCA racial relations committee. Kingman quoted Dudley as saying:

"I feel badly about this situation in Richmond, California. Of course, in order to change the rule, a two-thirds vote at our November convention would be necessary. That particular rule has been in force since 1916 when the PGA was formed, and such a situation as this one has never come up. I'm pretty sure something can be done about it."

Oakland Tribune columnist Alan Ward urged people to give golf another twelve months to come around. "It will come around," Ward said. "It has to."

But as the Tour moved on and after May left town, the issue died down and the lawyers began their work. The Oakland branch of the NAACP received a telegram from the national office pledging help, and that pledge was passed along to Rowell, the attorney hired by Spiller and Rhodes. Rowell wrote back to Thurgood Marshall, then the NAACP's chief legal counsel in Washington, who later became the first black U.S. Supreme Court justice, to lay out the case.

In the lawsuit, Rowell sought $5,000 for each golfer for a violation of a California law that said, "All citizens within the jurisdiction of this state are entitled to the full and equal accommodations, advantages, facilities and privileges of . . . places of public accommodation or amusement."

Whether that could be applied to professional golfers seeking to enter a golf tournament was another matter. But Rowell wrote that golf clubs signing contracts with the PGA, knowing that the organization discriminated against blacks, would therefore be accomplices to the discrimination. "If this point can be made to stick, it may well have the result of causing many golf clubs to think twice before they ever put on another PGA sponsored tournament," Rowell wrote.

The lawyer went on to describe that each golfer suffered another $100,000 damages each because the monopoly over the golfers' employment opportunities was similar to that of a union with a "closed-shop contract" that barred blacks as members.

Rowell then asked for help. He had already notified the three golfers that he wouldn't charge them his normal fee, but he needed help with the expenses to mount such a lawsuit. The early part of the case, including taking depositions and conducting an investigation, might cost about $250.

"It is apparent that the case filed on behalf of these three men presents novel and important legal points," Rowell wrote. "Likewise, it is highly probable that the case will be contested through every possible court."

About ten days later, Marshall's assistant wrote back, saying that Rowell first should seek help at the local level, adding that if the local branch was not able to provide assistance, "it is our policy to step in provided the issue is of national importance."

There, the paper trail disappears.

Whether Rowell sought help again from the local branch or the national organization is unknown. In fairness, the NAACP might be forgiven for focusing on broader horizons. In building its cases to desegregate schools and other public facilities, the troubles of a few men trying to break into the professional ranks of what many considered a minor sport probably weren't viewed as "of national importance."

The spring turned into summer, and the case dragged on behind the scenes. On the golf course, Teddy Rhodes qualified for the U.S. Open at the Riviera Country Club in Los Angeles. The 7,020-yard layout was the longest ever used for the open, and regarded as one of the toughest, but during a warm-up round on Tuesday, Rhodes's 67 was surpassed by no one, and matched only by Sam Snead. On the first day of the tournament, Rhodes shot a one-under 70 and was among only seven golfers who broke par, three shots behind coleaders Ben Hogan and Lew Worsham. He could play with anyone.

Meanwhile, the PGA, in court papers, denied all charges of discrimination. And the case was set down for trial on September 28.

But the case never got to trial.

A few weeks before the trial was to begin, Rowell asked the court for more time to prepare. Problems had arisen; not insurmountable problems, but problems. For one, George Schneiter, who had denied Rhodes and Spiller entrance to the tournament, had been traveling on the Tour for months and Rowell would not be able to take his deposition until early September, in Reno, Nevada.

The logistical problems of bringing the case were difficult for Rowell. Rhodes and Spiller lived in Los Angeles, when they weren't on the road playing in mostly black tournaments. In addition, the white golfers on the PGA Tour traveled outside California much of the year and their interviews for the lawsuit couldn't be completed for months.

It's also possible that the time and effort needed to mount his own congressional campaign, one that ultimately failed, also took its toll on Rowell.

On September 20, the case ended. Lawyers for the PGA, the Richmond Golf Club, and various PGA officials, and for Rhodes and Spiller, appeared in Contra Costa Superior Court. At Rowell's request, Judge Hugh Donovan dismissed the lawsuit. In court documents, the PGA and Rowell stipulated that there had been no discrimination and that no one had denied Rhodes and Spiller entrance to the tournament. It was legal boilerplate language that is usually part of the bargain in an out-of-court settlement: legal language that releases the PGA from any liability and gives it a public face-saving in exchange for some concessions behind closed doors.

Dana Murdock, an attorney representing the PGA, said in open court that the PGA would not discriminate or refuse tournament-playing privileges to anyone because of color. And Rowell said he consented to the dismissal after the PGA made a pledge that there would be no further discrimination. His clients, he said, weren't interested in making money but in "break[ing] down racial barriers."

Still the circumstances leading to the settlement—and the details of the settlement itself—remain hazy today. Spiller told Al Barkow that a crucial decision came shortly before the trial was to begin:

"Rowell comes down on the train to meet us before going to court, and says that on the train he met the PGA attorney and they worked out a deal where the PGA promised it would not discriminate against blacks if we dropped the suit. Rowell said that would be okay."

In fact, the PGA's own magazine, *Professional Golfer,* in discussing the conclusion of the lawsuit, never mentioned the organization's constitution, specifically Section 1, Article III, which allowed only golfers "of the Caucasian race" to become PGA members, and thus play in tour events.

Instead, the magazine pointed out that the Tour's tournament regulations contained no provisions that would restrict anyone from entering tournaments based on their race, creed, or nationality. Had the case come to trial, the PGA would have contended that Rhodes, Spiller, and Gunter were barred from the tournament solely because they had not met other requirements "which must be met before applicants are accorded playing privileges in PGA co-sponsored events."

In effect, Schneiter seemed to be saying he never mentioned race when he asked the three golfers to withdraw, even though the underlying reason the three could not be members was their race. It was a lesson in semantics Spiller would not soon forget.

The PGA said it fully expected the golfers to file applications for playing privileges in PGA cosponsored tournaments and for approval as tournament players, subject to approval by the Executive and Tournament Committee that December. There's no record any such approval was considered, however.

Seemingly, an opportunity had been lost to break down discrimination in the sport. As the year ended, the PGA had given up little. And the PGA's pledge went unfulfilled, or neglected. Instead of conducting "open" tournaments, which implied that the tournaments were open to anyone who could compete, the PGA changed many of the tournaments to "invitationals," which meant they were now exclusive events that required invitations to play.

Organization president Ed Dudley's statement earlier that year that "something can be done about it" had long since died out by the end of the fall.

It must have been small consolation to Spiller, Rhodes, and other blacks trying to play on tour, but something had actually changed. The plight of blacks in golf had been thrust onto the front pages of sports pages around the country. Many whites learned for the first time that blacks actually played golf, and that some of them excelled at it. They also learned that the problems with race and sports did not end when Jackie Robinson put on a Dodgers uniform; rather, they entered a new phase, when other sports were subjected to the same question: Why not?

Even in golf, why not?

"That was a turning point," Barkow said. "Not immediately, as you know. Their lawyer messed them up a bit. A lot. He trusted the PGA to follow through and they didn't. But it was a start and they had to make a start. And it got out. The word got out and it got into the system; people started thinking about it."

8

"We've Got Another Hitler to Get By"

Joe Louis, one of the most famous athletes of his time, climbed into the ring with the Professional Golfers' Association of America in 1952, and immediately threw a haymaker. It got everybody's attention.

"I want the people to know what the PGA is," Louis said. "We've got another Hitler to get by."

In one short remark, the Brown Bomber had likened the struggle by Negroes to play professional golf to the Nazi terror that had sucked the world into war, caused the the extermination of millions in death camps, and led to the combat deaths of millions more.

It was hyperbole at its most extreme, but Louis was no punch-drunk stiff; he knew the value of symbols. He'd been one himself.

For weeks in 1936, the talk of America was: Could Joe beat the Nazi? That Nazi was Max Schmeling, a strapping example of Hitler's "master race," a term that Negroes had become accustomed to hearing in their own country long before Hitler kindled his Aryan firestorm.

As Americans white and black huddled closely to their radios on June 19, 1936, Schmeling knocked Louis out in the twelfth round. Golf bore some of the blame.

Louis had been introduced to the game only several months before, but he was smitten. Living in New York with his first wife,

Marva, Louis was paid a visit by a young sportswriter named Ed Sullivan, from the *New York Daily News,* and he brought Louis some books on golf and a golf club or two. "I was swinging, slicing, hooking, putting around all around the apartment. Marva would get a little nervous, afraid I might strain myself, or break up the apartment."

When Louis decamped to Lakewood, New Jersey, to train for the Schmeling fight, the golf clubs came along, too. And suddenly Joe's new passion became a problem for his handlers. In the days leading up to the bout, when his trainers wanted him to relax and put on some weight, Louis set out for the golf course and got dehydrated in the sun. When his trainers wanted him to relax and go deep-sea fishing, Louis had other ideas. "I said to myself, 'Shit, I'm in top form, I'm going to play a few rounds of golf.' I needed that day like you need another hole in your head."

When he weighed in at the New York Hippodrome before the fight, Louis was at 196—down from 216 at the start of camp—and Schmeling weighed 192. The fight lasted twelve rounds, and it went in a knockout to Schmeling.

The loss hit hard. In Chicago, men in "Little Harlem" rioted. A girl in New York tried to drink poison in a drugstore. And for Jews, Louis had special significance, as a hero who could knock down the Superman myth. Art Buchwald, who grew up in Hollis, New York, and was glued to the radio that night, said the defeat was "the blackest day in Hollis." And in the rest of the United States, for that matter.

"Didn't train properly, and between the golf and the women and not listening to what [his trainer] Chappie said, it's a wonder I wasn't killed in the ring," said Louis. "I let myself down, I let the whole race of people down because I thought I was some kind of hot shit."

Two years would pass before he would get a rematch, even though he wrested the heavyweight title from James J. Braddock in June of 1937. But Louis's vengeance was swift. On June 22, 1938, the normally impassive Louis showed a fury that inspired a deer-in-the-headlights fear on Schmeling's face. Louis dropped the German to the canvas once, and again. Hitler's Superman lasted only two minutes and four seconds in the first round, and then recovered in a hospital. It was redemption—for America, for Louis, for Negroes. "It was a glorious night," said longtime *Baltimore Afro-American* sportswriter Sam Daly. "I can't use a better adjective than that."

As Louis went on to establish himself as the dominant heavy-weight boxer of the era, his love for golf only grew. He couldn't stay away from the golf course. When his children Joe and Jackie were born, he was on the golf course. It became a rare place where father and son could be alone; Joe Louis Barrow, Jr., first saw him hit a golf ball when he was three at a Chicago golf course now named Joe Louis the Champ Golf Course.

Louis soon became the patron saint of black golfers. For years, he had a black pro on his payroll—first Clyde Martin, and later Teddy Rhodes. And he helped other struggling pros whenever he could. He would also stand up for them at critical times.

He sponsored the Joe Louis Open in Detroit, and the pros were treated well. Walter "Chink" Stewart, a pro from Baltimore, arrived one year and was told his entry fee had already been paid. It was Louis, who had paid for everyone else, too. "He was that type of man," Stewart said. "And after the tournament was over he chartered a plane and flew a lot of the pros up to Canada for a tournament up there."

With golf came gambling, and his gambling was legendary. As Louis once explained, money wasn't something to bank and earn interest, but something to bring him and others pleasure. He had been one of eleven kids of an Alabama sharecropper who up and left when Joe was young. After his family moved to Detroit, Joe quit school to help provide for them.

"Maybe I felt this way because of all the hard times I'd had as a child. Maybe I'm a damned fool. Maybe I thought the well would never dry up. You tend to think that way when you're 23 years old and you've reached what I had reached."

Louis, as one wag put it, had made a lot of other people rich during his career. Some have estimated that he lost $500,000 on the golf course, and that estimate may be low. He was a magnet, not just for hustlers, but for others who wanted to get close to the champ and get a piece of him. One summer, he lost $90,000 to sharpies who raised their handicaps and bet wads of cash. Smiley Quick, the white hustler, boasted to pro golfer Doug Ford that, all told, he had taken $250,000 from Louis on the golf course. Louis loved a challenge and often overestimated his abilities on the golf course. Though he was never overmatched in the ring, his competitive juices often wouldn't allow him to admit he was overmatched on the golf course.

And when he did win, he often refused to take another golfer's money, especially a golfer who was struggling to make a living. He also understood pride, and sometimes agreed to matches with much better golfers, knowing they needed the money.

At Chicago's Wayside Golf Course, he lost $10,000 one day to a friend who owned a small cleaning establishment, only to come back to end up ahead $17,000. When the man was short $7,000, he wrote Louis an IOU with his cleaning business as collateral. Louis later tore up the IOU rather than take the business away from his friend.

He loved to play and he loved the action. Losing a match meant nothing to him; he'd double his bets and hope to pull off a miracle on the last hole. Sometimes he did.

"You start off playing maybe for ten, twenty dollars," said Eural Clark, the L.A. amateur who played frequently with Louis. "He'd do a lot of pressing. Sometimes we'd play thirty-six holes. He'd be down two hundred dollars or so coming to the last hole and he'd go double or nothing. And win."

Once, Clark was one up on Louis with one hole to play. On the par 4, Clark was on the green in two, but Louis had hit his second shot in the bunker. "I got it today," Clark said to himself.

It was so dark, they had to turn on the lights of the golf carts to finish the round. Reaching for a club to play his sand shot, Louis asked for someone with white shoes to tend the pin and help him see the cup. "You know, he blasted the ball right into the hole," Clark recalled, laughing. "I was sick, and he'd just laugh. People are just clapping, pulling for him. Made me sick. I'd hustled him all day, come to the last hole and he'd win it."

Louis became a good amateur golfer, shooting consistently in the seventies, and often entered the amateur division of the UGA National. He finally won the amateur title in 1951, beating a skinny sixteen-year-old from Texas, 2 and 1 in match play. (The kid's name was Robert Lee Elder.) Louis entered golf tournaments wherever he could and was the first black man to play at a number of country clubs across the country.

By virtue of his universal appeal to all races in America, Louis was constantly besieged with requests for appearances. As a result, the San Diego County Chevrolet Association, the sponsors of the San Diego Open invitational, asked Joe Louis to participate in the tournament, one of the first stops on the pro tour in 1952. Said a spokesman, "We are most anxious that Joe, one of America's true sportsmen, play in our event."

But a week before the tournament was to begin, its committee said it had been notified that the PGA rules banned Louis and two other Negro golfers who were attempting to qualify, pro Bill Spiller and amateur Eural Clark.

Eventually, Louis got a message from PGA president Horton Smith, telling him he couldn't play. "Well, the funny thing is, I hadn't thought about playing till then," Louis said in his autobiography. "But all this made me mad as hell. I called Walter Winchell and gave him the story. He said, 'Who the hell is Horton Smith? He must be another Hitler.' Winchell put the story on that night."

At 9:00 P.M. Eastern time, Sunday, January 13, from the ABC radio studios in New York, an announcer extolled the virtues of Richard Hudnut Crème Shampoo and then introduced Walter Winchell, who delivered his signature opening line.

"Mr. and Mrs. North and South America and all the ships at sea—let's go to press!"

In his rat-a-tat-tat style, Winchell informed his listeners about the pill overdose of an executive's wife, the status of a Mafia trial in New York, a fight between Zeppo Marx and a movie producer, an upcoming demonstration by Communists in San Francisco. Then he teased his audience with this line:

"Dan," he said, mentioning the name of a New York sports editor, "I have an exclusive I think on one of those unhappy discrimination stories. This time, concerning Joe Louis the ex-champion. Coming up."

With that, Winchell delivered his own version of the international news, in two-sentence bites, spiced with a poke at President Truman and a reference to Winchell's hero, General Dwight D. Eisenhower. After a few more items from Washington, he got down to the Louis item:

"San Diego, California—Joe Louis, the former heavyweight champion, has just been dealt a very hard blow.

"Joe was invited to play in the San Diego Open from January 17th to January 20th at the San Diego Country Club. The golf tournament proceeds going to the crippled children in San Diego.

"However, Horton Smith, the PGA President, would not give an OK to the ex-champion to play in that Open, because Joe Louis told me on the long distance telephone only a few moments ago, he is a Negro.

"Joe, thanks for telling me about it. . . . You of all people have known where I stand on such miserable things for a very long time."

The next day, along with his secretary Leonard Reed, Louis appeared in San Diego and paid a visit that evening to the *San Diego Union* sports department.

Louis sat in a swivel chair and talked boxing, with traces of an Alabama twang in his soft voice. Just a few months earlier, he had been fiercely beaten by the young heavyweight Rocky Marciano. At age thirty-seven, Louis now had a touch of silver flecking the stubble above his upper lip, and he confronted the question again: Was he done?

Louis dropped his chin and almost inaudibly said: "Don't think I'll fight no more." He said he hadn't intended to make an announcement until he returned to New York. "But I won't fight no more."

Of course, Louis had retired more than once before. In fact, he was really in retirement now, but he was constantly considering whether to come back. The story was still news, and it was played prominently in the *Union*. The bigger news, however, was his present task: to confront the PGA over its policy to exclude blacks and anyone else of color from tournaments.

Louis told the sportswriters that he would appear on the 1st tee at 7:00 A.M. the next morning, if necessary, to qualify for the tournament, even though he had one of the ten exemptions local tournaments were allowed to give. He did not doubt that the PGA would try to bar him from playing.

He had no beef with the tournament organizers or officials at the golf course. But he suggested they consider canceling the tournament if the PGA refused to allow the black golfers to compete— a suggestion that had no realistic chance, since San Diego had labored long and hard to get a pro tournament and wasn't about to jeopardize it now. Louis even dangled an offer to double the tournament's $2,000 pledge to a children's charity should the tournament face down the PGA with a cancellation.

This was Joe Louis versus the PGA, and he dared the organization to call his bluff. "I want to bring this thing out into the light. I want the people to know what the PGA is. The PGA will have to tell me personally that I can't play."

And then, almost as an afterthought, Louis dropped his bombshell in that dingy and smoky newspaper office. One of the century's most important and popular sportsmen turned his finger on a man who was a virtual unknown outside the golf world, and compared him to one of history's most loathed tyrants and mass killers.

"We've got another Hitler to get by. They're all working the same way. Horton Smith believes in the white race—Hitler believed in the super race."

Horton Smith's ascension to the PGA president's job had drawn mixed reviews among the touring pros—some saw him as a cold, calculating opportunist. But no one had ever compared him to Hitler, or even called him a tyrant.

Born in Springfield, Missouri, he quit the Missouri State Teachers College in 1926 to turn pro. The next year, he worked at three different golf clubs, perhaps an early indication of his drive and ambition, while he worked on his game. By 1928, he was ready to make some money on the Tour.

In 1928 and 1929, Smith won fifteen tournaments and at age twenty, was named the youngest rookie to the Ryder Cup team. He was regarded as the last man to beat golfing icon Bobby Jones, who won the Grand Slam in 1930 and then abruptly retired from active competition. That year, Smith edged out Jones to win the Savannah Open. In 1934, Smith won the inaugural Masters Tournament, and repeated the feat in 1936, with both victories forged in dramatic one-shot wins. As a player, Smith cut an elegant figure, with a slow, smooth swing and a sweet touch on the greens. The golf writer Herbert Warren Wind described him as a "wholesome, studious, finicky, and handsome young man."

But Smith had long been considered an introspective man, even a loner, and when he took the PGA presidency, some players harbored suspicions about someone who wanted both to compete against them and be their superior. The players' needn't have worried, though. The glorious and powerful job of PGA president paid no salary or benefits—Smith made a good wage as head pro at the Detroit Golf Club—while Smith no longer posed a serious challenge as a touring player, perhaps the victim of too much fiddling with and revamping of his once formidable swing.

"He had been a nonsmoking, nondrinking, nonswearing, twenty-four-hour-well-behaved young man winning or finishing high in golf tournaments, and it hadn't bothered him to be called a Boy Scout on the tournament circuit," PGA historian Herb Graffis wrote.

What some saw in Smith was a man who had developed organizational skills in the army and a practical business sense in his country club jobs. He might also bring some peace to the dissension-wracked PGA, an organization of about 3,000 members, mostly club pros, who each ran a business at their local clubhouses. The touring pros constituted only 10 percent of the membership and each of them prospered or failed under one simple maxim: Win or go home. They were not under contract to the PGA and as free-lancers, they chafed at anyone telling them how to do anything. As *Sport* magazine said in 1952, "Generally speaking, the glamour boys of golf are a free-wheeling, self-seeking band of individuals with nobody's interests at heart but their own. They pay their own way down to the last tip to the locker-room boy, and they must win to eat." Smith had succeeded as both a club pro and a touring pro—sometimes straddling both worlds—and was well equipped to address the problems of both.

But when he heard about Louis's comments in San Diego, they must have hurt him deeply; he'd risen to captain in the army during World War II, not exactly serving on the front lines fighting

Hitler, but a part of the effort nonetheless. When he heard about the mushrooming uproar in San Diego, Horton Smith had been president of the PGA less than two months.

Bill Spiller and Eural Clark played in two qualifying rounds for the San Diego tournament. Clark failed to qualify, but Spiller shot rounds of 77 and 75 and qualified by two strokes. Whether he would be allowed to tee it up at the San Diego Country Club during the $20,000 tournament, with the likes of Tommy Bolt, Lloyd Mangrum, Jackie Burke, Jr., Cary Middlecoff, and, yes, Horton Smith, was still unclear.

Smith, meanwhile, had been playing at Pebble Beach with touring pros and was flying to San Diego to try to iron out the problems. "I do not know the exact situation, and we can make no ruling on anyone who wants to play in the tournament until I've talked with the other six members of the PGA tournament committee and with the cosponsors in San Diego."

But Louis had warmed to the task. He played a practice round of golf, or, more accurately, sloshed through a round because of the heavy rains that made the play difficult. It was his style never to raise his voice in anger, and as he spoke to reporters who flocked to hear him take on the PGA, he wore that expressionless mask that betrayed no emotion.

Louis evidently knew what to expect when he arrived in San Diego. In fact, according to his autobiography, he had gotten a message from Horton Smith a week before, telling him that he couldn't play. But he decided to force the issue.

"I didn't expect they'd let me play when I came down here," he told reporters. "But I wanted 'em to tell me personally. I want to bring this thing out into the light so the people can know what the PGA is."

And in a comment that he would have to back away from, Louis said it was all or nothing.

"I'm not asking for anything simply because I'm Joe Louis. I won't let them lift the restrictions for me alone. Either the others [Spiller and Clark] will be permitted to play or I won't play either."

Why hadn't golf even given it a chance—as baseball did, at first, with Jackie Robinson—and allowed one golfer to compete on the PGA Tour? "So far, the PGA has done nothing. Absolutely nothing."

San Diego Union sports editor Jack Murphy watched with admiration Louis's rise to the fight. In his column, Murphy said: "His features were composed in the familiar expressionless mask he wore while bearing in for the kill against Schmeling and Conn and Baer. In that, he was the Louis of old.

"But he is none the less determined, a fact of life instantly recognized by the PGA. Smith and other members of the PGA's tournament committee quickly perceived that, in Louis, they have drawn no ordinary opponent. And the odds are that Joe will achieve his goal. The PGA, dependent upon public good will, dares not resist."

Even as Louis spoke, sentiment was moving through the tournament committee, which included golfers like Jackie Burke, Jr., to leave the decision up to local sponsors whether blacks could compete. This was the policy the United States Golf Association had adopted years before. "I believe that's the solution," said Burke. "That's probably what we'll do. The sponsors should have the final say-so. They're giving the party. We're here as guests."

Burke, like a number of white golfers of his era, had at least one thing in common with most black golfers: he, too, had started in the caddie pen. Even as the son of a club pro who'd been imported from the East to teach the newly rich Texans in Houston how to play golf, Burke started as a caddie and learned at an early age how to play dice and about every other game of chance while he waited for his next bag. "It was sort of a twelve-hour gambling casino. I didn't need much more education than that I got in the yard," he said. He'd also seen a number of Negro caddies who could beat any of the club members, but who never made it out of the pen. Men he knew by their nicknames: Steptoe. Hungry Joe. Sweet Young. Even Shorty Flanagan, "a half-crippled black guy who could beat them all." As a kid, Burke hadn't been allowed in the clubhouse either. And now that he was, he seemed to understand the impatience of those who could play the game but were still on the outside.

"That had been brewing out there a long time," he said years later. "I've always taken the view that if anybody can beat me, let 'em tee it up. I proposed to the PGA, they've got to be out there. I want to play against the best guys out there. I lived that."

As it was, the San Diego sponsors, who had invited Louis, appeared to be blindsided by the PGA rule and were forced to post a notice to all qualifiers: "Due to the inability of the PGA officials to be present before start of qualifying round, all entries qualifying will be subject to official PGA acceptance. In the event of non-acceptance, entrance fee will be returned."

In other words, blacks had no free pass until Smith arrived from Pebble Beach to sort it all out. As Smith was flying to San Diego, Louis was telling reporters: "This is the biggest fight of my life."

When he arrived, Smith immediately met with Louis and some of the Tour players. His decision was that since Louis was an amateur, he could be invited by sponsors to play, but that since Spiller was a professional, his case would fall under the PGA's rules, including the "Caucasians-only" bylaw. In Smith's view, he was merely following the rules and could not unilaterally sidestep the PGA's constitution. But the language served to trap Negro professionals in a perverted circle of logic. Spiller could not play in the tournaments because he was not a member of the PGA. And Spiller could not become a member because he was not a Caucasian. No matter how many other conditions of PGA membership existed—getting the support of two current members, for example, and working in a pro shop for five years—there appeared to be one hurdle he could never overcome. As long as that constitutional provision was unchanged, Negro pros were in a catch-22. If one thing was immutable, it was a man's race, although some in desperation tried to hide it, escape it, and even shed it like a lizard skin.

Among them was a baseball player who played for Branch Rickey during his days as baseball coach at Ohio Wesleyan. The story goes that in 1904, the team traveled to South Bend, Indiana, to play Notre Dame. There, Rickey said, he had to loudly protest before the local hotel would register the team's only black player, Charles Thomas, and only under the provision that Thomas share a room with Rickey. When Rickey stepped into the room, he found Thomas trying to peel the skin off his hands. "Damned skin . . . damned skin! If I could only rub it off." From that moment, Rickey vowed to try to change things in his sport.

Smith had started the meeting without Spiller, but Jimmy Demaret came out and told him what was transpiring. Once inside, Spiller met face-to-face with Smith, who to Spiller was just another mouthpiece for an unjust and unfair policy that was holding him back. "That Horton Smith," Spiller told Al Barkow years later, "he could talk a hole in your head, and he started this meeting without me. See, I was the guy doing all the rebelling and I think they didn't know how to talk to me because I wasn't a yes man. The fact that I was more educated may have had something to do with it, too."

It had been four years since Spiller had sued the PGA, extracted some vague promises, and seen virtually no progress. He had heard enough gibberish, semantics, and double-talk. It was time for change, and most of the players understood something needed to be done.

"I just don't think we had the brightest people in the world running the boat," Burke said years later. "However, Horton Smith wasn't like that—he was a bit of a politician, he was slow moving."

The conversation between Spiller and Smith didn't last long, but it sent the room's temperature up several degrees. Spiller's outrage radiated heat.

As Spiller told it, he confronted Smith and demanded the PGA remove the Caucasians-only clause and allow Negroes a chance to get some club jobs, play on tour, and utilize the PGA's job-placement service.

"Yeah, we've got a job-placement service, but golf is social and semisocial and we have to be careful who we put on the job," Spiller said Smith told him.

At that, Spiller said, he looked at Smith and issued a challenge.

"Mr. Smith, I heard a rumor that you made a statement that if you were as big as Joe Louis, you would knock me down. Well, if I hated someone that much, I wouldn't let size bother me."

Spiller's readiness to fight, literally, for his place on the white tour must have provoked a rush by the others in the room to intervene before anything got started. But Spiller felt he was being talked down to, and he wouldn't accept the same old excuses.

As a parting shot, he reminded the group of the lawsuit he and Rhodes filed in 1948. Burke and Leland "Duke" Gibson, a tour player who was on the tournament committee, stopped him at the door, asking for time to work out something. "Sure, but if you don't, I'll see you in court," Spiller said he told them. "You ran over me the last time, but you aren't going to do that this time."

Joe Louis had hoped for a knockout, but he decided to take what he could get this round.

Because he had been invited by the sponsors and was an amateur, and thus not subject to the PGA's rules, Louis was allowed to play, and play he would. But Spiller couldn't let it rest. On Thursday, as the tournament was about to open, Spiller stood in the 1st tee box and prevented the tournament from starting.

The incident was said to be brief, ending when Louis and others successfully talked Spiller off the tee. It's not known what was actually said to Spiller, but tournament director Frank Caywood explained—again—that Spiller was not a member of the PGA and could not play. PGA officials kept repeating that Spiller did not fulfill all the requirements of membership. But Spiller knew that even had those been fulfilled, his race would have barred him. "I've heard all this before and it still doesn't make sense," Spiller said.

So, the tournament began. Louis readied himself to play with Horton Smith and Leland Gibson. But negotiations continued until moments before their tee time.

As Louis stood by, his secretary, Leonard Reed, conferred with Smith and other PGA officials, and got some assurances that something would be worked out for the pros. As to Louis's remarks that likened Smith to Hitler, Louis said they weren't meant to be personal. "I'm opposed to what Smith represents—prejudice."

Louis, for one, had good reason to believe he had forced the issue by his appearance, bringing his presence to a matter that had stalled. Years later, in his autobiography, he would say the PGA had blinked. "We won that battle. We started playing and before we finished one round of golf, we received over 100 telegrams congratulating us on getting a chance to compete with white golfers."

But Smith could claim victory as well. He had snuffed out the fuse crackling toward the public relations powder keg. Photographers snapped pictures of him and Louis, together, shaking hands, and smiling. And he said something could be worked out, perhaps by adopting a system to approve a supplemental list of Negro players who could play in some events, provided the sponsors and local clubs agreed.

As it was, the Louis and Smith group drew the day's largest gallery. After all, it was Joe Louis, the most popular black athlete ever. As the threesome made the turn at the 9th hole, Negro waitresses in the clubhouse jammed into the pressroom, which had a clear view of the 10th tee. "That's our boy!" someone exclaimed as Louis prepared to hit his drive.

Louis finished with a 76, and Smith shot a respectable 73, after a horrendous start with a 6 on each of the first two holes. After the round, a Negro woman who had been in the gallery approached Smith and addressed him.

"Mr. Smith," the woman told him, "I came here expecting to hate you and everything about you. But after seeing you, listening to you talk to Joe and hearing what you propose, I now believe that anything you do in this situation will be for the best interests of all concerned."

"I sure enjoyed myself out there," Smith said. "Played pretty well, too, once I got that other business out of my mind. You know, I'm a golfer—this PGA job is something extra. I don't make my living working for the PGA. I earn it playing golf."

For his part, Spiller could not contain his feelings. Where was the progress? "I'm greatly disappointed in Joe," he told reporters after Louis and Smith teed off. Later in the day, in the locker room after their rounds, players like Demaret, Paul Runyan, and Joe Kirkwood, Jr., said they thought Spiller had a good case. "I play for money," said Spiller. "Joe, here, he just plays for fun."

At heart, Spiller was a gentleman, but when he was provoked by some injustice, perceived or otherwise, he didn't care if he made people uncomfortable, and even golfers sympathetic to his cause, both black and white, felt he sometimes went too far. He would speak up when speaking up was considered uncivil. This was the early 1950s, still, years before the Civil Rights Movement had picked up momentum. In a sense, Spiller was ahead of his time, in that his style would have been better suited to the sixties, not the early fifties.

"Because in those days, they believed in gradualism, that eventually it would happen," said Al Barkow, golf historian. "Even Louis. But that was the attitude of establishment blacks. They sort of accepted the idea, well, in time. In time it will come, slowly, the gradualist approach."

To his credit, Smith would work that weekend to forge a compromise with the black golfers that could live long past San Diego. Whether it was the promise he'd made to Louis or Spiller's not-so-veiled threat to go to court again, the two sides agreed on a plan.

A committee of five Negro golfers would be formed to maintain an "approved list" of golfers who were qualified to play in tour events. The committee would include Louis and Teddy Rhodes, as cochairmen, and Spiller, Eural Clark, and Howard Wheeler.

Negro golfers would be invited to PGA cosponsored tournaments, provided the sponsors invited them and the host clubs approved them. They also must be endorsed by the PGA tournament committee, the group of touring pros who met with Smith when he dropped into the San Diego maelstrom earlier in the week.

Read closely, the change left it up to tournament sponsors and host clubs to determine whether they wanted Negroes to play. But it was a start, a small beginning that Spiller and Rhodes thought—mistakenly, as it turned out—they had achieved four years ago with their lawsuit.

The PGA tournament committee unanimously adopted the change. Smith, Burke, and Gibson were committee members, and they were already in San Diego. By telephone and telegram, Smith got the approval of the other members—Harry Moffitt, the PGA's secretary; Chick Harbert, a player from Detroit; and Clayton Heafner, a North Carolina touring pro who had helped Charlie Sifford coming up—for their votes. One member, Dave Douglas, of Wilmington, Delaware, couldn't be reached.

And Smith also conferred with Spiller, who warily agreed to give it a try, before the compromise was announced late Saturday afternoon.

"I'll go along with this until the [PGA's] national convention in November," Spiller told reporters. "Then I want to see something done about that 'non-Caucasian' clause. I know definite progress has been made."

And it had.

Already, the Phoenix Open had agreed to become the testing ground for the new regulation. Even though the host club and sponsors had signed a contract for the tournament long before, the tournament said it would abide by the new regulation.

On Sunday night, 9:00 P.M. Eastern, Walter Winchell put his own postscript on the San Diego affair.

"Joe Louis, the former champion, just sent word from the coast— that the unhappy incident [at San Diego] got good results . . . Horton Smith of the PGA has agreed for the first time to allow six Negroes to play in the Phoenix, Arizona, Open next Tuesday."

Indeed, a number of golfers headed to Phoenix the next week, and teed it up to try to qualify. Louis had asked for seven invitations and got them. Spiller, Rhodes, and Sifford were the pros, and Louis, Reed, Eural Clark, and Joe Roach were the amateurs. They drove across the desert to Phoenix to play in their first white tournament that wasn't one of the three "opens"—Los Angeles, Tam O'Shanter, and the Canadian Open.

As they pulled into the Phoenix Country Club, however, they realized that some things had not changed. Their privileges at the tournament, for example, extended to the golf course, and not the clubhouse. They would be unable to change or shower in the locker room. The segregation extended to the golf course. The seven Negroes were sent off in two groups, first thing. But it didn't matter; they finally had a chance to show what they could do.

Louis was given the honor of teeing off first, since he had brought the matter to a head in San Diego. Sifford, Reed, and Clark followed.

Their euphoria didn't last for one hole. On the green, Sifford went to take out the pin and looked down into the cup. His face contorted into a mask of revulsion.

"I had the flagstick half raised," he recounted in his book, *Just Let Me Play,* "but I shoved it back into the cup. Somebody had been there before us. The cup was full of human shit, and from the looks and smell of it, it hadn't been too long before we got there that the cup had been filled. Obviously, someone associated with Phoenix's fanciest country club had known who would be the first to reach the green—the black guys."

How could this have been done, in full view of the clubhouse, with scores of tournament officials and greenskeepers preparing for a tour event? As the rage welled up in the four golfers, play was halted for half an hour, until the cup was replaced. But the message had been sent: this is what you can expect, even on the golf course. It had its intended effect, at least on Sifford, whose concentration was so badly destroyed, he failed to qualify. Louis fired an 81, and also didn't make it. "What a crude, disgusting thing to do to people," Sifford wrote years later. "Damn, all we were trying to do was play a game of golf and make a little bit of money."

By the time they all finished—with Spiller, Rhodes, and Clark qualifying—they were reminded again how welcome they were. They headed for their cars in the parking lot, because they weren't allowed in the locker room. Sifford remembered that Spiller dug in his heels and announced he was going into the clubhouse after all, to take a shower. Even over the protests of the other golfers, who warned him not to make waves, Spiller went in alone.

Within ten minutes, a white official approached Louis and told him that something might happen to Spiller if they didn't get him out of the shower. "He suggested that somebody might try to drown Bill. Joe shrugged his shoulders and gave us a what-are-you-going-to-do? look," said Sifford. "He had to go in there like a big black cop and tell Bill to leave."

For what should surely have been a moment of triumph for the black golfers, they found that they weren't exactly welcomed with open arms. They had to stay in private homes in the "black neighborhood." Even as the black waiters at the clubs waited for them to come to the country club dining rooms, they weren't allowed in. Spiller argued with Joe and Teddy about using the dining rooms and locker rooms "and I had to promise them I wouldn't go in the clubhouse for a while, until things got better." As if they needed reminding that some things hadn't changed much, a radio announcer wore a Confederate cap while reporting results from the scoreboard.

Clark dropped out of the tournament after an opening round of 81. Spiller did not make the cut, after shooting rounds of 79-77. Teddy played all four rounds, with a 77-71-75-79–302, finishing twenty-eight strokes behind winner Lloyd Mangrum and well out of the money.

Not to be denied, the golfers headed to Tucson. At the El Rio Golf and Country Club, Rhodes, Sifford, Louis, Clark, and Reed all qualified. The headline was that a relative unknown, Henry Williams, Jr., won the $2,000 first prize with a six-under-par 274. The other story was Jimmy Demaret's adventure on the par 5 18th hole. Demaret hit five shots out of bounds, and finished with a 14 on the hole. "Never have I ever taken a 14 for one hole until today," Demaret said, before dropping out of the tournament. Reed and Rhodes made the cut, but finished out of the money at 291 and 293, respectively.

And that, effectively, was the winter tour for blacks in 1952—Phoenix and Tucson, and then home.

The Tour now swung south into Texas, where none of the golfers would get invitations to qualify.

That same year, singer Billy Eckstine, Sifford's patron, embarked on a thirty-five-date concert tour of the South with Count Basie, and he noticed changes rippling throughout the country. On his first tour in 1945, his audiences were almost entirely Negro and the prejudice was manifold. By 1952, more than half the listeners were white. And while the audiences were often segregated, there was no separation in New Orleans, Miami, and Columbia, South Carolina. "It's not the old South any more," Eckstine said.

There were no such illusions in the golfing world. When Jimmy Demaret told Spiller to forget about playing in the South, at least for now, he understood. Play everywhere else, but just don't go south. At least not yet. And they didn't.

Could the PGA have done more to expand the opportunities for Negroes to play in the South? No doubt, and it's a vexatious question that haunts the PGA today (and one its officials seem to have studiously avoided, instead preferring to trumpet the breakthrough of Tiger Woods). Realistically, the Tour depended on good weather to play golf, and thus the South and the border states were critical to the Tour during the early part of the year. But the South was where blacks were especially unwelcome, perhaps in danger, even on the golf course. In the early fifties, before the Civil Rights Movement had gathered steam, strict segregation was still a legal, political, and cultural reality. *Brown* v. *Board of Education of Topeka,* the landmark Supreme Court ruling that struck down the so-called "separate but equal" standard in public schools, was still two years away. Golf, like any business, relied on local support from fans and sponsors. When it came to the South, the PGA had neither the incentive nor the fortitude to effect similar social change in its small corner of the sports world.

As time went on, the compromise that had been reached in San Diego appeared to be not much of a compromise at all. The fact that a group of Negroes were appointed to approve the qualifications of other Negroes struck many as another vestige of Jim Crow. Who did these men think they were, passing judgment on the fitness of others to play? Had any other committee been needed to approve Negro athletes' qualifications in other sports—baseball, football, tennis?

"Not only is the acceptance of membership on this committee a disgraceful thing," wrote Russ Cowans of the *Chicago Defender*, "but when you add to this the fact that there are some members on the committee who are not qualified to pass on the 'character and manners' of a dog, then the whole thing has the fragrance of a dead dog."

Cowans wired telegrams to Spiller and Louis, urging them to decline membership on the committee. He also sent one to Horton Smith, denouncing the proposal. And his word carried some clout, not only because he was sports editor of the *Defender*, but because, for a time, Cowans had served as Louis's personal secretary, and was one of the first black reporters to provide extensive coverage of golf.

But he needn't have worried. The Negro committee would have little chance to make an impact. Few invitations came their way, other than from the three tournaments they had become accustomed to playing in over the years. San Diego was an exception, but according to Sifford, he was not allowed to play again at Phoenix and Tucson until 1959. Even Louis, as the only acceptable black for many tournament sponsors, got discouraged, and he stopped accepting most invitations.

The players, as usual, were forced to play where they could, and to wonder whether any black golfer could make a living, full-time, playing golf. As the decade of the fifties wore on, black golfers were lucky to get a chance to qualify in a meager ten to fifteen of the PGA Tour's schedule of more than forty tournaments per year.

The black tournament circuit was an option but couldn't feed a family. Rhodes and Spiller were pushing forty, an age when most tour players began making provisions for a soft landing at some country club. Sifford was several years younger, but he had passed thirty, no raw rookie. He was reaching his peak, with few places to show it.

9

Running to the 1st Tee

D r. Hamilton M. Holmes, Jr., his two sons, and a family friend
drove to the Bobby Jones Municipal Golf Course in Atlanta
and plunked down their money. But a leisurely round of golf was
not in the cards for them that summer day.

It was 1951, and Negroes were not allowed to play on public golf
courses in Georgia. But Dr. Holmes, his sons, Alfred "Tup" Holmes
and Oliver Wendell Holmes, and their friend Charles T. Bell decided to force the issue. And force it they did.

Dr. Holmes had made sure they had brought a lawyer along
with them. And, to rebut any arguments that Negroes had never
been admitted before, they sent a friend ahead to see whether he
would be allowed to play. He was a Negro, but sandy-haired and
light-skinned, and thus admitted without hesitation.

But their arguing did no good; the Holmeses and Bell were
turned away because they were clearly Negroes. And that rejection
launched the first in a series of legal challenges to a sinister web of
Jim Crow laws that were routinely invoked to bar blacks from
using public golf courses and other recreational facilities across
the South. Soon thereafter, in North Carolina, Florida, and Virginia,
blacks denied access to public courses chipped away at segregation
with lawsuits or protests, often getting arrested for their trouble.

What Dr. Holmes, his sons, and Bell could not predict was that
their simple act would result in a four-year fight before they were
legally entitled to play a public course in Atlanta. Their case would

land in federal appeals court twice and finally reach the Supreme Court of the United States before the issue was settled.

Even among some blacks in Atlanta, the lawsuit was considered an uphill fight. Tup and Oliver's sister Alice kept hearing from friends: "Why y'all doing this? Don't rock the boat. Try to talk Tup out of this; he's a hothead." A prominent black Atlantan who frequently did the mayor's bidding discreetly approached their lawyers and asked them to drop the lawsuit.

After futile discussions with the city, a lawsuit was filed in district court in 1953. It might have been resolved in 1954 had the four golfers been willing to accept a judge's ruling that, yes, they were entitled to play on public courses but under the "separate but equal" standard that had prevailed in America for more than fifty years. The judge ordered the city to come up with a plan that allowed blacks to play, and that also preserved segregation. The city came back with a solution: blacks could play on public courses every Monday and Tuesday.

But the men said no. They wanted to play every day, like anyone else. Their remaining option, a long shot, was the Supreme Court. The court had given them some reason to hope, with a decision just a few months earlier. That May, in *Brown* v. *Board of Education,* the Court had struck down the decades-old "separate but equal" standard in public education.

On November 7, 1955, the Supreme Court ruled against the city of Atlanta in *Holmes* v. *City of Atlanta,* in line with its rulings on desegregation, including a Baltimore case involving public bathing and recreational facilities. The Court sent the case back to the local federal court to determine how to end the segregation.

The mayor of Atlanta finally ordered the city to comply with the Supreme Court decision. "We have but two alternatives: to comply with the court order, or close down and cease operation of our golf courses," said Mayor William B. Hartsfield.

"Should we close the course, it would deprive nearly 70,000 white players and 100 city employees of their jobs and their rights in order to deny a few dozen Negro players the use of the golf links. Atlanta has never provided a separate but equal golf course for Negroes because such an expensive project could never be justified to our taxpayers in terms of the few Negro citizens who play golf."

The governor of Georgia, Marvin Griffin, was disgusted that the city had "chosen to throw in the towel," but he grudgingly acknowledged that there was nothing he could do about it. It was now inevitable; black and white folks would be playing on the same golf courses.

But not right away.

Dr. Holmes, who by that time was seventy-one and a respected physician in Atlanta's growing black middle class, had helped bankroll the legal fight but favored caution about exercising his newly gained rights on Atlanta's golf courses. There had been hints of trouble—including talk that some would pack guns in their golf bags in the event of protests. He himself had received a telephoned threat warning him to stay away from the golf course.

"We decided to put the game off completely," said Dr. Holmes. "We have plenty of time, and we'll wait until after the holidays. Some of my friends were anxious and suggested that we wait. We want to avoid friction."

But Tup, Oliver, and Bell would not wait. They were of a different generation, a bit more impatient than their elders. Tup, one of the best amateur golfers, black or white, in Atlanta, won the conference golf championship three times while at Tuskegee

Institute. He did not back down easily, having served as a union representative at Lockheed before he started selling insurance. Oliver, his older brother, was a World War II army veteran and an ordained minister. And Bell, a college graduate himself and a veteran, had become a successful real estate broker in his family's business, Bell Realty, which was housed in the Bell Building.

Tup and Charles had played many a round together, at the nine-hole Lincoln Country Club, one of the first black-run country clubs in America and an important social center for blacks in southwest Atlanta. As a golf course, however, it had its limitations, utilizing about thirty-five acres of unused land at Lincoln Cemetery. One of the holes swung down alongside the burial grounds. (Dr. Holmes and Tup are buried there.)

"Many times we would be shooting and it would end up alongside a grave," recalled Bell. "We'd have to say, 'Bless you, sister, bless you, brother, I have to shoot my ball.'" But the course wasn't much of a test: its holes were short, its greens small, its upkeep minimal. Those limitations and an unwillingness to improve the grounds, in part, drove Dr. Holmes, his sons, and Bell to look elsewhere in Atlanta to play.

On Christmas Eve, the men headed out to North Fulton, an eighteen-hole public course challenging enough to serve as tune-up for some of the pros who played the Masters in April. It had a nice clubhouse, a locker room, and showers. "As soon as we played, they pulled them out," said Bell. "They cut off the showers. At every one of the municipal courses, they cut 'em out."

When the men got out of their car in the parking lot at North Fulton, a white golfer who had pulled up moments earlier noticed them.

"He looked around and saw us; he got his pull cart, slammed his trunk, and ran up to the clubhouse ahead of us," Bell said. "He alerted the pro and others that we were coming. We just assumed he said, 'The blacks are coming,' or 'The niggers are coming.'"

At midmorning, the three teed off without incident. "They seemed to hit a good ball," said assistant pro Hank Whitfield. Right behind the threesome were two other Negroes, T. D. Hawkins, a bank teller, and Arthur Peterson, a real estate broker who worked at Bell's office.

The Holmes brothers said one group of golfers in front of them stopped, asked them how they were doing, and compared scores. Someone else told them, "Fellows, we are glad you are here."

Perhaps the biggest scare came on the 4th or 5th hole, when a crush of media found the golfers. From their standpoint, said Bell, the cameras looked ominous. "I thought it looked like a shotgun from a distance. But we didn't panic. They took pictures and asked us how we were playing. These white players—some were Jewish, some were Gentiles, they were upper middle class. They were not rednecks."

That afternoon, in the *Atlanta Journal,* the news story started this way: "Five Negroes played golf on Atlanta's North Fulton course Saturday."

In another time, that sentence wouldn't have had a shred of news in it. But in 1955 in Atlanta, no one needed to read the second sentence: "They were the first Negroes to play on a public course since the city was ordered on Thursday to open golf facilities to them."

What the newspaper didn't report is, that same day, other blacks played at some of the other municipal courses in Atlanta. "That was a fact, and that's what I strategized, playing on those other courses," Bell said. "They were dwelling on the people who initiated the suit. They forgot about those others."

Those others included Zeke Hartsfield, one of the best black golfers of his time. As a kid, he caddied for the great Bobby Jones at East Lake course, but found that he couldn't play much golf in the South. He and other blacks spent their formative years learning golf on a nine-hole course in Decatur, Georgia, that was built in the backyard of a black fortune-teller. And one day in 1939, Hartsfield wondered why it wasn't his right to play at Candler Park, just as it was the right of whites to play there. His boss, a white baker in Atlanta, urged him on. And Hartsfield teed off without incident and played two holes before he was reminded that he was different somehow. On the 3rd tee stood the police, ready to handcuff him.

"They had so many policemen over there, you'd have thought I'd killed somebody," Hartsfield said, laughing during a 1990 interview. "I was released after the owner of the bakery told them to let me go. They [the police] always listened to white men with a lot of money."

It wasn't until sixteen years later that Atlanta's public golf courses were desegregated. Hartsfield was living in New York with his wife, Birdie, and heard one afternoon that beginning the next day, anyone could play on Atlanta's public golf courses. A few hours later, he was on a night train to Georgia. He got a cab at the train station the next morning and went straight to Adams Park. He remembered running to the 1st tee.

Mayor Hartsfield, no relation to Zeke, tried to appease his white constituency by suggesting that the Supreme Court ruling applied only to golf courses, and would not be applied to the city's other recreational facilities. And the governor continued to sound the alarm that it wouldn't end on the golf courses; it was only the beginning.

"This is but a foretaste of what the people can expect in those communities where the white people are divided at the ballot box and where the NAACP holds the balance of power on election day," the governor said.

As for the Holmes brothers and Bell, they soon returned to the golf courses, and played one, then another, and another, until they had played every public golf course in Atlanta.

10

Just Another Golfer

Bill Wright nearly broke down into tears. He'd had a chance to qualify for the National Public Links Championship, and he'd blown it. It was 1959.

As he sat in the clubhouse at the Wellshire Golf Course in Denver, going over in his mind the thirty-six-hole qualifying rounds, the twenty-three-year-old Wright couldn't get two things out of his mind: his sorry performance on the final hole, and the promise he had made to his father that he would make it, that he would qualify.

Moments earlier, on the final hole, Wright had faced a short par-5 that left him an easy chance for a birdie and a good chance for an eagle, since he could reach the green in two. And he had reached the green in two, but three-putted for a par, and a thirty-six-hole total of 149. Wright knew that he needed a 148 to make it.

When he thought back over the last few days, his finish was no great surprise; he hadn't played well since he arrived in Denver from his Seattle home. In practice rounds, he had sprayed the ball and his putting touch had abandoned him. Steve Swain and Cliff Brown, two other guys he'd paired up with in practice rounds, had no trouble fleecing him for a couple of bucks each round.

The disappointment was most profound because of his dad, Robert Wright, who had patiently passed along his love for the game to his son. With his angular, six-foot-two, 175-pound frame and his athleticism, Bill would go on to play basketball at Western

Washington College of Education, and team with the great Elgin Baylor in Amateur Athletic Union (AAU) tournaments. But he had the raw tools to become a good golfer, and he had the attitude. After finally luring Bill out to the golf course during his son's sophomore year in high school, Robert Wright pointed out the junior champion.

Bill turned to his father and said: "Give me a year, and I'll beat 'em."

"It will take longer than that," his father said.

"Give me a year."

His father was right; it would take longer. But young Bill learned quickly, playing often with his father and picking up tips by watching the Seattle area's best golfers. The impatience of youth, however, always stirred just below the surface.

"I didn't take it seriously. My dad, he's calm, never blows up. But me? Well, I quit golf once because I just didn't have the maturity up here," he said, pointing to his head. "My dad was patient and I soon got over being temperamental about the game."And slowly, the game took hold. And slowly, Bill joined his father, Robert, as a golfer to be reckoned with at the public golf courses in the area.

Seattle was not insulated from the problems of access blacks faced all over the country. At the time, African American, Japanese American, and Chinese American golfers were forced to form their own golf organizations, because the clubs associated with the public golf courses would not allow them to join and play in their tournaments without first winning their own segregated tournaments.

Robert Wright often qualified for those tournaments, but it didn't deter him from trying to fight the segregation that plagued public golf in the Pacific Northwest. As a result, Wright was not the most popular man at Jefferson and west Seattle golf courses.

Robert and Bill Wright remained a formidable pair. Father and son had barely missed qualifying for the Public Links in 1958. And while Robert missed again in 1959, Bill made it through the local qualifying round. It made no difference to him that some of the white golfers who also qualified for Denver didn't want to get on the same plane with him or play a practice round with him. Bill had made it to Denver, and he was ready to make good on his promise to his dad.

The Public Links Championship was run by the United States Golf Association, the country's oldest national golf organization, which established the rules of golf in America and conducted a number of national championships, including the men's and women's U.S. Opens.

Unlike the PGA, it had no long, shameful legacy, no Caucasians-only clause. In fact, even in its early years, the USGA acted with some distinction, when president Theodore Havemeyer faced down a boycott against John Shippen and Oscar Bunn during the 1896 U.S. Open.

Nevertheless, the USGA, whose executive ranks were dominated by the white and wealthy, was in no great hurry to transform the game of golf into a redoubt of racial equality that outpaced other institutions of the times. Although Shippen ended up playing in several opens around the turn of the century, the USGA was marked by timidity in later years. In 1938, for example, the USGA's executive committee, chaired by president A. M. Reid, reviewed an entry for that year's U.S. Open. What survive are the committee's terse notes.

"An entry for the Open Championship was reported from Mr. James C. Hamilton of Rockville, Conn., a Negro. Mr. Reid said that

Mr. Lavitt had communicated with him regarding the entry; Mr. Lavitt apparently being the sponsor of Mr. Hamilton. On a motion by Mr. Sweetser, seconded by Mr. Rainwater, it was resolved that Mr. Hamilton's entry not be accepted."

No other records survive to elaborate on the discussion of Hamilton's entry. On the other hand, the minutes reflect nothing to distinguish his entry, and thus a reason for disqualification, except his race: Negro.

The USGA never adopted a racially restrictive clause, but it occasionally bowed to the unwritten rules of segregation that prevailed at many of its member golf clubs. In 1942, the Hale America Open tournament in Chicago, which was affiliated with the USGA, turned back the entries of seven Negroes. When the golfers appealed to USGA headquarters, the organization bowed to the wishes of the host club, Olympia Fields Country Club.

In 1952, the Miami Country Club informed the USGA "that it would not permit Negroes to compete in the 1952 Amateur Public Links Championship on its course."

Tacitly condoning the exclusion, the USGA refused to intrude on a member club's "prerogative" and submitted to the demand from Miami. That exclusion meant that some fine local Negro amateurs had their clubs taken right out of their hands. At the time, the Publinx, as it was known in its abbreviated name, was a national stage for many Negro golfers, who were relegated to public links and found few opportunities in the pro ranks.

Seven years later, a shy, lanky college kid out of the Pacific Northwest fashioned the most eloquent counterpoint to that most unsportsmanlike behavior in sport, during the Publinx in Denver, Colorado.

As Bill Wright sat alone, stewing over his disappointing per-formance, conversations from nearby tables began to penetrate his funk. "I made it!" said one golfer at a nearby table. But it couldn't be: the man's score was higher than Wright's! Bill slowly began to realize that he had miscalculated, and that the cutoff number wasn't 148, it was 150. He had slipped into the final field of sixty-four golfers, after all, and by one stroke.

Now, the college senior faced some of the best amateur golfers in the country. And from here on in, the tournament was match play—one-on-one matches that meant the winner advanced and the loser went home. With his little canvas bag that held only twelve clubs—two woods, nine irons, and a putter—Wright faced the daunting prospect of five grueling days to capture the National Public Links Championship.

For his first match, Wright would face one of the best amateur golfers in the field.

Mat Palacio, Jr., a forty-three-year-old car salesman from California, had barely missed being the low qualifier with rounds of 69-69, a far cry from Wright's two rounds of 74-75. As they stepped to the 1st tee, Bill was literally shaking from nerves. It was his first big tournament. Palacio, on the other hand, was a tournament veteran. At nineteen, he had won the California state amateur title, the north-ern California championship two years later, and the Pacific North-west tournament in 1941. As if he needed any additional incentive to win, Palacio was playing Wright on his fifteenth wedding anniversary.

It made no difference.

Wright quickly settled down and rediscovered his putting stroke. He birdied six of the first twelve holes and went on to overwhelm Palacio, 5 to 4. After the round, Palacio confided to Wright that he didn't intend to go home; he wanted to stay and watch the rest of the tournament. "Bill," Palacio said, "you're gonna win this thing."

Palacio also gave Wright a putting tip—"You got to slow it down a little bit"—and a caddie. Dave Bucher, a local high school kid who had been carrying Palacio's bag, now picked up Wright's little canvas bag. "I'd never had a caddie before, even in a tournament, and I wasn't sure I needed one then," Wright said later.

His confidence restored, Wright gained momentum with victories in his next three matches. He beat Bobby Kay, of Toledo, Ohio, 3 to 1; Wallace Smith, a forty-two-year-old police officer from Pontiac, Michigan, 3 to 2; and North Dakota State University golfer Don Kristofitz, 5 to 4.

Wright had won four 18-hole matches, and reached the semifinals, only to confront a former Publinx champion and a deep fear of the unknown.

Don Essig III had won the championship just two years earlier. He also was a member of the golf team at Louisiana State University, where athletes were prohibited from competing against blacks. Rumor had it that Essig felt compelled to call his school to get permission to play Wright, although Essig dismissed the talk. He was representing his hometown, Indianapolis, he said, and not LSU. Nevertheless, Wright was unsure how well he would perform, and whether he would encounter the kind of gamesmanship that could turn the match ugly.

He soon dispelled any doubt about his performance. Over thirty-six holes, Wright had twenty 1-putt greens, a mind-boggling accomplishment. Essig kept close as they came to the final hole. He was one down and needed to beat Wright on the hole to force a playoff. As they teed off, that prospect seemed more than likely.

Wright sliced his drive badly, and it arced straight for Colorado Boulevard, out of bounds and a penalty that would cost him a stroke and put him back on the tee again, hitting three. But the ball struck a tree and bounced back onto the course. Wright drained a twelve-foot birdie putt to halve the hole and take the semifinal match one up.

That set him up for a thirty-six-hole final with Don Campbell, a thirty-three-year-old insurance salesman and a former club pro, from Birmingham, Alabama, who had been reinstated as an amateur. Campbell was no tournament rookie either; he'd won more than thirty-five amateur events. And again, there was more to think about in a match with Campbell—another white golfer who came from the Deep South.

Earlier in the week, Cliff Brown, the promising black amateur from Cleveland, had barely lost to Campbell in a third-round match; Campbell had holed a birdie putt on the 2nd hole of sudden death. And Cliff Brown was no slouch.

He would go on to win the pro division of the UGA National in 1965 and compete for several years on the PGA Tour. Slender, with reddish hair and freckles, Brown was called Red Devil by some friends, as much for his fun-loving, hard-drinking ways as for his complexion. He also talked a good game. "Look here, look here," he would say to get someone's attention, "ain't no motherfuckin' thing that scares me," and then erupt into his trademark cackle that would fill a room.

Brown couldn't shake the disappointment he felt about his match with Campbell. In fact, Brown told Wright that it was more than that birdie putt in sudden death that beat him. Brown had once caddied for Campbell in Florida and hadn't been able to clear his mind of the notion that Campbell was still in charge, even when locked in a one-on-one match.

"I caddied for him, and I was still a caddie," Brown told Wright. "If you meet him later on, don't let him be in that dominant situation."

Wright brought no such psychological baggage with him to the match. While he sometimes hit his irons thin, sprayed his drives, and chipped too boldly, Wright's putter remained white-hot. He bolted out to a quick start, winning four of the first five holes, before Campbell started to chip away at the lead. But it was too late, and Wright prevailed 3 to 2.

"I was thinking of guys not being particularly nice to me," said Wright, referring to his two final opponents. "But I found Essig and Campbell very kind to me." When the two finalists entered the locker room together, and alone, Campbell shook Wright's hand again. "I have to hand it to you, Bill, that was a good round, and you withstood everything I had to dish out," said Campbell.

Thus, Bill Wright became the first black man to win a major tournament title in the United States.

He had become a crowd favorite over the week. Wright could sense the otherwise polite galleries were pulling a *little* bit harder for him. He had gained their respect for his sportsmanship, at one point politely rebuking the gallery for moving while Essig hit a shot, causing him to fluff it. "Some of you folks bothered him on that shot," Wright said to the fans. "It was very unfair. Please give him a better break so he can play his regular game."

He was the tournament rookie, at times unsure of the rules and protocol of a major championship. But at the end of a grueling week, which began with 18-hole qualifying rounds on Monday and Tuesday, followed by two 18-hole matches on Wednesday and again on Thursday and 36-hole matches on Friday and Saturday—167 holes of competitive golf in all—Wright stepped forward and took the Standish Cup, signifying the nation's finest municipal links golfer.

The ceremony was memorable not for what tournament chairman Emerson Carey said—he proclaimed Wright "another fine champion" in a long line of tournament winners—but for what he did not say. Carey never mentioned that the reserved young winner was a Negro, and the first Negro to win a major golf tournament at that.

Wright liked it that way. He had experienced a tournament that was about sportsmanship and fair treatment by officials, fans, and other players. For a week, it had been about golf, nothing else.

It was only when he got a phone call from his hometown paper that someone articulated that Wright's win was more than another name on a silver trophy. "How does it feel," the reporter said, "to be the first Negro to win the Public Links?"

"Call me back," Wright shot back, and hung up.

This wasn't about race. When he had stepped on the golf course each day, it finally felt like it was a fair world. Race—finally—did not seem to be a factor. Sure, he was the first Negro to win the National Public Links Championship, the first to win an integrated national championship of any kind. But for a week, on a Denver golf course in 1959, Wright's reality had been this: he was just another golfer, competing at the highest level, overcoming long odds, and finally prevailing.

11

"I Am Somebody!"

As if to signal a whiff of change in the air, golf gained an unlikely convert in 1961, a man famous for his cigars. And it was not Charlie Sifford.

Fidel Castro took a few of his buddies out for a round of golf at the Colinas de Villareal Golf Club, a course across the bay from Havana.

Politically and sartorially, it was a surreal event. Up to then, the Cuban revolutionary had treated the game with scorn, calling it the pursuit of the "rich and exploiter of the people." He was reported to have plans to convert the golf club into a workers' social center.

But this day, photographers captured Castro on the first green, clad in his signature olive-green military fatigues, beret, and black boots, an ensemble that would have made Teddy Rhodes and Jimmy Demaret wince.

And just like a foolish eighteen handicapper, Castro bragged about his game after winning the 1st hole. (His score was not reported by the state-run media.)

"I could win over Kennedy easily," he said about the U.S. president, who was known to have a pretty fair game, sometimes shooting in the 70s. Not to be outdone, his playing partner, Major Ernesto "Che" Guevara, won the 2nd hole and said he was sure he could beat former president Eisenhower.

Caddies who carried their bags told a different story: Guevara won the round with a 127 and Castro soared somewhere past 150. "They couldn't even beat you," sixteen-year-old Delio Rodriguez told a reporter.

Was it too much to dream that at a time when an avowed Marxist had taken up the most bourgeois of games, a reform, not even a revolution, might sweep through the ranks of American professional golf? Would the game, long held to be the province of the privileged and white, finally rebuke its segregationist language? Spiller, Rhodes, and Sifford could only hope so.

But golf in America always seemed a world removed from the changes in society as a whole, and decidedly so. Whereas in Scotland, golf was also a game for the middle class, in America, it was a game for wealthy gentlemen. Even as the decade of the sixties rocked virtually every other social institution in America, the upheaval caused barely a ripple in the country club establishment. Perhaps because of cost, investment of time, and demand for large tracts of carefully landscaped property, the golf establishment remained the province of the upper class. Other sports such as baseball, football, and basketball had no such requirements. If there wasn't a diamond, a field, or a court in the local public park, you improvised.

Some explain golf's aversion to diversity not as a prejudice, but as an inflexible rejection of change itself. Golf was rooted in tradition, and change could be a direct challenge to that tradition. In a sense, it represented status, and once attained, it must be protected, or risked being devalued.

"They were protecting tradition," said Bob Rickey, a sporting goods executive for thirty years. "There were a few deep Southerners, where prejudice influenced them. At that time, there were several presidents (of the PGA) in a row [who were] Northerners. Golf people are funny people, they are great traditionalists. Don't tamper with the game. It wasn't racial prejudice really. It was more tradition."

In fact, the PGA elected a new president every two years, and they came mainly from northern states. Were they bigots, or simply traditionalists who felt that one should wait while an entire society became accustomed to the idea? Was it naïveté? Because they saw no blacks at their clubs, how could there be a problem? Certainly, it was a circular logic that kept the PGA from changing.

As Teddy Rhodes talked to a writer from *Golf* magazine that year, he was giving most American golfers their first real exposure to black pros—not to mention Teddy Rhodes, arguably the finest black golfer of his time. Even the most avid follower of the PGA Tour probably hadn't seen a Negro compete and certainly hadn't watched a Negro golfer on television.

But that exposure had probably come too late, at least for Teddy Rhodes. He was now nearly forty-eight, and his health was beginning to fail him.

He continued to compete but had no false hopes. He had won, by rough estimates, 150 tournaments, mostly black tournaments. The most PGA events he had been able to play in was 11, in 1956, but he turned forty-three that year. In 69 Tour events, he finished in the money in 24 and had nine top-twenty finishes. The largest check he earned in a white event was $1,500, in the early fifties, for a fourth-place finish at the Labatt Open in Canada. He had shown flashes of what he could do—a first-round 70 in the U.S. Open in 1948—but he never had enough chances. His four UGA National pro titles—in 1949, 1950, 1951, and 1957—didn't begin to describe his impact among other golfers, both black and white.

He remained the most amiable and respected ambassador of the Negro pros, someone whose philosophy still, in 1961, was to accept progress wherever it could be found and leave no hard feelings. Now, years after Rhodes and Spiller had tried to push their way into white professional golf, Rhodes explained that he was more comfortable doing things another way:

"We colored pros make a great point of giving assurance with everything we say or do that we are not trying to force ourselves into the facilities, such as showers, men's rooms, bars, restaurants, or card rooms, at the various golf clubs. To do otherwise would provide the very material bigots seize upon. We always try to put over the simple truth: We will be content to be allowed to make a living at the thing we do best—playing golf. We will always be happy to find a place to eat and sleep where we will be welcome, and there are more such places all the time. Colored people are making great progress."

What was striking about these comments in 1961 was that while Rhodes preferred to stay out of the spotlight and take opportunities as they came, he stood out by virtue of his golf game and his behavior. His was not the broken-down caddie swing, but a smooth, effortless, and rhythmic pass, honed by untold hours on the practice range and by instruction wherever he could find it. Besides, getting angry can ruin most golfers' concentration, something Rhodes had found out for himself.

"Teddy told me that to get angry was the equivalent of losing your game," activist Maggie Hathaway told one writer. "Getting angry made him so nervous that sometimes he drew his putter back and couldn't bring it forward."

He was admired, and not just for his swing. He was a classy, sometimes flashy, but never garish dresser. He would have stood out nonetheless, because he cared about how he played and how he acted, not just how he looked. Sometimes he played the front nine in one set of clothes, disappeared into the clubhouse at the turn, and emerged with a whole new outfit in which to finish the round. He may have picked up that idea in his youth, when as a caddie at Belle Meade in Nashville, the club manager would change outfits every four or five hours.

"A sucker couldn't give me a suit at the store, not off the rack," said Joe Roach, Sugar Ray Robinson's golf pro for many years. "Slacks, the best of shoes, the best of everything. Ted was the same way. I was the same way. Even the guys that was supposed to be broke. They was still getting along as far as their appearance."

Teddy had a lot of nicknames, and one of them was Rags. It might have been for the clothes he wore as a kid. Another explanation is the more obvious reference to his penchant for matching his friend Jimmy Demaret, the dapper and gregarious white pro, as a sharp dresser.

For many, clothes were as deep as their style went. Not so with Teddy, and countless young Negro golfers took their cue from him.

"He always walked with his head up," said Harold Dunovant, who became a club professional at a number of golf courses. "Never seen him walk with his head down. Something like: 'I am somebody!' Ted, he did a lot to help my character. I think so, because I've always been a little mean type of person. My mother once told me, when I was seven years old, I wouldn't live to be twenty because I was too mean. 'Boy, somebody going to kill you before you get twenty years old.' The way he [Rhodes] carried himself, that influenced me. Aw, man, he was something else. Not only classy, he had personality. I ain't never heard Teddy knock nobody, say nothing bad about nobody. Ninety percent of those pros always knocking each other. All I ever heard Ted say was trying to help somebody."

To a whole generation of younger golfers, he had another nickname: Uncle Ted, that avuncular soul who always had time for others, even if they weren't worthy of it. Like his old boss, Joe Louis, Rhodes would typically buy a pair of golf shoes for himself and buy another pair for a younger golfer nearby. That included times when Rhodes gave some tough advice to younger golfers who had scraped and saved to get to a tournament, then missed the cut by a dozen strokes and came looking for Teddy for gas money to get back home. He'd give them the money but first give them some advice.

"Look, old buddy, I'm going to give you a certain amount of dollars and I'm gonna give you some advice. You go home and practice." And the unspoken message, delivered in a sympathetic package from Uncle Ted: "Don't come back out here until you got the game."

Rhodes, while he possessed just a fifth-grade education, was well spoken. "You would think he had a college education," Dunovant said. "I had never even thought about Teddy's education because I always thought he had one. He was never at no loss for no words, I'll tell you that."

And now that the professional golf world had opened up, time had passed Teddy Rhodes by. He was now the éminence grise of black golf. And the writer from *Golf* magazine put it to him straight.

Golf magazine: How good do you think your chances really are for winning one of the big tournaments?

Rhodes: To level with you, I think I have hardly any chance at all. They kept me standing around on the outside for too long—over thirty years. I'm now forty-seven and over the hill as golfers go. But I think I've contributed a little something to the struggle to have my people given a fair break in golf.

Rhodes betrayed no bitterness; it wasn't his nature. He was optimistic for the golfers who would follow him. He had grown up doubtful that any of his race would play in the same arenas with whites, in boxing, baseball, football, basketball, tennis, track. But he'd lived to see the likes of Joe Louis, Jackie Robinson, Jim Brown, Bill Russell, Althea Gibson, and Jesse Owens.

"We may yet see in golf what there has been in practically every other sport—a colored champion," he said.

12

"We Just Don't Want Them Near Us"

By this time, Spiller knew he was a marked man, for his audacity, for his refusal to take his medicine quietly, for his confrontational style. Years earlier, he couldn't wait for better opportunities to arrive for teachers in Oklahoma, and now he couldn't wait for the PGA to take its sweet time to let the best golfers—no matter their color—tee it up against each other. His directness led him to openly ask the questions no one else would. His impatience made him anathema to PGA officials, who branded him a hothead, a troublemaker.

One year at the Los Angeles Open, he asked the tournament starter why blacks were always paired together. The starter said it was because they had to deal with the players from Texas. Spiller shot back: "I thought this was the L.A. Open, not the Texas Open. If they don't want to play with us, tell 'em to go to hell back to Texas!"

The starter's microphone happened to be on, and Spiller's frustration echoed around the 1st tee and beyond. As he recounted the story decades later to Al Barkow, Spiller noted that the crowd clapped and whistled.

Not only was Spiller loathed by tour officials, but those who befriended him were warned that they weren't helping their careers any. "The PGA told me—I used to travel with Spiller—they told me to stay away from this guy," said Pete Brown. "They said if you ever want to try to play on the Tour, you got to stay away from this guy. He's bad news. They hated his guts."

Rickey, the MacGregor sporting goods executive, had met Spiller and befriended him in the fifties and given him and other black pros golf clubs. Rickey remembered attending a PGA meeting in California and encountering Spiller picketing a satellite golf tournament in Long Beach. Spiller was standing outside the entrance, with his clubs beside him, carrying a sign that charged racial discrimination.

"There's your goddamn buddy, leading the goddamn picket line," said some white pros, needling Rickey.

If there was added urgency, it was because Spiller wasn't a young man anymore. At forty-eight—the same age as Rhodes, although with fewer health problems—he had passed his physical peak as a golfer. It had been more than a decade since he and Teddy had sued the PGA. But he wouldn't give it up.

Whoever would listen, and even those who had heard his lamentations already, were subjected to his bitter broadsides against the PGA and its leadership. As an educated man—particularly in the early fifties, few of the white tour players had a college education—Spiller couldn't understand how the PGA felt it could put anything over on him.

He continued to play and to give occasional lessons at courses around Los Angeles, and to hold a series of jobs. He was raised at a time when any self-respecting man was always the provider—even though his wife, Goldie, held down a steady job with the water department. With three kids to feed, his pride and his family's needs made him force down another bitter pill: Spiller still caddied.

John Shippen
in 1913.

Bill Wright (left) accepts the trophy for winning the
1959 United States Golf Association Amateur Public
Links championship.

Charlie Sifford playing his way to the 1969 Los Angeles Open title.

The smooth swinging Ted Rhodes in 1948.

Bill Spiller, the man who challenged the Professional Golfers' Association's "Caucasians only" rule.

Pete Brown celebrating his victory at the 1970 Andy Williams San Diego Open.

In 1975 Lee Elder became the first black man to compete in the prestigious Masters tournament. Elder earned his way in to the competition by winning the Monsanto Open.

Joe Louis was a better boxer than golfer but his celebrity brought attention to the exclusionary policies of the PGA.

Calvin Peete won eleven PGA titles in the 1980s, a total surpassed only by Tom Kite.

Joe Louis (right) works on his putting stroke under the watchful eye of Bill Spiller.

Lee Elder celebrates his winning putt at the 1974 Monsanto Open.

Nat "King" Cole (right) presents the Roy Campanella Professional trophy to Charlie Sifford (center), winner of the North-South Negro Golf Tournament, as Ted Rhodes looks on.

Calvin Peete and caddie Dolphus Hull celebrate Peete's victory in the 1985 Tournament Players Championship.

George May, golf promoter extraordinaire, gives a final word of advice to golfers at the Tam O'Shanter tournament, one of the first competitions to invite the participation of black golfers.

Joe Louis in 1951.

Eural Clark (left), Ted Rhodes (center), and Charlie Sifford at the 1952 Phoenix Open tournament after Rhodes posted a score of 71.

The Spiller kids grew up on the west side of Central Avenue, on East 122nd Street, in a postwar tract house Bill bought with $7,000 he had won from Joe Louis on the golf course. Pamela, the only girl and the youngest, was treated differently from Bill junior, the oldest and first son, or even James, the middle child. She was Daddy's girl, and she preferred to go shopping with her dad because he would get her what she wanted, while Mom would be more practical.

When Dad was home, the TV or the radio was always tuned to sports, but he was usually out, since they lived just a few miles from the Western Avenue Golf Course, where Dad played. Pam wasn't allowed to play golf. She went to a few tournaments, but her relationship with the game was distant and it was something her friends would tease her about, that her dad played a lazy man's sport.

"All you do is walk around and hit a ball," they'd tell her, sneering.

But still, he had the time to spend with her, even to go to PTA meetings at her school. "He was Mother of the Year," Pam said. "Since he had the time, he got the award."

It was a warm relationship, but one that did not include lots of talk about other things. No frank talk about family finances. She never really knew her parents' ages. And when Bill junior read Alex Haley's *Roots*, and tried to trace the family tree, his mother wouldn't talk about it and his father couldn't. "He was from that generation; we were told what to do, and you didn't ask questions," Bill junior said.

As the firstborn son, Bill junior was born into a whole different set of expectations than his brother and sister. He constantly heard the old bromides, especially how kids had it so much easier nowadays.

Over and over again, the father told the son about his fight to play golf, about sticking his neck out to no avail. But what young Bill didn't understand until later was how that fight bred a bitterness that dominated the family's life.

"I grew up with that, but I didn't understand it. I didn't know why he was angry, come home angry, be slamming things, throwing things, breaking things, yelling at my mom, yelling at us. And it was all because he'd had a bad day. I didn't know why, then. Later on, you look back and you're told things."

When Bill senior took his oldest son out to play golf, Bill junior resented it, because it wasn't something he wanted to do. On the golf course, however, he saw his father transformed; for Bill senior, a good day on the golf course was a great day. The golf course was where Spiller was in his element, where his passion was expressed, where he excelled.

As a young kid, Bill junior was often the fifth in his dad's foursomes, with people like Charlie Sifford and Teddy Rhodes and Pete Brown. He liked Charlie because he smoked those cigars. He liked Teddy because he always had a nickel for candy, and because he talked *to* you, not *at* you. And Pete, man, Pete could hit the golf ball farther than all of them. They played at Western Avenue, and later at Rancho Park, and then at Hillcrest Country Club.

Spiller was not a member at Hillcrest, but it was a place that treated him well and allowed him to make some money under the table, by caddying and giving some lessons, unofficially. Also, it was a place that knew about exclusion. It was a country club started by Jews in Los Angeles who weren't welcome elsewhere.

"I played with just about everyone that was famous," Bill junior said, "but the only reason I did was, I was a little kid that no one minded. My dad would bring me. 'This is my son and he can play and I'm proud of him.' I remember riding in limousines with Lucille Ball and Desi Arnaz and playing with Jack Warner and Tony Curtis and Kirk Douglas."

Hillcrest was a place where Bill junior could play and caddie a little himself. He got to know the sons of members and played in tournaments with them. When he turned thirteen, they even threw him an honorary bar mitzvah at the Wilshire Temple.

At the golf course, young Bill took some pleasure in watching his father, because there, Spiller was recognized as good at what he did. Friends and hangers-on would gather around Bill senior, and they appreciated him, understood him, valued what he did.

"He really had a love for the game," said Bill junior. "He was a Jekyll and Hyde personality. When he was on the golf course, everything was right, even if he was having a bad day. At the snack bar on the ninth hole, I could eat whatever I wanted if he was having a good round. And then we would spend *hours* in the clubhouse afterwards, with him holding court."

There were some bad days. One of them was when young Bill, at age thirteen or fourteen, finally beat his father at golf by shooting a 72 or 73. There was no rite-of-passage pride from Bill senior, rather an anger from someone who never liked to lose, didn't know how to lose, even to his firstborn.

For his part, young Bill began to resent playing a game he didn't choose, and being told what to do. This was no different, in many ways, from most father-son relationships. The father had his idea of what the son should be doing with himself, so why not take him to the office, as it were, and teach him a few things?

There was something else going on, too. Young Bill, playing with his father, became part of the hustle. He was a perfect cover. Who would think a father, out for a friendly game of golf with his young son, would be looking to hustle the other members of a friendly foursome? "I didn't know this until I was an adult and thought about it," Bill junior said. "That's why I was there!"

At Hillcrest, Spiller was hauling a member's bag one day when he was asked why he wasn't trying out for the Tour. Harry Braverman's question triggered Spiller's sad tale, but this time he got more than just sympathy. Braverman said he had a friend who might be able to help. Spiller should write a letter to Braverman's friend, Stanley Mosk, the attorney general of the state of California.

For years, blacks had to fend for themselves when they challenged the status quo. Spiller and Rhodes, of course, filed their ill-fated lawsuit in 1948. Sifford said he had consulted Joe Louis and Billy Eckstine about the possibility of a lawsuit, and at one point, the NAACP had approached Sifford about filing a lawsuit, according to former tour official Joe Black.

Things seemed different now. In fact, a number of people made sure that the issue received increasing attention and wouldn't fade into the background.

Jackie Robinson, for one.

Robinson, retired from baseball, had found his voice against discrimination through his syndicated newspaper column. And sometimes he wrote about golf, a game he loved to play but viewed as a last vestige of outright racism in sports. And Robinson's voice lent more momentum to the cause, specifically a move to grant Charlie Sifford membership in the PGA. In 1960, he wrote that it was time the U.S. Civil Rights Commission look into the PGA's exclusion.

"Undoubtedly, the time has come for action," Robinson wrote.

Sifford was sometimes referred to as the "Jackie Robinson of golf," a title he alternately declined and accepted. Sifford once said his task was tougher than Robinson's because Jackie played a team game, while Sifford played in a game of individuals. It was another comment by Charlie that rankled other blacks, Spiller among them, who had been fighting for acceptance and suffering greater consequences for their activism.

In some ways, though, Sifford was right. Jackie had Branch Rickey, a white man who was part of the baseball establishment and wanted to change the sport from within. And Rickey prepared Robinson, as much as he could, for his trial by fire in the big leagues. When he first summoned Robinson to his office, Rickey fingered a copy of Papini's *Story of Christ*, and asked Robinson if he could turn the other cheek, not fight back, when other players hurled the worst slurs at him.

"Mr. Rickey, do you want a ballplayer who's afraid to fight back?" Robinson asked.

"I want a ballplayer with guts enough not to fight back," Rickey replied.

After Jackie's first season with the Dodgers, though, Rickey released him from that edict to always turn the other cheek. Suddenly, Robinson was arguing bad calls with umps, jawing back at players in the other dugouts.

That competitive fire did not wane on the golf course. During a round with black amateur Eural Clark, Robinson and Clark were waiting in the fairway for a foursome that was taking its sweet time on the green. As Clark remembered it, the hole was the par-5 he could reach in two shots. Impatient by the dithering up ahead, Robinson ordered Clark to hit anyway, and his ball rolled up onto the green. As Clark and Robinson watched, one of the beefier members of the group scooped up Clark's ball and tossed it off the putting surface.

"C'mon," said Robinson to Clark, who saw in Robinson's eyes what big-league catchers saw when he came barreling for home. "I'm gonna get this big sucker, here."

"Jackie got up in this cracker's face," said Clark, "and said, 'I want you to go get that ball and put it right back where it was.'" After a few tense moments, some mumbling and muttering under his breath, the man did just that.

What Robinson also realized, without Rickey telling him so, was that he had to be better—in every part of his life, and not just as a ballplayer. Black sports historian Doc Young, writing about baseball in 1945, said that "after [centuries] of residence in America, the Negro had to be college-bred, one of history's greatest all-around athletes, as honest as Jesus, as clean as laundered white-on-white, as pure as Ivory, as emotionless as the Sphinx, as cool as the Sky Blue Waters . . . merely to get the chance to play the sport which had, before him, boasted of all sorts of people of foreign extraction, rowdies, drunkards, temper tantrum throwers, wastrels, and called them heroes because they could hit a ball or catch a ball or field a ball."

Another piece of advice Rickey gave Robinson was that he marry his girlfriend, Rachel Isum, whom Jackie had met at UCLA. (In early 1946, they did get married.) Rickey was prescient enough to recognize a powerful sexual undertow that could potentially scuttle his whole plan for Robinson. Black men posed a threat to white men.

The threat was no less powerful in golf, where, unlike major sports such as football, baseball, and basketball, fans wandered around on the playing field and could get quite close to the players. In addition, golfers usually had the run of the clubhouse—bar, locker room, dining room—where they routinely rubbed elbows with their fans. Intrinsic to golf was the social aspect, which the major sports never had to consider. Football, baseball, and basketball players returned to their insulated world, their own locker room where the outside world was barred, once the game was over. Not so in golf, and it was a considerable subtext for PGA officials.

Doc Young remembered a meeting at a Southern California country club with Spiller, Rhodes, Sifford, and "several liberal PGA members," who said the social aspect of the game was the toughest obstacle in their effort to help the black pros. "These liberals, including one or two PGA officials, actually respected Sifford, Rhodes, and Spiller, the latter a college man, personally and professionally," Young said. "'We'd love to have you play,' was the gist of what they said, 'but . . .' They didn't have to diagram the *but*."

It's no wonder that Spiller's decision to crash a country club dance after the Bakersfield Open one year was considered not just bold, but dangerous. The black players were not allowed in the clubhouse, but Spiller went back to his motel, showered, put on a coat and tie, and returned to the club.

"He went into the clubhouse and asked the [club] president's wife to dance with him," said Frank Snow, one of Spiller's golfing friends. "He said she got up to dance with him."

It wasn't talked about much, but a widespread view went something like this: Even if you decide to let 'em play, don't let 'em socialize. (Black players routinely changed clothes out of the trunks of their cars, because the clubhouse was off-limits to them.) No telling what it could lead to.

"I think it's that old philosophy, the thing that had a lot to do with Jackie's entry," said Sam Lacy, the eminent sports columnist for the *Baltimore Afro-American*. "They were afraid that a black guy coming into what was normally a white culture, what had been for so long, that he was going to be disruptive or chasing people he shouldn't chase—women. . . . Branch Rickey said, 'Marry the girl.' Just like that. And that was the reason, because he knew that society was going to be rebelling if Jackie came in and was a potential pursuer."

If it wasn't clear enough, a 1963 *Newsweek* magazine poll plumbing Americans' feelings about race relations quoted one California woman with startling bluntness: "We don't hate niggers," she told an interviewer. "We just don't want them near us."

The history of blacks in professional golf is not simply an unending struggle for acceptance on the white tour. It includes the effort by black teaching professionals to make golf more accessible to anyone, black or white, who wanted to learn the game. Among them was Harold Dunovant, a bear of a man with a booming voice who accompanied James Black and Junior Walker out to Los Angeles in 1963. When he was made an assistant at Western Avenue in early 1964, the *Afro-American* headlined its story: "L.A. Club Hires Tan Golf Pro." Dunovant would eventually hold either assistant or head pro positions in California, Ohio, Louisiana, New York, and North Carolina.

In Nashville, there was Joe Hampton, who as new head pro, helped open the city's first golf course to blacks in the 1950s, a nine-hole spread called Cumberland. He remembered his remarks at the opening ceremony to be short and sweet: "Regardless of race, creed, or color, I want everybody to come out here and play this golf course." He later saw Cumberland transformed into a championship-quality eighteen-hole course that was named after his longtime friend Teddy Rhodes.

And in Chicago, Robert Horton was still teaching students in 1999, after sixty years as a golf instructor. At age eighty-one, Horton was patiently correcting his students' hooks and slices at the Joe Louis Driving Range.

Among this group was a man known to his friends and students simply as Loosh.

Lucius Bateman, who taught at a driving range in Alameda, hard by the San Francisco Bay, took a scrawny little white kid named Tony Lema, gave him a job at the range, and helped turn him into "Champagne" Tony Lema, who won the British Open in 1964 and was headed for a sterling career until his 1966 death in a plane crash. There were dozens of other kids like Lema, and Bateman was never one to turn his back on a kid who asked for his help. To some of them, Bateman was the closest thing to a father figure they had.

"If kids who don't have any money ask for my help, I give them all I can," he told an interviewer once. "I just ask them for one thing in return: to try. I do the rest. I get to know them and they get to know me."

Born in Louisiana, Bateman soon moved with his family to Biloxi, Mississippi. When he was old enough, he began caddying at the Edgewater Hotel and Golf Club there, and eventually became a solid player while he worked his way up to becoming head caddie master.

After a hitch in the Air Force, he returned to Mississippi to polish his golf game and try the Tour. He soon realized there were no opportunities on the white tour and moved to the Bay Area, which he'd visited while in the Air Force. While a shipyard welder in San Francisco, Bateman made his mark on local golf courses.

In fact, the same week in 1948 that Spiller and Rhodes were denied entry to the Richmond Open, Bateman was down the road a few miles, matching the course record at Alameda Municipal Golf Course, shooting a 63. The pro there asked him to help with the junior golfers, and that eventually landed him the teaching job at Airway Fairways, the driving range along the east edge of San Francisco Bay.

"His passion was teaching, managing that place, but more importantly he loved kids," said Dick Lotz, who played on the PGA Tour from 1964 to 1977. "He was not a married man, but he loved kids and liked to teach kids."

At age twelve or thirteen, Lotz met Bateman, and eventually went to work for him at the range, enduring the sour face Loosh made when he saw Lotz swing a golf club. Lotz's older brother John was already working there. Lema, John McMullin, and the Lotz brothers were just a few kids who were turned into good golfers by Bateman. To those kids, he was much more than a golf teacher, this mild-mannered man in the white Hogan cap; he was an ambassador for the game and a role model.

"Some of the kids who worked the range might have been troubled kids in the community," said Dick Lotz. "He would go down and bail 'em out and give 'em a job and try to get 'em on the right track. He was more than just a golf guru."

In 1965, Bateman told a reporter that his main regret was not being able to interest many black kids in the game. "Colored boys don't think it's their sport. When Joe Louis was heavyweight boxing champion, all of the colored youngsters wanted to be fighters.

It would be the same with golf if a Negro pro came up who could rival Arnold Palmer."

Ironically, the few black kids who did show up at the range eventually stopped coming, said Lotz. One of the fathers explained that he would be ostracized, bringing his kid to a man whose only interest was teaching a white man's game.

Bateman must have shaken his head. He had been denied opportunities to play professional golf back in Mississippi because he was black, he had been passed over for pro jobs at country clubs because of his race, and he had been denied membership in the PGA because pros at driving ranges didn't qualify. What he wanted to do was teach the game to any kid who would listen and work hard. Dick Lotz was one of them. "He was like my second father," Lotz said.

Black golfers had another ally, whose persistence was inspiring and occasionally irritating. Maggie Hathaway seemed to be the only one who knew it was the sixties on the lush, tree-lined fairways of professional golf. She was a wakeup call to tournament directors and white golfers who evidently hadn't heard of Dr. Martin Luther King, Jr., or civil rights marches and protests.

A slender copper-skinned woman with the erect bearing of a stage performer, Hathaway came to Los Angeles and tried to become a movie star. The daughter of a Methodist minister, she grew up in a place that was not on most maps of Louisiana, where, she claimed, they didn't keep birth certificates of blacks, where they wrote your name and birthdate in the family Bible, where people could be a gumbo of black, Choctaw Indian, and whatever other strains wove through their family tree. What hers yielded was a proud, dignified, and sometimes irascible woman who became one of golf's few activists.

She landed some small parts in a handful of movies. And her most memorable moments on screen might have been as Lena Horne's legs. Miss Horne was a beautiful woman, but it was Maggie's legs when the script called for a shot of the star's legs.

One day, Maggie went out to Griffith Park Golf Course, met Joe Louis, and fell in love—with golf. She'd never picked up a club in her life, but Louis made her a wager: hit a shot up onto the green, and he would buy her a set of golf clubs. It was one of those bets that Joe didn't mind losing—he had helped lots of golfers by losing to them rather than giving them handouts. But Maggie had found a game she would love for life, and soon learned there were injustices to fight.

With her friend Sammy Davis, Jr., she helped establish the Beverly Hills branch of the NAACP. And when she went to work as a golf writer for the *Los Angeles Sentinel* in the early 1960s, she added press credentials to her Screen Actors Guild card. She also found a soapbox.

When she applied for membership in the all-white Western Avenue Women's Golf Club and she was rejected, her friend County Supervisor Kenneth Hahn talked her out of a lawsuit, but he moved to suspend the activities of such clubs at public facilities until they accepted blacks. When the women finally relented, however, Hathaway was not among the golfers admitted.

She began picketing golf tournaments in California in 1955, except the L.A. Open, which had allowed blacks to play since the forties. Still, her press credentials as the *Sentinel*'s golf columnist provided her an opportunity to make Palmer and Nicklaus and Player and any number of other pros squirm, by asking questions about race relations and discrimination:

"Why don't you help Sifford and Spiller and Rhodes get into the PGA?" "Will you vote for Sifford to get into the Masters?" "Mr. Player, how does it feel to play with blacks in America?"

She fought for Spiller and she fought for Sifford and anyone else who didn't get fair treatment. When crooner Bing Crosby neglected to invite Sifford to his annual "clambake" tournament up the coast in Carmel, she threatened to picket. The negative press caught Crosby by surprise. "I lost his friendship when we picketed," she said. But the next year, Sifford got his invitation and Crosby invited the Mills Brothers when he couldn't find any white pros who would play with him.

In her column for the *Sentinel*, called "Tee Time," she delivered her own pastiche of news, plaudits, opinions, asides, and admonitions about the golf world and those who traveled in it. Along the way, with Sammy Davis, Jr., she began the NAACP Image Awards, which were televised across the country to recognize excellence by blacks in various fields of endeavor.

And she had, as she said, a twenty-four-hour-a-day job, leading picket lines, taking pictures, writing columns, trying to get Charlie Sifford and Pete Brown and Bill Spiller and Teddy Rhodes and Lee Elder into tournaments. Sometimes, she lent an ear to Spiller and his problems, over a drink at the Western Avenue Golf Course. "Maggie, I'm an educated man. I have a degree. Why can't I play?"

"But this man couldn't play golf; he was a redcap down at the train station," said Hathaway, sitting a few feet away from where she and Spiller had sat. "He was embarrassed. He stayed angry. He lived angry. He was hurt day and night. He never stopped complaining that they wouldn't listen. Plus, he kept playing."

And Hathaway kept pushing, pushing for answers, pushing for results, pushing for fairness. "She was a dude, I'll tell you," said former touring pro Jackie Burke, Jr., with admiration. But, like many who push, she wasn't universally respected, even among blacks. She was like Spiller in that she couldn't keep quiet about unfairness in golf, and some couldn't abide her for that reason. Bill Wright, the 1959 Publinx champion, said Hathaway, like Spiller, was unfairly branded as contributing to the problem. "You're causing all these problems for us," they would say. "Bill, if you be quiet, Maggie, if you be quiet, they would let us in."

But Maggie, like Spiller, couldn't be quiet, not about this.

Sifford may have been the first to seek the help of California attorney general Stanley Mosk, sometime in 1959. He had been introduced to Mosk at Hillcrest by Billy Eckstine, and he later spelled out his problems with the PGA in a letter to the attorney general. "He merely asked me to help him," Mosk said.

According to Sifford, Mosk contacted the PGA to confirm that they openly discriminated against blacks according to their own bylaws. If so, Sifford, as a resident of California, was a victim of that discrimination, unless the organization could show that there were reasons other than race for his exclusion from the PGA.

Within months of having met Mosk, Sifford said, the PGA offered to make him an approved tournament player. Whether there was a direct connection between Mosk's interest in the PGA and Sifford's changed status is unclear. But the organization must have realized that Mosk, as California's chief law enforcement officer, could make things very uncomfortable. The PGA was also getting a constant drubbing in Jackie Robinson's nationally syndicated newspaper column. J. Edward Carter, the PGA's managing director, told Sifford, "Robinson hit us pretty hard, didn't he?" In fairness, Sifford had his supporters within the PGA. Dugan Aycock, a

North Carolina professional on the PGA's executive committee, had known Charlie since Sifford was a ten-year-old caddie, and felt he deserved to play in PGA tournaments. And Carter apparently offered to line up paid exhibitions for Sifford and assist him with problems in the South.

The PGA wasn't making Sifford a member, but offering the kind of tournament-playing privileges it had granted to the postwar wave of pros who hadn't worked in pro shops and only wanted to play on the Tour. The approved-player classification could be granted to golfers who were sponsored by two PGA members and had the game to compete on the Tour. Then each application was given a case-by-case review. For more than a decade, Sifford said, he had met those conditions, but for some reason, he had not passed the review.

Once granted, a pro could become a full member of the PGA after five years, provided he had played in at least twenty-five tournaments each year.

Sifford had earned it. He was the most consistent black professional in the game and had already won an unofficial PGA event. In 1957, after a sudden-death playoff with Eric Monti, Sifford captured the Long Beach Open and a $1,700 first prize. It allowed the Siffords to put a down payment on their dream house in Southern California.

And beginning in 1960, Sifford tried to make the most of it. He was able to play in seven tournaments at the start of the year, including the Crosby and in Palm Springs, and finished in the top fifteen on four occasions. But toward the end of February, he was forced to head back to Southern California, because tournaments in Baton Rouge, New Orleans, Puerto Rico, Pensacola, St. Petersburg, Palm Beach, and Wilmington, North Carolina, refused his applications to play. The southern swing of the Tour still seemed off-limits to a black player, even a card-carrying black player, and that made it nearly impossible to play those required twenty-five tournaments a year.

But in early April, a small crack appeared in the wall.

Sifford got a call inviting him to play in the Greater Greensboro Open. Mostly through the efforts of Dr. George Simkins, head of the local chapter of the NAACP and an influential figure in Greensboro, North Carolina, Sifford was invited to play at the Sedgefield Country Club and thus become the first black to play in a PGA tour event in the South.

"We know Charlie and we like him," said a spokesman for the tournament. "We think the time has come to do this. We're not looking for special honor or credit and we do not want to make a big to-do. We prefer to consider Sifford's try the normal, proper thing and let it go at that."

But, of course, it was a milestone, and it wouldn't pass by unnoticed.

It was a moment mixed with both exhilaration and fear of what could happen to a high-profile—uppity, to some—black man in those parts. Sifford said he probably wouldn't have accepted, but for his wife, Rose. "This is what you've worked for," she said. "You will do fine."

And she was right. On a wet and windy first day, Sifford fired a three-under 68. He was the first-round leader of the Greater Greensboro Open.

Sifford was relaxing that night, staying in a private home, when he got a telephone call. As he described it in his book, *Just Let Me Play,* the caller had a white man's southern accent.

"Charlie Sifford?"

"That's me."

"You'd better not bring your black ass out to no golf course tomorrow if you know what's good for you, nigger. We don't allow no niggers on our golf course."

"I tee off at 10:15 in the morning. You do whatever it is you're going to do, because I'll be there."

"You'd just better watch out, nigger."

Click.

Sifford, nonetheless, showed up the next day and teed off at 10:15. Within moments, he heard the voice he'd heard on the phone the night before. "Nice shot, Smokey. How ya going to play the next one?" What followed was a round in which a dozen hecklers followed him from the 1st hole until the 14th, when the police came to take them off the course. At times, they would stand within a few feet, screaming at the top of their lungs. They yelled taunts in the middle of his backswing, surrounded his ball with beer cans. Although a PGA official joined Sifford a few holes into the round, admonished the hecklers, and stayed between them and the golfer, their taunts echoed across the fairway. And, in Sifford's memory, the rest of the gallery stood silently by.

At the end of the day, Sifford fell out of the lead and into third place, with a one-over 72. Sifford has called it one of the greatest rounds of his life, under the circumstances.

He finished out the tournament with scores of 70 and 75 to finish fourth and collect $1,300, a decent payday for any pro. "My job's tougher than Jackie Robinson's was," Sifford told reporters. "He had a set salary. I have no sponsor. I have to finance my own way. He had a team backing him. I'm playing alone."

He put his clubs in the trunk of his Buick and drove to Texas, for the next week's tournament in Houston. He thought he had earned his stripes on the PGA Tour, after the week he had had in Greensboro. He had seen the worst, and he had survived, even succeeded.

At the end of his two-day drive, Sifford walked into the clubhouse at the Memorial Park Golf Course, a public course in Houston where the $40,000 Houston Classic was held. And he was told the sponsors didn't want him to play there, and there was nothing the PGA could do about it. No one had bothered to tell Sifford in Greensboro, before he had made the long drive, locking his car at night to sleep on the side of the road. No one seemed to care that he had a PGA card to play. What could he do? Sue them? A group of Negroes picketed the golf course during the tournament because of his exclusion, but Sifford decided he would drive on to the next tournament, the Texas Open invitational in San Antonio.

This time, he didn't even get past the gate, where the guard didn't have to check the list of players before turning Sifford away. Sifford turned around and drove home to California, no doubt thinking not so much about how far he had come, but about how far he had yet to go.

13

Four Fewer Words

Stanley Mosk wasn't a golfer; tennis was his game.

But his interest in golf would help provide momentum for the reform that blacks had been seeking for decades. As the highest law enforcement official in the state of California, he had an opportunity to effect change. And Mosk, for black golfers, turned out to be the right person in the right job at the right time.

A white liberal who would ultimately ascend to the California Supreme Court, Mosk had a track record that gave encouragement to blacks. In the 1950s, as a superior court judge in Los Angeles, Mosk had ruled a deed's restrictive covenant against a Negro couple to be un-American. As attorney general—and a popular one at that, having been elected in 1958 with more than a million-vote margin—Mosk had the power to make things very uncomfortable for the PGA, especially with the championship due to be played in Los Angeles in 1962.

The year before, he had taken the bold step of warning the PGA about sponsoring racially restricted tournaments on public golf courses in California. Such tournaments using public facilities in California, said Mosk, would be blocked.

It was a move that already had consequences in California. The Southern California delegation to the PGA faced the cancellation of its thirty-seven-year-old sectional tournament because of Mosk's edict about public courses. In the fall of 1960, the delegation went to the PGA's national convention with a proposal to alleviate the situation: strike the Caucasians-only language from the PGA constitution. The convention overwhelmingly rejected the motion, 67–17.

Now, in 1961, Mosk was upping the ante.

He threatened to take on the PGA if it staged its championship on even a *private* golf course in California. The championship, scheduled to be played at the Brentwood Country Club the following summer, was now in jeopardy.

"I have advised the national PGA officials that their activities under a constitution restricting membership to 'professional golfers of the Caucasian race,' whether on a private or public golf course, violates both the public policy and the laws of California," Mosk announced.

It would be a tougher fight to win if the tournament was played on a private golf course, as opposed to a public course supported by taxpayer dollars. But it was a risk Mosk said he was prepared to take. "I believed then, and believe now, that society and the law can ultimately defeat overt bigotry every time."

"I advised the PGA people they could not discriminate. They, of course, said they were limited by their provisions limiting participation to Caucasians. I said, 'Well, if you insist on enforcing that provision, I will go into court and get an injunction.'"

At the PGA's midyear meeting in May, the pressure on the organization was having some effect. Its executive committee announced, in a vaguely worded statement, that it had withdrawn the tournament from Los Angeles. "Under present conditions in California, the PGA did not feel that it would be possible to conduct a successful tournament of the magnitude of the PGA championship in that state," said president Lou Strong.

In fact, the PGA faced not only an activist legal authority in Mosk, who could continue to make noise and perhaps take legal action, but also opposition from a sponsor, the L.A. Junior Chamber of Commerce, which announced it would withdraw from the PGA Championship.

It was one of the few times a sponsor had, directly or indirectly, used its leverage with the PGA on behalf of blacks, rather than lobby against their participation. But as a longtime sponsor of the L.A. Open, the Junior Chamber had supported a tournament that had for years allowed blacks to compete. "In the meantime, it is our intention to continue to stage the L.A. Open under our existing contract which guarantees the right of entry to all players, regardless of race, color, or national origin," the chamber said in a statement.

Public sentiment, reflected in the sports press, seemed to be turning against the PGA, with more and more portrayals of an organization that, at best, was out of step with society and, at worst, approached Neanderthal status.

"The PGA is far behind the times if it thinks that racial segregation still has a place in sports," intoned *Sports Illustrated,* perhaps the most influential sports publication of its day, in May 1961.

"Professional basketball, baseball, and football have long permitted Negro athletes to play, and all these sports have thrived in consequence. It's time that the PGA put its musty store in order, too."

Mosk, meanwhile, was not satisfied just to drive the PGA's championship out of California. He wrote the attorneys general of other states to tell them what he had done and to seek their support. Most of them, he said, pledged to do the same if the PGA attempted to stage its segregated championship in their states.

"But somehow," Mosk said, "Pennsylvania slipped through the cracks."

Indeed, by mid-June, the PGA had found a new site in New-town Square, outside Philadelphia. The Aronimink Golf Club had agreed to take the 1962 championship, and both the PGA and Aronimink were putting the best face on the move.

"The PGA is happy and proud to be able to take its National championship back to the Philadelphia area and to conduct it on an outstanding golf course such as that at Aronimink," Strong said. "All of us in the PGA will look forward with anticipation to our return to Philadelphia, where the enthusiasm of the golfers in the vicinity is unsurpassed anywhere." The PGA's public relations seemed to have a dazzling effect on at least one hometown newspaper. The *Philadelphia Inquirer* gave top billing in its sports section to the news of the 1962 PGA championship coming to its backyard but never mentioned any of the circumstances surrounding the tournament's move from California.

The NAACP, however, was quite willing to remind people. In a letter of protest to the president of Aronimink, W. W. K. Miller (a development the *Inquirer* dutifully reported, but at the bottom of its fourth page of sports), the organization registered its distaste. "We are extremely unhappy that Aronimink has decided to make itself a party to the continuing un-American practices of the Professional Golfers' Association," the letter said.

But the PGA continued to deny it had beat a retreat from California, a position that amazed Mosk and others. "It does shock me they would try to rewrite history," said Mosk, in a television interview more than three decades later. "But I suppose when one discriminates, he is likely to find any excuse in an attempt to justify it."

And the PGA suggested that Charlie Sifford had been denied entry in that year's PGA Championship not because he was black, but because he hadn't played good enough golf to get in the tournament, as other golfers had had to do under the rules.

"It is unfortunate that the NAACP did not take the trouble to learn the facts before making these unwarranted charges," Strong said. "If officials had taken a moment to ask Charlie Sifford about the PGA championship, he could have given them the facts and cleared the air."

In a technical sense, the PGA was right. Sifford had not qualified under its criteria. He had not finished among the top-twenty point leaders in the PGA in 1960, he had not finished among the top-twenty money winners in 1961 through the Masters in April, and he had not finished among the top-twenty-four finishers in the 1960 PGA Championship.

What Strong did not say was that Sifford had just secured a provisional touring card in March 1960, so he was three months behind other golfers. He was also at a disadvantage in the South, where most tournaments refused to invite him to play. And as to the third criterion, he was not allowed to play in the 1960 PGA Championship, so finishing among the top twenty-four was an impossibility.

It was a classic example of the conundrum blacks constantly faced, on and off the golf course. The ground under their feet always seemed to shift as soon as they were able to stand up. Rules were often met with suspicion, because they were often used to keep them out rather than to create an orderly, fair process, as whites contended. They were guises that denied them opportunity. Like Sisyphus, blacks kept pushing the rock up the hill. But, unlike that character from Greek mythology, blacks occasionally made it to the top with their rock, only to face yet another hill, and then another.

Finally, there seemed to be a plateau in sight.

Whether it was Mosk, or the L.A. Junior Chamber of Commerce, or the constant beat of criticism from heroes like Joe Louis and Jackie Robinson, or merely an attitudinal change that came with the passage of time, the PGA, amid the back-and-forth accusations about the 1962 championship, took a step to change its bylaws in that spring of 1961.

At the same time in May that the executive committee announced that the 1962 tournament would be moved, it announced that it would recommend that the Caucasians-only clause be removed from the organization's bylaws. The membership would vote on the recommendation at the annual meeting in November.

The membership had voted on the same proposal the previous year, and it had gotten trounced. But things were different this time. The secretive and powerful executive committee voted on the proposal this time, and announced its recommendation in a rare public statement. The vote to remove the clause was unanimous.

The move, said president Lou Strong, was "in keeping with the realization of changing world conditions and coinciding with principles of the United States government."

Six months later, at the forty-fifth annual meeting of the PGA, Lou Strong stood before the delegates at the Diplomat Hotel in Hollywood, Florida, and received a deafening ovation, one of the most rousing ever seen at an annual meeting.

And no wonder. The forty-eight-year-old club pro from Rochester Country Club had presided over one of the organization's best years ever. It was a new, golden era in golf.

A new PGA National Golf Club, with two championship eighteen-hole courses, was under construction. A new PGA headquarters was on the drawing board. Membership had risen to an all-time high of about 5,000. Prize money for the pro tour would grow to nearly $2 million in 1962.

Speaker after speaker lauded Strong, whose election to a second one-year term seemed equal parts love-fest and coronation.

"Lou," said Howard J. Youngman, honorary president at Strong's club in Rochester, "I want you to know and I want the PGA to know how happy and proud we are to have you as our golf professional."

Almost as an afterthought, the delegates took up two amendments to the constitution. One eliminated the requirement that members be residents of North or South America. The other removed four words—"of the Caucasian race"—from the PGA's membership requirements, the four words that had effectively denied an entire generation of black golfers the opportunity to answer a defining question in their lives. "Can I compete with the best?" "Can I make a living at this game?"

Without fanfare, the delegates voted 87–0, and the two amendments were approved.

After eighteen years, discrimination de jure was banished from the PGA's bylaws. Discrimination de facto would persist, only in subtler ways.

Somehow, it seemed fitting to many blacks that Gary Player won the 1962 PGA Championship.

That year's championship, of course, had been ignominiously forced out of Los Angeles when California attorney general Stanley Mosk said that any organization practicing discrimination would be barred from using the public recreational facilities in his state. With the Caucasians-only clause still intact, although in its last days, the tournament was moved to the Aronimink Golf Club in Philadelphia's wealthy suburbs. As for Player, he came from and still lived in South Africa, where racism was codified. And he had come to play golf in a country that still excluded many blacks from competing in his profession. At first blush, if there were a tournament to match a man, it was the PGA Championship and Player.

Player had been enjoying tremendous success on America's professional tour. Player was in the middle of a magnificent run. At five feet seven, 150 pounds, he was compact but powerful, one of the first golfers to bring an athlete's training regime and diet to his sport.

In 1958, he had finished second at the United States Open at Southern Hills Country Club in Tulsa. In 1959, he won the British Open at Muirfield, the second-youngest player to do so. In 1961, he captured the Masters Tournament, the first foreign player to do so. And now in 1962, at age twenty-six, he had won the PGA Championship, again the first nonresident to take the prize.

Accounts of Player's win spoke of his steady putting. They spoke of his triumph over Nicklaus and Palmer and a surging Bob Goalby, whose twenty-five-foot putt to tie on the final hole slid two feet past the hole. There was no mention that the championship had been moved from the Brentwood Country Club in Los Angeles to Aronimink.

Soon enough, Player would become a symbol to many blacks, and not for his golfing excellence, but for apartheid in his country and civil rights in the United States. By virtue of his success in places American blacks weren't allowed to compete—the Masters and the PGA tournaments, for example—Player would be the target of hostile questions and worse.

At first, he insisted he was merely a sportsman, not a politician, and thus not inclined to answer for his country's policies. But while he refused to criticize his country, Player tried to help black golfers behind the scenes. He had seen the kind of treatment Sifford had gotten at the Greater Greensboro Open, where he was badgered by beer-guzzling crackers who screamed at him for several holes before they were escorted off the course. When Sifford, in frustration, had slammed his pencil down on the table at the end of the round, Player had shook his head and sympathetically asked him:

"Laddie, how can you play like this?"

Player himself would find out.

14

"Laugh at 'Em and Keep Goin"

P ete Brown made the long walk up the 1st fairway at Farmington Country Club and onto the green, where his ball had dropped, softly, ten feet from the hole. This wasn't the time for Brown to pause and reflect on the long journey that had gotten him here. He had other things to think about first: the line and the speed of that putt, which could win him his first white-run tournament, the 1962 Michigan Open.

Six years earlier, on a bitter winter day, at a hospital barely an hour's drive from this lush layout west of Detroit, a doctor told the frail and immobile Brown he'd be lucky if he walked again. At the mention of golf, the doctor shook his head and told Brown to find another line of work. Finally, after a year in Herman Kiefer Hospital, Brown went home. Unable to stand from the pain at first, he gradually got stronger, and his muscles began to remember how to repeat his fluid compact swing, which had impressed the best black golfers of the time—Charlie Sifford, Teddy Rhodes, and Bill Spiller. A few years after he left Kiefer, Pete Brown was walking down the fairway again, a black man with a dream of playing for big money on the PGA Tour.

By the late fifties, Brown was all the way back, playing well on the loosely knit circuit of black tournaments. He won in Houston, Dallas, Chicago, and Asbury Park, New Jersey. In 1961, he even captured the United Golfers Association's National Open—the black tour's championship—in Boston. In 1962, he tried to repeat in Memphis, but trailed badly going into the last day, when everyone played thirty-six holes. That morning, Brown's wife, Margaret, awoke wide-eyed.

"I dreamed you shot 66-66 today!"

"Well, stop dreaming," Pete said derisively.

In fact, he shot 66 that morning and matched it with another 66 in the afternoon, winning easily.

The Michigan Open was something different. Just opened to blacks, the tournament was more than a shot at a $1,000 payday or a top finish in a predominantly white championship. Winning at Farmington could be a sign to other pros that Pete Brown was ready for the PGA Tour.

Tom Talkington, a thirty-seven-year-old club pro from Ann Arbor, held the lead after three rounds, but Brown caught him with a 68. "We had never heard of Pete Brown up there. He just showed up," said Talkington. "I remember his golf swing. Stylish, really stylish."

Talkington played first, chipping from just off the green to within a few feet for his par. Brown circled the hole, gauging the speed and line. He settled over his putt, and the crowd stopped stirring, realizing that the tournament could end right here. On this warm, cloudless August day, all was still as Brown got ready to pull back his putter blade and stroke the putt.

"Hey, nigger! What are you doing?"

Brown stepped away from the ball. The spectators froze, unsure how to react. The shout had violated one of golf's commandments—silence while players were striking their shots. The words were a sacrilege, like a brick through stained glass.

Brown had handled drunks, hecklers, and rednecks before. He'd grown up in Mississippi, where you were lynched for looking twice at a white girl. But this was a big tournament in Michigan, not the Deep South. Brown and other black golfers would learn this bitter lesson, over and over again: a more complicated racism operated up north, where a thin veneer of civility barely covered resentment roiling underneath.

"Guys in the South, if they didn't like you, they'd tell you," Brown said. "Guys in the North, they'd hide it."

Not this day. Brown backed away and saw that a group of white teens driving on the road along the 1st hole had spotted him, slowed down, and seized the opportunity. As the youths roared off, Brown shook his head. (Talkington, however, did not recall the moment.)

And then he laughed—out loud.

The crowd joined him, nervously. The tension melted away. The moment passed.

His birdie putt skirted the hole and he had to settle for par. No matter. Two holes later, Talkington made bogey on the par-3 3rd hole, and Brown's par putt raced eight feet downhill, spun around the cup, and dropped in. He had won on the third playoff hole, but he had won a small triumph on the first.

"If they say something, laugh at 'em and keep going, and they'll quit," the soft-spoken Brown explained years later.

That attitude—smile, laugh, keep walking—won him a lot of admirers, many of them white partners who witnessed the abuse Brown and other black golfers endured. "He didn't make a big fuss about anything," said Bob Goalby, a white golfer who was occasionally paired with Brown. "If he shot 77, he didn't bitch. If he shot 67, he might smile. He had a good demeanor. He didn't get too high or too low."

Brown was a stark contrast to his friend Charlie Sifford, who played with a cigar clenched in his mouth and seemed to wear the bitterness of the years. Unlike Brown, Sifford rarely smiled on the course and sometimes stopped to confront those who baited him. He also said things that didn't endear him to other black golfers, many of whom endured the same struggles he did. Years later, when a *Wall Street Journal* reporter called him to ask him about the success of Lee Elder, Charlie declined to be interviewed.

"I'm the Jackie Robinson of golf," he told the reporter. "You should be doing a story about me."

Charlie had a sharp edge, but it drove him, pushed him through the days when blacks were turned away from golf tournaments. "Charlie was mean," Pete said, his voice rising in amazement. "He would fight, literally fight." On occasion, he would pause on the tee and clean his fingernails with a knife he carried with him. He might just have been cleaning his nails or he might have been delivering a message to stay away, if you had any plans to make trouble. For the most part, he kept a lid on his temper. He had to. Just as Jackie Robinson was forced to endure the taunts, the insults, the death threats, so Charlie and other golfers would have to endure their fair share as well. Still, Charlie and Pete couldn't have been more different.

Pete Brown was born in 1935 in Port Gibson, Mississippi, near the Louisiana border, to Etta Brown and her husband, George, a sharecropper, carpenter, and Baptist minister. After the family, including three other boys, moved to Jackson, Mississippi, Pete gravitated to Livingston Park Golf Course, the city's only public golf course (which barred blacks from playing). Like other boys in west Jackson, the black neighborhood where the Browns settled, he didn't see golf as a game. Their games were basketball, football, and baseball. Golf meant carrying a white man's golf bag for money. At eleven, he joined some of his buddies from the neighborhood who went to work at Livingston Park. "I decided to go out there with them to see what was going on."

He quickly moved from caddying to the locker room and then to the back room at the pro shop. Meantime, golf became more than a job. Although he wouldn't play his first full round until he was fifteen, sharing a mismatched collection of clubs, Brown and his friends would sneak onto the course early in the morning, playing the few holes that couldn't be seen from the clubhouse. Or they'd make their own golf holes by mowing abandoned fields and using sticks as pins. When work was slow around the golf course, Pete and his friends would chip balls for hours, a routine that contributed to his accomplished wedge play on the Tour. By the eleventh grade, he had dropped out of school. "I was exposed to the golf course all the time. I spent most of my time there. You caddied for the good golfers. You would learn all the shots they would make. You got to know the game by listening to them. We got ahold of some clubs and tried to do what they were doing."

They'd also heard about a course in New Orleans, a three-hour drive down Highway 55, which let blacks play on Mondays and Fridays. Pete and his friends would leave town by 3:00 A.M., roll into the parking lot by sunrise, play thirty-six holes, and drive back to Jackson that night.

Along the way, Pete Brown found out he was a natural.

At eighteen, he borrowed a set of clubs and caught a ride to Houston for the Lone Star Open, a black tournament, and competed against Spiller, Sifford, and Rhodes, all three several years his senior and trying to scratch out a living on the black tour. The kid didn't seem to be intimidated; he chose to play in his first official tournament as a professional, not an amateur. "Some of the guys tried to talk me out of it. I didn't need a trophy, I needed money."

He shot 73 for four straight days, finished second to Sifford, and collected his first paycheck as a pro: $250. It whetted his appetite. He came back to Houston the next year and won the Lone Star, beating Sifford and Spiller.

The buzz had started about the young Mississippi kid who could play. Spiller came through Jackson and picked up Brown for a northern swing. In Chicago, Brown watched a few black pros and Joe Louis play in the Tam O'Shanter, one of the few white tournaments that allowed blacks to enter. In Detroit, Brown entered the UGA's National Open and finished second and then went home to Jackson.

By then, a successful black businessman named Randolph Wallace, who had grown up poor in Mississippi, took notice and made Brown an offer. "If I came to Detroit, he would pay my way through school, college, all expenses," Brown said. "All I had to do is teach his family and play with him."

Brown headed for Detroit and arrived in the middle of a cold northern winter. Wallace put him up at one of his hotels, the Randora (which combined Wallace's first name with his wife Dora's), and the Mississippi boy quickly learned about the big city, living and working odd jobs in a hotel where black entertainers stayed while in town.

Within days, Brown also learned that blacks weren't allowed to play on Detroit's public courses. And within a few weeks, Brown fell ill. The doctor told him it was probably strep throat.

"But I never got better. I got worse. I started losing the feeling in my fingers, my toes. I couldn't swallow. I was really getting weak. I was losing my eyesight. I was still at the hotel, going to the doctor every day. He didn't try too much. Finally, I went to the doctor one day, same office. Another doctor there, a young foreign doctor, he came in. He looked me over, looked in my eyes, and said, 'Man. I got to get you to the hospital.'"

In 1956, few blacks worked at Kiefer Hospital, a big complex just northwest of downtown. Fewer were admitted as patients. Brown felt neglected, especially as he watched doctors work feverishly on a young white boy in the same room. Brown was virtually paralyzed, the muscles around his joints lifeless. The doctors said it might be polio or infectious mononucleosis, but they never knew for sure. Or if they did, they never told Brown.

For the first and only time in his life, Brown considered suicide. He was helpless, in a hostile institution, in a strange city, with few friends and no family. "If I could have gotten to the window, I would have jumped out. But I couldn't move," he said.

"I didn't tell my family, noooooo! I didn't want to tell them. I didn't want to worry them. They found out later." His patron, Randolph Wallace, paid the hospital bills and periodically phoned Brown's family in Mississippi. And he'd lie; "Pete's fine," Wallace told them. By then, Pete had dropped nearly 50 pounds, from 170 to 122. The doctor offered little encouragement. "He told me to find something else to do; I wouldn't play golf again. He told me I couldn't walk. I just couldn't see myself in the wheelchair. I kept trying. I didn't give up."

Finally, he was able to move a toe, and then another, and then his foot. "After they found I could move some muscles, they worked on me like mad. I walked out of the hospital after about a year."

Advised to move to a warmer climate, Pete went back to Jackson. He hurt so bad, he could barely stand, but he took his old job at

Livingston Park. He thought about playing again, but it was months before he could swing a club, and when he did, he nearly fell down trying. "It was five years before I could even attempt to run," he said. "I didn't know how."

During his slow recuperation, some friends introduced him to Margaret Grisby, home visiting her family in Jackson. When he took her out to dinner, she found him different from other men she'd known in Jackson: soft-spoken and reserved but somehow more mature. Margaret's mother found him to be different from the other boys, too. Margaret came home one evening and there was Pete in the living room talking to her mother.

"What are you doing here?" Margaret asked.

"Well, I'm here to take your mother out to dinner," Pete said.

For their second date, Margaret chose a short skirt and heels. Pete picked her up and took her to a place in Jackson she'd never seen before: Livingston Park Golf Course. They were married in April 1957.

Tour veteran Dan Sikes had been through enough Sundays on the Tour to know strange things could happen. He was familiar with the final, wrenching day of a tournament, when even the best golfer's nerves got rawer, muscles got tighter, knees got weaker. He had lived the magical side of Sunday the year before when he won the 1963 Doral Open. He'd suffered through the cruel side, too, when he lost the 1962 Houston Classic, in a playoff to Bobby Nichols.

Now, at the 1964 Waco Turner Open, he wasn't sure how this Sunday might turn out. Sikes had finished his round, trailing Pete Brown by one shot, and stood behind the 18th green, a par-3, waiting for Brown to finish. Brown stepped to the tee and hit a three-iron left and short. He was faced with a tough up-and-down for par and the win. Sikes told his caddie, Perry Bales, to get ready for a playoff.

By the time he reached his ball, Brown knew he needed par to win his first PGA tour event and gain a little security and, just as important, a year-long exemption to play on the Tour. He also knew he could make history that day. He could be the first black to win a PGA tour event.

This wasn't just any tournament. This was Waco Turner's tournament. This wasn't one of those events that was named after two huge, faceless companies that had merged yesterday, the way the PGA tour events would someday get underwritten.

Waco Turner was not just a person, he was a character. He and a PGA tournament were a clash of cultures, akin to a Texas barbecue at Buckingham Palace. You had to admire the spirit, but it was sheer hell for the traditionalists.

Waco (after the Waco Indians) Turner was an ex-teacher who struck it rich—real rich—when he exercised some options on land surrounding an oil field. You could see some of his wells from his golf course in Burneyville, Oklahoma, near the border with Texas. While he didn't exactly wear six-shooters on the golf course, he did carry a .22 rifle and a shotgun on the rear floorboard of his Cadillac. And one day he decided he'd like to have himself a golf tournament; so the Waco Turner Open became one of the more unusual stops on tour for several years.

"When you woke up in the morning, he'd want you to have a bourbon with him," said Jack Tuthill, the PGA's longtime tournament director.

He was a cowboy version of George May—flamboyant and generous to the players. He liked to do things his way and wouldn't brook criticism of his tournament or his golf. He had run the tournament at a country club thirty miles to the north for three years, until people started telling him what to do. So he moved it down to an 800-acre spread his daddy had owned, and built his own course. One player made the mistake of calling it a cow pasture; he was promptly shown the front gate. It was Turner's golf course, and he let you know it, sometimes by buzzing players on the course with his twin-engine Cessna. When he was on the ground, he liked to drive his Cadillac around the golf course, crisscrossing fairways toting the rifle and shotgun to pick off turtles that ate the fish in his lakes.

Some called the tournament the Poor Boy Open, in part because it came on the same date as the Tournament of Champions in Las Vegas. You had to win a PGA tournament the previous year to get into the Tournament of Champions; even the previous year's winner of the Waco Turner Open went to Vegas. The rest of the golfers went to Burneyville, not exactly a garden spot, but most were grateful for the chance.

Every day of the tournament, Turner would reward the golfers with cash for every birdie, eagle, chip-in, low round, you name it. This year, the total purse was $20,000, but he handed out another $19,235 in bonuses.

A few years earlier, he asked Tuthill to accompany him to the bank to get some cash for the daily prizes.

"It's Saturday," Tuthill said. "The banks are closed."

"I got my own; I'll open it." Turner said.

Pete Brown, on the final hole of the final day, had a tricky, twenty-yard shot off bare, hard ground to get close enough to win. "It's probably one of the hardest shots in golf," Brown said. "Dirt, no grass. I took the wedge. That shot, I played around the club-house [in Jackson] all day. I was familiar with the shot."

The ball landed two and a half feet from the pin, and Brown tapped the putt in. As the gallery applauded, Sikes's caddie put the driver back in the bag; no playoff. Brown had calmly stroked in the biggest putt of his life and became the first black to win an official PGA tournament and $2,700. But he grinned later, saying, "I'm still shaking." Waco Turner knew that Pete could now play in Ben Hogan's tournament at the Colonial in Texas, a place not hereto-fore very accommodating to black folk.

"You want me to go with you?" Turner asked.

"I think I can handle it," Brown said.

"Take my number. If they give you any shit, you call me."

At home with the kids, Margaret hadn't heard the news by the time Pete called from the tournament. In those days, most golf tournaments weren't televised.

"How'd you do today?"

"Well, I won," Pete said, matter-of-factly, as though this day was like any other.

But Pete knew this was different. He had captured the UGA National twice, in 1961 and 1962. He'd won a bunch of other black tournaments. But this was a seventy-two-hole PGA tournament.

He had accomplished something no other black golfer had.

15

Hustling

Even in 1967, Lee Elder had to scramble. As he headed out on the grind of the black tour, he knew he might be winning some tournaments, but he'd be making some money by hustling, too. It had been that way for years, hustling for a buck. It had been that way since he was a boy.

Born in Dallas, Texas, Robert Lee Elder was one of eight kids in his family. His daddy, Charles Elder, a coal-truck driver, was drafted into the infantry during World War II, and left Lee's mother, Sadie, a widow. When she died not long after, Lee was shipped to Los Angeles to live with a widowed sister.

He was twelve.

Within a couple of years, he had dropped out of Manual Arts High School in Los Angeles, looking to support himself. Since many of his friends were caddies, he thought he'd give golf a try, first cutting classes to make a dollar or two caddying. He was also sneaking onto golf courses at night, before being run off by park patrols.

Elder bounced around Southern California, working in Lloyd Mangrum's golf shop and in the locker room at a San Bernardino country club. Then he met a golfing hustler named Moses Brooks.

Elder had already been hustling at golf courses in Los Angeles, but he became so taken with Brooks, he accompanied him back to Dallas and became the man to beat at Tenison Park Golf Course. Elder worked nights at the Hostess bakery, washing those pans that held the Twinkies, then wandered over to Tenison, known far and wide as a nest of hustlers and golf sharks. Occasionally, a white guy named Alvin Clarence Thomas would be there. He was better known as Titanic Thompson, the most famous hustler in America.

Tall and lean, and said to usually wear an undertaker's expression, Thompson was in his early sixties, but he had lost little off his game, the game of winning money at almost anything, from trap shooting to poker. And, like any good hustler, he did his best to eliminate risk when he took a bet. He had told a judge so, when he was hauled into court to answer a charge of operating a game of chance.

"Your honor, this charge couldn't be right. There wasn't nobody in that room had a chance but me," Thompson wrote years later in an autobiographical magazine article.

You had to be some kind of hick, hermit, or both not to have heard of him. Thompson won nearly $1 million in a poker game in San Francisco with Nick the Greek as his partner. He had married four times. (One of his wives, Nora, had filed for divorce claiming the gambler's life was too dangerous and transient. She later married gangster Pretty Boy Floyd.) Thompson said he shot and killed five men and was responsible for the drowning of another, although he claimed that all were justified. He considered himself the best golfer of his time, having beat Byron Nelson with a 29 on the back nine to win a "nice bet," as he called it.

Humility wasn't one of his strong suits, and befitting a man with an adjective for a first name, Thompson claimed he was a natural golfer. It was during that long-running poker game with Nick the Greek that Thompson got serious about the game, taking lessons in secret. He claimed he even stayed out of the sun as much as possible when he played, to avoid a tan and raising suspicion.

"A year or so earlier I had been driving from Tulsa to Pitcher, Okla., and had stopped at a drink stand and was watching a fellow hit golf balls. I borrowed his club and drove one 300 yards the first time I ever swung at a ball. His club was left-handed, and I was right-handed, but I will tell you this about golf—if you are right-handed, you ought to play left-handed, and vice versa. I could play scratch either way, but for pure accuracy I am better left-handed."

Thompson claimed he won $1,000 betting he could hit the ball 500 yards; he won, by teeing up the ball on a par-5 outside Chicago in the dead of winter and hitting out onto an adjacent, frozen lake. On at least one occasion, Thompson took a knife to the cups on each hole, raising them slightly so that only a putt hit squarely in the center would go in. In the first full round of golf he ever played, Thompson claimed, he won $56,000—and was paid cash on the 18th green. He played with a young Ben Hogan and gave him some pointers and took on Dutch Harrison as a partner for a while.

But he didn't like to leave anything to chance. He'd show up on the 1st tee with his arm in a sling and have a sudden recovery by the time he stepped up to tee off. Against one strapping young golfer, who hit monstrous drives, he allowed him to hit three tee shots on each hole and pick the best one. As Thompson told it, the boy beat him for the first several holes, "but by about the 12th hole he was worn out from all that swinging, and I clipped him easy."

At Tenison Park, Thompson took a shine to the young Elder. And Elder began caddying for him. Meanwhile, Elder's game improved. At age fifteen, he first broke 80 at Tenison, a pretty good test for a muni course. (The neighborhood could be a little rough, though. Lee Trevino remembered when he and another fellow got held up on the course. Before handing over the cash, Trevino counted out the money he owed his competitor, saying, "Now we're even.")

And Elder said he knew for sure when Thompson—called Ti by friends—liked him and trusted him. During a poker game, Thompson got down to his last $2,000, having already lost at least $10,000. He asked Elder to take his car and go fetch more cash from Thompson's wife. "Meanwhile," Elder said, "he'd just bluff along with little bets until I got back. Ti told me, 'Don't worry about anything. Just drive regular and don't worry.'" Elder, of course, was scared to death. Thompson's wife handed him a little paper bag and he drove back fretting about getting caught in traffic or getting pulled over and having to explain what he was doing driving somebody else's car and what was in that little brown bag on the front seat. He made it back, and Ti thanked him.

With Elder, and lots of other talented golfers he spotted, Thompson's scam went like this: Elder would pose as Thompson's caddie. At some point during his match, Thompson would turn to his opponent and say: "I bet even my caddie can beat you!" Of course, the stakes would be increased, and when Elder defeated the mark, he and Thompson would split the winnings.

When asked why he never turned professional, Thompson scoffed and said pros couldn't make in a year what he could make hustling in a week, particularly in the early days of the Tour. Hogan, Harrison, Paul Runyan, and Bobby Locke all agreed that he could have been a great champion. "I didn't care about tournaments. I wanted the cash."

Money was that siren song that lured many a golfer—including black golfers scrambling to make a living—into a hustler's life. But at first, hustling was a necessity, a part of life, for most golfers trying to make a living on the fringes of the pro tour. To Negro golfers who, try as they might, had no opportunity to play on the PGA Tour and barely made expenses on the UGA circuit, it took on much more importance. Even if they won a tournament, many black golfers had to lend each other money to get to the next stop. The winner, it was often understood, would pay the motel and food bills for that week with his riding buddies.

They often hustled during the week and played in tournaments during the weekend. The stakes for the weekday games might range from $500 to $2,000, and you weren't guaranteed to win, particularly if you were playing on one leg or on your knees just to get some action from wary competitors. Winning wasn't always accompanied by sheer unvarnished joy. Elder knew that well.

"I felt bad taking a guy's money. I knew he had no chance, but if it wasn't me, somebody else would do it. I told quite a few lies— 'Man, I can't play, you've got to give me some strokes'—but this was the only way I could get a game. I knew it was dishonest, but there are times when you have to forget about dishonesty when you want to survive," Elder has said.

He felt he could win a number of ways. He could play standing on one leg or on his knees. He once won a game wearing a rain suit in ninety-five-degree weather. (A friend had wrapped him in towels soaked in ice water beforehand.) He also won a fair amount of money betting people he could beat them playing with a cross-handed grip. Few knew he used the unorthodox grip during the early part of his career, until Teddy Rhodes had him change it.

Usually there'd be some long nights before one of those matches. When he lived in Washington, Elder would head to the driving range at East Potomac, a public course near the Capitol and the only one open at night. Long practice sessions helped him shoot a 38 for nine holes while balancing on one leg, or drive the ball 155 yards from his knees and shoot a 41 for nine holes.

For a high school dropout whose parents had died before he saw his twelfth year, it was a way to make a living, if you didn't mind living without health insurance or a pension. In fact, there was no guarantee of a paycheck this week, or next, or the next after that. Many golfers leaned on their families for help. The wives of players often held down full-time jobs to earn predictable income. Spiller's wife, for example, worked for the L.A. Department of Water and Power. Rose Sifford once wrote her husband, Charlie, not to worry about his family at home, just to worry about playing good golf. She would get a job, and she did. The risk of hustling for men with families was so much greater. Lose, and a bunch of mouths went unfed.

Nonetheless, hustling was the only way some golfers could afford to stay out on the UGA circuit and even some whites could try to break onto the PGA Tour, particularly as they tried to get established. They might miss the cut in a PGA tournament and head to a UGA event on the weekend to make some money, along with some side bets along the way.

Seemed like everyone had to learn the hard way. At most of the munis where the blacks could play, hustlers were always hanging around, waiting for a game. And each had his favorite shot, one he'd practiced thousands of times and could execute in his sleep. Pete Brown heard about one who could throw a key in a lock, from five or six feet away. Three-Iron Gates, a white golfer, could get his ball up and down in two from anywhere in a bunker. "And he could hit a three-iron two hundred and eighty yards," said Brown, "play all his shots with that club, and shoot pretty close to par."

Fat Man Stanovich hung out in Los Angeles, and he took on most of the touring pros who came to town. Befitting his nickname, Fat Man was so big, you didn't think he could play golf. "Just huge. He couldn't play in the tournaments at all, but he could damn near make whatever [score] he wanted to win, if he was playing a guy," Brown said.

No one had a hometown record like Trevino in El Paso. Nobody beat him there. He'd play anybody with a Dr Pepper bottle (and not any other bottle, since Dr Pepper bottles had a flat edge and were easier to hit). Even Thompson was humbled by Trevino when he helped bankroll a young pro named Raymond Floyd to play him in El Paso.

As the story goes, Floyd traveled to the windblown course in west Texas where Trevino shined shoes, tended bar, shagged balls, and did whatever else needed doing, and lost the first two days and nearly the third if he hadn't eagled the last hole. Both men went on to have pretty good careers on the PGA Tour—Trevino won six majors and Floyd four.

There were hustlers like Trevino all over the country. One was Potato Pie.

His real name was George Wallace, and he played out of Atlanta, and he liked sweet potato pie and red sodas. He had a cross-handed grip, and loop at the top, but he hit the ball straight down the fairway and could putt like his life depended on it. "That ball didn't know but one way it could go," said Felton Mason, one of the golfers who used to ride with Pie.

Potato Pie would travel anywhere for a game. He went to Oklahoma and played some oilman for a week. He brought home $60,000 to pay for his house. But he liked to have a traveling partner. Out of the blue, Mason would get a phone call from him. "Man, can you catch a plane?" Pie would say. "I'll meet you in the airport and let's ride."

"Just go around and look for games," Mason said. "Wherever we'd stop, we'd look for their best player and say, 'Come on.' We'd start off in Columbus, Georgia. We'd always start out there. We used to trim 'em there, then we'd go to Flint, Michigan, play there for awhile; Indianapolis, play there awhile; go to Cleveland, stay there awhile, and maybe get on the turnpike and go to Philadelphia, and play there awhile."

One of the reasons Pie liked a traveling partner was that he couldn't read. The road signs, a menu, nothing.

"For years, I didn't know," Mason said. "I would be at the table to have dinner or something. He's got that menu, you know. 'Whaddayou think?' I'd say, 'Man, I don't know. Shoot, this surf-and-turf look good here.' He say, 'Goddamn, that sound like a winner. I think I'm going that way, too.'"

The best hustle took some time to set up. You headed out to a course, carrying a little bag with just seven or eight clubs, and waited for a game, sizing up the action, the competition, and the pigeons. You might pick up a game and hit the ball badly and lose a little cash to your playing partners. You'd praise your opponent's game and tell him you wanted to try again. And you'd lose again, all the while praising his game.

You'd start to look desperate and get mad at yourself, telling him you wanted to play for serious money. By then, he's seen your game two or three times already, and it hasn't improved any. And he agrees to play for $1,000.

At that point, you decide whether you want to win right then and there or lose again and try to get him back for one more game, for $3,000, $4,000, or more. The most successful hustle can last for days, after losing that $1,000 match. Elder once said that's the time to go for drinks with the pigeon, who's all pleased with himself. Then someone he doesn't know is your friend joins the conversation.

"Don't tell me about your big match," says the friend. "That ain't big. I don't think either one of you guys has the guts to play a real big match."

That's the time to let the pigeon talk and if he runs true to human nature, he feels stung and he puffs up and says he's got the guts. And he'll play the big money, next day, same course. And that's when you take him. "You take him ever so close, a hole or two or a stroke or two," Elder once told a reporter. "But you take him. And then you go somewhere else."

Inevitably, times would come when you wouldn't come out on top. If you didn't have the money, you had to be prepared to leave town quickly. Hustling wasn't exactly a gentleman's game, where the winners knew the losers and could always collect on an IOU sometime in the future.

And you always faced guys playing on their home course, with their friends around them, playing the round of their lives. Sometimes, you'd have to shoot a 64 or 65 to win. Some say making a four-foot downhill putt to win the U.S. Open is pressure; playing with no cash in your pocket and having to shoot a 65 is pressure, too.

While in Los Angeles, Elder was among a group of hustlers who frequented Fox Hills Golf Course. "That's where they used to hang out," said Pete Brown. "And you could get out there anytime; you would find 'em all. They were sitting there waiting, like buzzards."

According to Brown, Elder once lost a substantial sum, and his creditors came calling at the L.A. Open. Elder told them, "Wait, I'll be back in a minute," and jumped over the back fence of the golf course.

"They was ready to kill him," said Brown. "Because he was such a great golfer, that's the only reason he's living. He would be dead."

After Elder was drafted, he got a chance to play golf in the army, winning the post championship at Fort Lewis, Washington, and finishing second to Phil Rogers in the All-Service tournament in 1960 and second to Orville Moody in the Sixth Army Championship. He came out of the army in 1961, ready to play golf for a living. By the mid-sixties, there were about twenty tournaments on the UGA circuit, with the first-place prize rarely above $1,500. You got money if you finished in the top ten; if not, you'd go home empty-handed. So the side action was always brisk: either players were betting on themselves or there were always people around willing to bet on you or with you.

As the sixties wore on, Elder became the man to beat on the UGA tour.

He won the UGA National at Langston in Washington, D.C., in 1963, and again the next year in Indianapolis. And then in 1966 in Chicago, and again in Miami in 1967.

He won the Gate City Open tournament in Greensboro, North Carolina, the first five years they held it, including 1967. That year, Elder won eighteen out of the twenty-two tournaments he competed in. He had developed his game, with the help of people like Teddy Rhodes. With Sifford and Pete Brown playing on the PGA Tour pretty regularly, there was no golfer who could match Elder on the black circuit.

But one young golfer from North Carolina felt otherwise. James Black had an attitude, and he also had a game.

Thirty years later, James Black had been humbled by the years (he was now fifty-seven)—by open-heart surgery, by God (dressed in a dark suit and tie, on this day he was headed to church). He had hooked up with the Police Athletic League to teach young kids about life by teaching them about golf.

But there was no modesty—false or otherwise—when Black talked about his abilities as a young golfer. In his prime, he said, no other black golfer dared challenge him one on one, man to man. "Okay?" Black said, pausing for emphasis. "There's not one black that would say: 'C'mon, I'll play you for some money.' Never in my life—never. Never . . . in . . . my . . . life. All of 'em."

For a man who shot up like a comet on the white tour in early 1964 and disappeared over the horizon less than two years later, James Black was a mystery to some, a tragedy to others. James Black could have had a name in golf that resonates the way Tiger Woods's does today.

He had come to New York City and hooked up with a couple of other golfers from North Carolina who wanted to go to California to play professional golf. They piled into Harold Dunovant's car and headed west—the older, more experienced Dunovant, Black, and James "Junior" Walker, who'd had lots of success in tournaments around the New York City area.

Walker was from Rocky Mount, North Carolina, but realized he had to go north if he wanted to get serious about playing golf, in part because there the opportunities for blacks were greater. "They got no public courses for me in Rocky Mount," he said. "I left because I had to play." Some of his friends had gone to New York City, and now at twenty, Walker wanted to go there, too. "Yes, you can go, if you stay out of trouble," Walker's mother told him. He took a variety of jobs—at a factory, a garage—but kept gravitating to Jimmy Taylor's golf school on Seventh Avenue in Harlem. Word spread at public courses around New York City and in New Jersey that Walker played much bigger than he looked. The five-foot-eight, 140-pound kid could drive the ball, and he had a nice touch with the putter, too.

Dunovant, from Winston-Salem, had taken a liking to the two younger golfers and had helped them with their games. He enjoyed helping other golfers. Black golfers, Lord knew, needed lots of help with their games, and there were few to step forward and teach them. Dunovant had learned a lot about the swing over the years, and would spend a lot of time correcting the grips, stances, and swings of many black golfers. His apprenticeship had included hours of watching Teddy Rhodes hit balls from the shade of some tree, each ball, one after the other, landing softly within a foot or so of the other.

Dunovant had a car, some knowledge, a 300-pound frame, and a voice that sounded like it came out of a megaphone. When they got to California, Dunovant looked for a club pro job, while Walker and Black practiced, played, and looked to the New Year.

James Black was twenty-one, with a world of promise ahead of him.

At five feet eight, 165 pounds, he had a game that belied his youth, a classic swing that produced crisp and accurate long irons, length off the tee that approached the longer hitters in the game, a jeweler's touch with the wedge. And he could putt.

"James Black was the best player in our race then. Better than all of them. He had everything. He had the swing, the distance; he had all the shots," said Jim Dent, who played with Black and went on to become a star on the PGA seniors tour. "For me looking at it today, and looking at it back then, he had it all."

After months of struggling, things started to break their way as 1963 gave way to 1964. For one, Dunovant landed a job as assistant pro at the Western Avenue Golf Course, the last of the county-owned golf courses to desegregate their pro shops. And after failing to distinguish himself in some local Southern California tournaments, Black qualified for the Los Angeles Open, the first PGA event of the year.

Still, there were ominous signs for the 1964 season's first golf tournament, the Los Angeles Open. For one, the PGA had stepped in to alter the qualifying format for the tournament; in effect, it split the card-carrying pros and non-card-carrying pros into two groups to qualify, which seemed to cut at the heart of the open format. The card-carrying pros, in effect, had twenty-eight spots to play for, while the others had only seven. It was a format that brought back fears that, once again, golfers who were trying to break into the PGA, especially blacks, faced a system that was erected to discourage them.

At the golf course itself, Rancho Park, vandals had struck Sunday night, four days before the tournament was to start, and hacked up ten greens. Conditions were considered by many pros to be less than ideal to begin with, since it was one of the most heavily played municipal golf courses in the country. But tournament officials scrambled to repair the damage—nearly 7,000 square feet of turf on the greens were destroyed.

The vandals had apparently scaled the fence Sunday night and used golf clubs and shovels, carving swastikas in nine of the greens. By Monday, a crew of fifty men was replacing the damaged turf with sod from a nursery on the course. "They are doing such a good job of repair that I don't think the putting will be bothered very much," said Joe Black, the PGA's tournament supervisor. "Maybe this will affect the winning score by a stroke or two, but no more. We will try to place the pins on undamaged areas of the greens, as much as possible."

Nevertheless, overflow galleries and a financially successful tournament had been virtually guaranteed by the decision of one man to attend: Arnold Palmer.

Other golfers, with some awe in their voices, called Palmer the King. He was the Tour's top money winner in 1963, and had captured the L.A. Open in characteristic style, sinking a fifty-foot putt on the 17th to help lock up a final-round 66. But that wasn't all. Palmer had won seven tournaments in 1963 and was the leading money winner. In fact, in his pro career, he'd already won forty tournaments, six of them majors.

Palmer was about more than wins, though. He had transformed and transcended golf, bringing excitement to a sport that many TV viewers found as compelling as watching paint dry. With his hard-charging style, leathery face, muscular forearms, and slashing swing, Palmer's appeal broadened beyond the country club set to a cross section of America. In short, Palmer was made for TV. And TV meant more money, bigger purses, larger galleries, and, in a serendipitous spiral, more money. He was a man's man, throwing down his cigarette and hitching his pants as he considered his next miracle recovery, an athlete in a game that had a reputation for having few. He was also sexy, attracting legions of women, many of whom knew little about the game with the little dimpled ball until they saw Arnold Palmer on television.

Jack Nicklaus and Gary Player were skipping the Los Angeles Open, but it didn't matter. Palmer would play, and that was enough to muster a sizable army of fans. Arnie's Army, they were called.

For good measure, the Tour's other top players, including U.S. Open champ Julius Boros, had committed to Los Angeles. "Champagne" Tony Lema, a promising young golfer who liked to treat reporters to bottles of Moët & Chandon, also would play. He even dropped by the press tent on Wednesday—New Year's Day, 1964—for some bubbly out of a paper cup.

James Black was an unknown. As a Negro in a PGA tournament, you couldn't help but stand out, but Pete Brown, Lee Elder, and Charlie Sifford had qualified for Los Angeles that year, too. Black had never played in a PGA tournament before and certainly had not distinguished himself in Southern California tournaments since coming west; in the Montebello and Gardena Valley opens, he had finished out of the money. He'd seriously considered hopping a Greyhound bus for home.

At the L.A. Open, he was just a twenty-one-year-old from North Carolina, already married with three kids, who had to drive down to Yorba Linda to qualify. That day didn't start auspiciously. On his way to qualify, the car broke down. As his taxicab pulled up to the golf course, Black heard his name announced on the 1st tee. "I swung at the first golf ball with my street shoes on," Black said. He shot a 78, but it was good enough to qualify on a day when the wind nearly bent the palm trees in half.

The story that first *day* of the Los Angeles Open wasn't Palmer, or Lema, or any other established pro. It was Roger Ginsberg, twenty-five, who had joined the Tour the year before and hadn't won much money ($5,351). He had passed on a pitching tryout with the Dodgers to stick with golf. And that first day (the L.A. Open began on Friday), he was the leader, carding four birdies and no bogeys for a 67.

The curly-haired Bronx native of Jewish-Italian descent was delighted with his round and happy about his putting and wasn't bothered by the greens. "To me, they were just fine," he told reporters, with a wide grin. He made no mention of the swastikas that were still faintly visible.

Black teed off in the final group with two other unknowns, but he got constant glimpses of golfing royalty and its entourage. The mighty Palmer was playing three groups ahead, and most of the 10,000 fans at Rancho swarmed around him as he marched through his one-under round of 70. The distant roars of the gallery periodically filtered back to Black's group.

As the sun dipped into the Pacific five miles to the west, Black was still on the course. In fact, he was having a decent round by the time he got to the 8th hole—his penultimate that day, because he had teed off on the back nine. He had bogeyed two holes, but birdied three others, and was level with Palmer at one under, and three behind the leader.

Then he hit the 8th green, a par-5, in two and two-putted for a birdie. With a par on the last hole, he'd card a 69 and be just two shots back.

Black drove well on the 9th, but a curtain of darkness was dropping fast. After beautiful summer weather, midwinter darkness came quickly. He was eighty yards from the hole but had to walk up to the green to locate the pin. Moving quickly, Black pulled out a wedge, lofted the ball into the air, and never saw it again. It had disappeared into the darkness, and it had disappeared into the hole, for a 3, for an eagle. For a share of the lead in the L.A. Open.

There were few at the 9th green to appreciate the shot—even if they could see it. And for some of the wire service reporters, Black's heroics in the dark were a problem. They'd already sent their stories around the country, anointing Ginsberg the first-round leader. In fact, Black's name had been mistakenly erased from the scoreboard. But Black's 67 was real, and the new wire service versions got sent. United Press International summed it up: "Ever hear of Jim Black? Or Roger Ginsberg?" In the next morning's *Los Angeles Times,* one headline said: "Ginsberg, Black (Who?) Lead Open."

It was a nice showing for the kid. He got some attention, some ink, a prominent place in the first-day stories, and even some space in newspaper sidebars. "The handsome Negro caddied for eight years in North Carolina and decided this winter to get out of the snow and play golf in a warmer climate," the *Los Angeles Times* said. (The clippings weren't enough to get him through the contestants' gate the next morning, however. He had to go through the caddies' entrance.)

Besides, first-round leaders tended to be one-day wonders; they gradually slipped back into the pack and then into obscurity. After one brilliant round, they became footnotes by tournament's end. Sometimes their only mention was in the tiny newspaper agate that listed all who finished.

That pattern seemed to be repeating itself with the two first-round leaders. Ginsberg bogeyed the first three holes Saturday, and Black bogeyed four holes on the front nine, but both recovered somewhat to finish with 74s. "Jim Black, who must be the longest shot ever to share the first-round lead of this tournament, came back courageously after an outgoing 40 with a 34 for 74," said the *Los Angeles Times.* "Under the pressure this young man must have felt, it was a fine effort." Still, both men had dropped four shots out of the lead.

After a torrid 66 in the third round, Paul Harney vaulted into the lead on Sunday. Black shot 73, and was five shots back. Ginsberg receded further, with a 79.

On the final day, Harney clung to a one-stroke lead and collected the $7,500 first prize. Black fired a respectable even-par 71 for a share of ninth place and a $1,550 check. (Ginsberg also shot 71 and finished in the middle of the pack, winning $43.)

Black seemed to be on his way. There was talk of a sponsor, maybe even a PGA-approved player's card. And Palmer himself waited for Black at the 18th to tell him he admired his game. Would he like to use his line of golf clubs?

Although he was unable to talk his way into the next week's tour event in San Diego—he had no player's card yet and the tournament had already allotted its eight exemptions—this new kid, this handsome young Negro, had brighter days ahead. One *Los Angeles Times* sportswriter gushed that Black "is off to a runaway start as the rookie of the year."

James Black had always shown promise. He'd started as a caddie and played wherever he could, with his buddies in an open field, burying a tin can for a hole and using a fishing pole for the flagstick. Even at age fourteen or fifteen, he didn't lack for self-confidence. He told the old man who employed his mother as a domestic that he could play, that he could even beat him.

"Why don't you let me play with you and win some money?" Black asked him.

"How good are you?"

"I could shoot par golf or better."

He got his chance the next week. Black started off slow, bogeying the first two holes. "And I birdied the next eleven holes in a row. In a row. *In a row!* He wanted me to let up."

And now this kid from the projects in Charlotte started playing on country club layouts, too, because he was that good and because there were plenty of people who thought they could beat him—a black kid—especially on layouts where the only blacks worked in the kitchen. "I've been to country clubs where they'd introduce me to the head guy in the locker room, the head cook," said Black. "They'd tell me, 'You were the first one.'"

He started hanging out with gamblers, with men who would bet lots of money on him, with men who would rent a motel room and then sneak him in late and out early before anyone saw the Negro.

He learned to play all kinds of bets. He could throw a golf ball the length of a football field, from one end zone to another, through the goal posts. He'd win money on the putting green, using his foot to putt, while his opponent used a putter. He learned to hit every shot out of a paper cup, and win. "You can hit the ball further because of the spin," Black said. "You can put overspin on it so it'd come out faster." They were gimmicks, but gimmicks that would win bets—like closing his mouth around six golf balls.

His golf game wasn't gimmicky. By age fifteen, he said, he had broken 60 on an eighteen-hole round. By age sixteen, former touring pro Clayton Heafner would let Black use his golf clubs and hit balls off the 10th tee at Eastwood Country Club in Charlotte.

"You got a great pair of hands and a good pair of feet," said Heafner, who had helped another black kid, Charlie Sifford, twenty years earlier. "Golf is a hands and feet game." Heafner—who'd damn near won the U.S. Open, twice—sat by a clubhouse window and watched Black swing. "I worked at it, from sunup to sundown. I used to hate to see the sun go down and loved to see the sun come up," Black said.

If there was an advantage to being a black man on a golf course, it was that you often didn't have to establish the gambler's psychological advantage: getting the other guy to think he can beat you, and to put money on it.

"Most white people feel that black people can't play golf," explained Dunovant. "See, we go into a town; a white boy couldn't beat me blindfolded, but he would bet because he was white. He ain't gonna let no black man beat him. That kept us going. We beat a lot of white boys who thought he could play because he was white and we was black. Just as simple as that. You'd be surprised. We'd always say: '[Not] all white people can play golf. Find some that can't play.' But they were white and they thought they was supposed to beat you."

Black also played the circuit of white satellite tournaments and black tournaments, and gambled other days. He won under the most difficult of circumstances. One year at the Skyview Tournament in Ashville, North Carolina, Black won the three-day tournament hobbling around with a plaster cast on his right ankle, according to both Black and Dunovant.

"I was playing five other guys best ball, black guys," said Black. "And this guy hit me on the ankle with a three-iron. I [had] birdied five straight holes. And he said, 'You're not going to birdie another one.' That was it. I had birdied five in a row, the first five holes. It wasn't a lot of money; we were betting twenty-five dollars a man. You got to be careful who you bet, because everybody can't stand to lose."

Black played with some of the best money-players of his time, including Fat Man, Three-Iron, and Titanic. Occasionally, he'd hook up with or play against Bo Winiger and Al Besselink, and

Dutch Harrison and Smiley Quick and Herman Keiser, tour players or former tour players who, as a point of pride, never shied away from a bet on the golf course.

In a gambling game in St. Petersburg, Florida, at the Airco Golf Course, Black was fifteen under par after seventeen holes. And then quit. He said he'd already won the bet.

Still, there were many obstacles. He put it another way. "A lot of inconvenience being black. It was so inconvenient being black." Like a number of black golfers, he got death threats, and learned that for years, an FBI agent followed him around. How does he know? The agent, he said, wrote him a letter after he retired.

"And I thought he was a salesman. You know what I mean? I would see him, he'd come up, and we'd talk, and then it looked like he disappeared. I'd go to another spot and I'd see him. He liked golf."

Perhaps one of the biggest "inconveniences" occurred when he won a satellite tournament in the Midwest somewhere—he couldn't remember where. But as he told it, he won the tournament and a $5,000 check. He cashed the check and headed out of town, but was stopped at a police roadblock and arrested. By coincidence, just about the same time he had finished at the golf course, someone had robbed a bank in town. (Black had the $5,000 in winnings and quite a bit more from other wagers he'd won that week, he said.) The mayor, who'd handed him the check, came to the jailhouse and vouched for him.

Black was especially proud of his performance over the years in the UGA National, at the junior, amateur, and professional levels. In 1964 and 1968, he won the professional championship. These were accomplishments he achieved, straight up, no con. And it was a source of great pride to Black that no black golfer could beat him in an honest betting game. "Charlie [Sifford], Ted [Rhodes], none of them would bet Black," said Dunovant.

By the middle of 1965, less than two years after he took the first-round lead at the L.A. Open, Black virtually disappeared from the Tour.

It might have been the difficulty getting a sponsor—even Mose Stevens, who helped about every promising black golfer who came through Los Angeles, didn't like Black's cocky attitude, his independent streak. But finding a patient, reliable sponsor was a problem all struggling pros faced.

Black came to a friend, Bobby Mays, who had played on the black circuit for several years, looking for a place to live.

"Man, I might not be out here long," Black told him.

"Why?"

"Last two checks [from his sponsors] were bad checks. No money in the bank."

"Don't worry. Stay out there."

But Black went back to the bank, and the checks had still not cleared.

It might have been the pressures from home, because Black had a wife and three kids to support. And it might have been the difficulty of playing tournament golf at the highest level, where you played the course, not the other three guys in your foursome.

"This is what you're thinking about when you're gambling," said Mays. "You got money in your pocket; you really got to get down and play. But playing in tournaments, to me, you're just walking in the park, no thinking. When I'm playing in a tournament, I'm just hitting the ball, going from one hole to the other. But when you're betting and you're betting a guy like a ten-dollar Nassau, and you say, 'Oh, wait a minute, I'm three down, I gotta get a press,' you're counting your money as you go. Hey, that make you play—a guy trying to take money out of your pocket."

On tour, every week you faced the best players in the world to win top purse of $5,000 or $10,000. In 1963, Palmer was the leading money winner with $128,000. Playing the hustle, you could make $10,000 in one round, $50,000, $60,000, a year easy, if you were good.

And Black was good.

"Best gambler you ever seen in your life," said Mays. "This guy'd go out, he'd shoot 63, 64, 65, like nothing. Every round."

But Black said that on three or four occasions he put in the fix—purposely losing tournaments to win a bet. He lay down, he claimed, and in the process helped Elder win a tournament or two.

"No, I was letting him win, because I was making more money. Well, people were betting on me, that I could beat him—a lot of money. He would still win the tournament; I'd finish second. I was letting him win. I got somebody else to make the bets for me [on Elder]. I learned those things from Titanic, [Fat Man] Stanovich." He did it, he said, to survive, at a time when expenses for a week were a couple hundred and a tournament win wasn't much more than that.

"One on one, I never did that stuff. In those tournament spots, I saw that I could win more money; when a tournament win was $500, I could win $5,000.

"Once you get that reputation, then nobody wants to be around you, anyway. Good players don't have to do that. All the time, head to head, I was that good a player where I did not have to put myself in that position. You still got that thing of character and integrity.

That's why I could go and be around people that bet money and stay in their company all my life. Only time I did that, I'm surviving."

If true—and those close to Elder insist that Black merely lost, and not to win a bet—it certainly takes some luster off Elder's streak. "Just about all of us knew Black was lying down. Picking up, hitting some of those crazy shots. All that was a fact," said Dunovant.

But more than potential unfulfilled, it was integrity compromised, cheapened, tainted. And so the question arises: How do we know when he lost a tournament to win a bet, or just plain lost? Whatever the truth, professional sports have always worried about the gambling element. Boxing, baseball, basketball, and football have all had their gambling scandals. And the PGA understood that its game also attracted an element that wanted to tip the odds in its favor. Al Besselink got fined for betting that he would shoot a 66 the next day at a tour stop in San Diego. He won the bet—he shot a 65—but lost his argument with the PGA.

The history of golf is filled with tales of men who started out hustling but never relinquished the dream of winning in pure competition. Perhaps it was Black's inability to give up a gambler's life for a shot at a higher form of victory that cost him the place in golf history some thought he was destined for.

"I was living in the fast lane, but there was no management," Black said of that period. "I didn't have any agent to manage me, manage the money. I would say within a ten-year time, from the late fifties through the sixties, I made over three million dollars gambling."

Any left?

"None of it," he said.

By the fall of 1967, Elder was ready. He had the game and enough money in the bank to try the Tour. In October, he went to Florida and joined 104 other golfers at the PGA of America's third tournament players' school. It was grueling; the players played eight rounds on the East Course at the PGA National Golf Club in Palm Beach Gardens. The 30 lowest-scoring golfers got their tour playing cards for 1968. The school was twice postponed by rain, and the weather during the days they played was not ideal. But at the end, low-scoring honors went to the youngest player in the field, nineteen-year-old former British Amateur champion Bobby Cole from South Africa, who fired a 572 aggregate, or four under par. Gibby Gilbert was the runner-up, and one stroke behind him were Ron Cerrudo, a member of the Walker Cup team that year, and Deane Beman, a two-time winner of the U.S. Amateur. Also qualifying were Bob Murphy, a former U.S. Amateur champ, and Tony Jacklin, a member of Britain's Ryder Cup team.

And there, smack in the middle of the qualifiers, was Robert Lee Elder, from Washington, D.C., at ten over par. After an opening round of four-over 76, Elder settled down for rounds of 73-74-73-74-70-73-73.

Elder had a good start to his first full year on the PGA Tour, taking home a paycheck from each of the first nine tournaments he entered, a PGA record. He had become a respectable presence on the Tour, although still relatively unknown to the majority of white Americans who casually followed golf.

Then one day, Elder found himself on national television in one of the most gripping golf dramas anyone could remember. At the American Golf Classic in early August, he was thrust into a sudden-death playoff. He certainly could pick his spots. At the Akron,

Ohio, tournament, the course was one of the Tour's toughest layouts, the long Firestone Country Club. When he went to the 16th tee to begin a sudden-death, nationally televised playoff, he was joined by 20,000 fans, tour veteran Frank Beard, and a golfer who was on his way to becoming the game's best ever, Jack Nicklaus.

The 16th was aptly called the Monster because it was a grueling 625-yard par-5. A few hours earlier, Arnold Palmer had fallen out of contention when he carded a triple bogey 8. But Elder stepped up to a thirty-five-foot birdie putt and promptly drained it, sending his wife, Rose, into a spontaneous head-over-heels back flip from a sitting position. Elder stepped back and watched Beard miss his chip and drop out of the playoff. Nicklaus, who would not break so easily, stroked a twenty-foot birdie from the short fringe.

On the 17th, a 385-yard par-4, Elder missed a birdie putt, and Nicklaus reminded Elder that he was Nicklaus, and not some two-bit mark. He put his approach shot in a greenside trap, blasted it out, and ran in a long putt for par. On the 18th, Elder saved his par-4 to halve the hole, and he could sense many in the crowd were pulling for him. And as he and Nicklaus were driven back to the 16th in a station wagon, he was beginning to think he could win.

The tension kept rising, and television ratings kept building. This was no ordinary playoff.

"Seldom have spectators been so emotionally excited," wrote Lincoln Werden of the *New York Times*. "They yelled, 'Come on, Lee,' and others . . . yelled, 'You can do it, Jack.' Nicklaus and Elder 'did it' in that they became engaged in the keenest golfing playoff duel of the year."

At the 16th, Elder bunkered his third shot but sank a six-footer for a par-5. Nicklaus's birdie putt was short by a few inches. They walked to the 17th, the fifth playoff hole. On the fifth sudden-death hole, the 17th, the 390-yard, uphill par-4, it finally ended. Elder hit his second shot fifteen feet past the pin. Nicklaus dropped his within eight feet. Elder's birdie try had grazed the edge of the cup and stayed out, but Nicklaus's didn't. He had won his second straight tour victory and the $25,000 purse. Elder and Beard got $12,187 each.

"Oh, how sweet it could have been" was the way one sportswriter put it. But Elder had given as good as he'd gotten, playing the role of overmatched underdog to the Nicklaus 24-karat Golden Bear legend. His performance had come under the harshest glare, the pressure of a nationally televised playoff that made the most seasoned tour veteran's throat go dry. And suddenly, here was an appealing, photogenic *black* golfer, and he had given TV viewers a dose of drama and a shot of adrenaline.

Frank Lett, Jr., a golf writer and UGA official, had just finished playing golf in Michigan and was sitting around the television with forty or fifty other golfers, black and white. "It seemed like everyone to the man (black and white) was pulling for Lee to win it," he said. In fact, at the next tour stop, Rose said, Nicklaus's wife, Barbara, sought her out and told her, "I want Jack to win all the time, but I was pulling for Lee."

Elder, in newspaper terms, made great copy. Physically, he resembled a popular TV personality, the comedian Flip Wilson. What's more, he traveled with his wife–business manager, an attractive and loquacious woman, and their miniature poodle, Zsa-Zsa.

"Elder did more for Negro golf in 45 minutes than everybody else put together had done in 45 years," said Maxwell Stanford, president of the UGA. It was a gross exaggeration, yes, but one borne of the excitement and enthusiasm over a riveting performance. Elder was a black golfer for an age when television had become a pivotal reason the prize money continued to climb on the PGA Tour. To the sporting world, Elder seemed to have appeared out of nowhere, the right man for the right moment.

But the truth was more complex. At thirty-four, Elder had been around competitive golf a long time. He was a PGA rookie, but a tough, seasoned rookie.

16

"You Know, a Shank'll Jump on You"

Spiller had won dozens of black tournaments and had matched Hogan with a first-day 68 at the Los Angeles Open. But by the time his playing days were behind him, his highest finish in a white tournament was fourteenth, in the Labatt tournament in Canada. When the sixties rolled around and the Caucasians-only clause was erased, Spiller essentially told the younger players that they needed to take advantage of what he and others had begun.

Still, the desire to play on the Tour burned in Spiller's gut long past the age when most golfers mellow, lose interest, or shrug their shoulders and realize the game belongs to younger golfers. Spiller never let it go.

He made a living with jobs on and off the golf course. For some years, he ran his own doughnut shop (Mrs. Spiller's Old-Fashioned Doughnuts), at the corner of Century and Normandie. It wasn't a particularly safe part of town, especially if you ran a cash business and had a drive-through window. People could drive up, stick a gun through the window, and ask for cash—and occasionally did.

His love was on the golf course. And after work—at the dough-nut shop, he would start work at 4:00 A.M.—he played. He was well known enough that people recognized him at golf courses all over Southern California—in Palm Springs, in San Diego, and around

Los Angeles. At Tamarisk in Palm Springs, one of the Marx brothers stopped by to say hello. "Wherever we went, it didn't matter which course we were on, someone would recognize Bill and come over," said Bud Garnier, a regular playing partner. "After a while, it almost got annoying. You'd be playing a round and a guy two fairways over would come over and say, 'Are you Bill Spiller?'"

But it wasn't enough to be recognized. Now in his fifties, he still wanted to put his dreams to the test. So in October 1967, Spiller went to Florida for the PGA's qualifying school—at fifty-four, the oldest golfer trying to qualify that year. He finished well out of the hunt. (He was nineteen over par after the first five rounds; there is no record, however, to show whether he made the cut after the sixth round to play the final thirty-six holes.)

The following year, he had a choice of qualifying schools, created by a division between the players and the PGA that had grown to near irreparable proportions. Many of the Tour players formed a new organization, the American Professional Golfers, which planned to sponsor its own tour in 1969, and the PGA be damned. By the fall of 1968, the whole matter had been thrown into court, forcing tournaments around the country to take sides.

It proved a windfall for players who sought to join the Tour. In the fall of 1968, the PGA had its qualifying school as usual, and the new organization, the APG, had its own qualifying school, too, played at the Doral Country Club in Miami.

Spiller, at fifty-five, headed for Miami to give it another try.

He was competing with hundreds of golfers half his age. His hair was graying and he was balding on top. Some of his playing partners in Los Angeles started calling him the Medicine Man, because of the pills he had to take for various ailments.

But he still had a fair game, although it had some serious hiccups. Known as a tremendous putter in his early days, he struggled on the green, as many players do, when he grew older. "He never showed his age on the golf course, except for his putter," said Garnier. "He lost total control. He would have a six-inch putt and you could bet he'd miss it. From tee to green, he was as good as anybody."

One day at Western Avenue, Garnier came into the clubhouse shaking his head about Spiller's problems. Sitting there, Charlie Sifford had little sympathy. "I'm not gonna feel sorry for him, because that son of a bitch has made enough long putts for anybody," Sifford told Garnier. "It's nature catching up to him."

Perhaps more troubling and unpredictable was Spiller's periodic bout with the shank. An embarrassment to any accomplished golfer, a shank is a serious mishit that sends the ball off the toe or heel of the club, usually at severe angles.

Physically, a golfer can easily make corrections to eliminate the shot. But it can also reemerge just enough to prey on his perpetual insecurity over his swing. The shank can pounce at the worst possible moment, particularly when a golfer is near a bunker, a thick grove of trees, a creek, a pond, or an out-of-bounds stake—and occasionally on the 1st tee, in full view of the putting green, pro shop, and clubhouse. It makes other golfers turn away, half out of sympathy, half out of fear that it is catching. For Spiller, it was an ugly reminder that golf could sometimes humiliate you and almost always mess with your head whenever it wanted to.

"Nobody would want to play with him because of it," said Curtis Sifford, a former tour player and Charlie's nephew. "Nobody would want to watch it. He never knew when it would come up."

"He was up in age," said James "Junior" Walker. "You know, a shank'll jump on you. When you're playing, you don't know when you might shank it."

Still, Spiller had a game and his pride. He was determined to play on the Tour, perhaps be the oldest golfer to come out of the qualifying school successfully. And he would do it at the Blue Monster, the players' nickname for Doral, which was plenty long and had plenty of water to avoid. The players were to compete for several days, playing a total of 144 holes.

And so Spiller played well and came to the last several holes needing only a steady finish to qualify, according to friends and golfers who played in the same qualifying school. Despite the odds—racism, false promises, vindictiveness by the PGA, and now age and uncertainty—Spiller, it appeared, would become a tour player.

It was not to be.

Pete Brown remembered Spiller telling him that he arrived at a short par-5 over the water. "He hit a good drive, laid up—perfect. A little wedge shot over the water to the green." But, remembered Pete Brown, the shank returned.

"He shanked it three times into the water and missed qualifying by one shot. He made a big number on that hole—nine or ten or something."

Eventually it sunk in for Spiller. There would not be a next time.

"He never tried again," said Pete Brown, his voice barely above a whisper.

17

The Masters?
"I Hope You're Right!"

As the day dawned on the Los Angeles Open, the first stop on the Tour in 1969, Charlie Sifford got good news and he got bad news.

The good news came with that morning's *Los Angeles Times.* Sports columnist Jim Murray, in his inimitable style, praised Sifford and skewered golf's establishment, especially the Masters Tournament. Murray said that before Charlie, golf was essentially "the recreational arm of the Ku Klux Klan. Pro tournaments had periodically allowed blacks to play, only to point to their lack of talent when they didn't score well during their rare chances. But Charlie double-crossed them. Charlie could play this damn game all right. Charlie was competition. The Masters, which loved to invite some obscure golfer from Formosa but never invited a black American, ought to send a car for Charlie."

Murray may have cheered Sifford that morning, but Charlie's physical condition did not. Like a lot of golfers who played regularly, Charlie had his share of ailments. He was considering surgery on his hands because of a painful infection in his fingers caused by a manicure years earlier.

Even worse, Charlie had come down with the flu and had considered withdrawing from the premier tour event in his adopted hometown. He had been coughing all that week and was tossing down antibiotics to get ready. It had gotten so bad that week that he'd given up his trademark cigar. He usually smoked four or five per round, often to calm his nerves, but not this week.

Sifford was fond of the tournament. It was in his backyard and it had allowed blacks to play before virtually any other. He also knew the layout at Rancho Park. The course on Pico Boulevard, which had hosted twelve of the previous thirteen L.A. Opens, had been the source of some grumbling from the pros, but mostly over the clubhouse and driving range, which had recently been refurbished. The pros generally liked the 6,827-yard par-71 track. Arnold Palmer had won there three times (1963, 1966, and 1967). "On the whole, it is an exceptional course, and it is always a great experience to play it," said Billy Casper, who won in 1968 at a different course.

As the first day of play began, another black golfer, James "Junior" Walker, a three-time winner on the UGA circuit in 1968, was the early leader with a 67.

Growing up in Rocky Mount, North Carolina, he got to shag balls for the legendary Betsy Rawls and carry Jackie Burke, Jr.'s, bag. But at age twenty, Walker decided he wanted to go to New York City, where his opportunities to play golf were much greater than in the segregated South. "I asked my mother, 'Could I go?' She said, 'Yes, you can go, if you stay out of trouble.' And so I went to New York in '59. I decided I wanted to go there and get a chance to play golf, without runnin'. I used to run on the golf course." He turned professional in 1962 and moved to Southern California in 1963.

At Rancho that day, Walker went out early, when the course was wet, and played long. Nonetheless, he birdied five of the first seven holes. Tour rookie Grier Jones, who had been the national collegiate champion the previous year, and tour veteran Dave Hill later turned in 66s. But the day became Sifford's, although that didn't become apparent until well into his round. He finished the front nine with a one-under 35, then missed eight-foot birdie putts at both the 10th and the 11th. Then his luck changed.

Sifford hit a one-iron to within four feet on the 12th and sunk the putt. On the par-5 13th, he holed a forty-yard wedge shot for an eagle. It was then he realized the day might be special, and the normally dour Sifford smiled broadly. A fan in his gallery noticed.

"How come you smiled?"

"What did you think, I was going to cry?" Sifford replied.

Sifford birdied the next four holes, rolling in a fifteen-footer for a birdie on the 17th to complete the run. He had played the back nine in a stunning 28, for a 63.

It was Charlie's lowest competitive round since he fired a 63 in the opening round of the 1955 Canadian Open. That day in Toronto, Sifford had been standing nearby when Arnold Palmer came off the course, expecting to see his name at the top of the leader board after shooting 64. "How the hell did Charlie Sifford shoot a 63?" Palmer blurted out, looking at the scores. Sifford turned around and said: "The same way you shot 64, Arnold Palmer." Palmer looked over and laughed. But nearly fifteen years later, at the Los Angeles Open, Sifford repeated the feat.

"Give that old man a saliva test," quipped Dave Hill, a friend of Sifford's.

By the next day, Sifford was hoarse from the flu, but he managed an even-par 71—two bogeys, two birdies—to maintain a two-shot edge over the field, led by George Archer, the six-foot-six, rail-thin ex-cowboy. "I feel better, but I still was trying for another 63," he said.

By Saturday, still no cigars. He was coughing so much, he threw away a postbreakfast stogie. But he fired another 71, with one birdie and one bogey, and increased his lead to three strokes at 205. While he was grinding, a South African, who started eight strokes back Saturday, shot a 66 to tie Dave Hill for second place at 208. The thirty-four-year-old Harold Henning, who had played on the U.S. circuit for fourteen years, was playing in only his second L.A. Open.

The question was: Could Sifford hold on for one more day?

It's unusual for a golfer to lead for three rounds, rare to lead a tournament all four days, start to finish. Lloyd Mangrum was the last to do it in Los Angeles, thirteen years earlier.

"Whatever is going to happen is going to happen," Sifford told reporters as he came into the clubhouse. "I feel I'm playing good enough to win, but I'm not worrying about it. I'll do the best I can. I can't worry about the other fellow's score. If you do that, you'll hurt your own game."

By Sunday, Charlie had warded off the flu with, as his wife, Rose, said, "about fifty different kinds of pills." He had carried the lead without his cigars and with a swing that could be described as economical, using his muscular arms and wrists. It was no country club swing, but closer to a powerful lunge that left him with an off-balance finish and at times a nasty hook.

"His swing was nothing to get drunk over," wrote Jim Murray. "Off the tee, Charlie ends up with his hands crossed, his legs crossed, and sometimes his eyes. He looks like a guy who has just fouled off a low, outside 0-and-2 pitch. But when Charlie gets around the green and smells money, he's like a surgeon."

That week, Charlie had also found something to help replace cigars. Around his neck he was wearing a "praying hands" medallion he'd been given at a testimonial dinner. He'd been fingering it all week for luck.

And so, on Super Bowl Sunday, with Joe Namath's Jets and the indomitable Baltimore Colts preparing to meet later in Miami, the day began with a golf tournament in Los Angeles.

As is customary for the leader, Sifford teed off last on Sunday morning, at 11:45 A.M., with his friend Dave Hill and Australian Bruce Devlin. Playing one group ahead was Henning, the South African who had closed fast on Saturday.

Charlie started fast. He rolled in a four-footer to birdie the par-4 1st hole. He saved par with one putt on the 2nd. And on the 208-yard par-3 3rd, Sifford dropped a twenty-foot putt for a birdie. He was ten under par for the tournament and felt as though he could close out the tournament on the front nine.

But while the temperature started to drop, Sifford's putts didn't. When he missed the greens at the 5th and 6th, he took bogeys and finished the front nine just one shot ahead of Hill and Henning. Since his eight-under back nine on Thursday, Sifford had been a model of consistency, shooting conservative, even-par golf.

When he bogeyed the tough par-3 12th, he dropped into a tie with Hill and Henning. Playing one hole behind Henning, Charlie must have heard the roar on the 13th green, when the South African took the lead for the first time by dropping a twenty-foot birdie putt.

Playing under enormous pressure for so many years, he might have wilted this day; it would have been understandable. He was forty-six, after all, weakened by the flu and the chill of a January day. It would be an honorable finish, at second, or even third. Charlie, in fact, had already shed the rap of a slow finisher one Sunday in 1967, when he fired a 64 to win the Hartford Open and become the second black man to win a full-fledged PGA tour event.

Instead he answered with a twenty-foot birdie 3 on the 16th, setting off a raucous cheer from the gallery. Sifford made a six-foot putt to save par on the difficult par-3 17th. And with Henning and thousands of others watching at the 18th, he two-putted from about forty feet to make par and send the tournament into a playoff. (Devlin's twenty-foot birdie hung on the lip of the cup, or he would have joined the two men.)

Thousands of fans rushed to the 15th hole for the beginning of the sudden-death playoff, in the chill and the encroaching dark. Though the tournament estimated it had lost $15,000 in gate receipts to those who stayed home for the Super Bowl, word must have gotten around that Sifford was in a playoff. "There were so many people here for the tournament," said Junior Walker. "I'd never seen so many people for the tournament."

Sifford had learned from playing the 382-yard par-4 earlier in the day about playing the proper club into the green. He'd hit a wedge and left it short. This time, his nine-iron settled forty-two inches from the cup.

Henning had missed the green with his second shot but chipped to within par range.

As Charlie calmly cleaned the green in preparation for his putt, his caddie, Jay Haney, pulled the pin, ran to the edge of the green, and dropped to the ground. Tears were streaming down his face and he was wringing his hands. Maggie Hathaway, the golf writer for the *Los Angeles Sentinel*, overheard the caddie talking to himself. "He should not be here, but I made two mistakes today by advising him wrong on two putts," he said. Sifford had been known to fire a few caddies in his day. But, Hathaway wrote, as she and others tried to console Haney, "the roar of the century went up to the skies and echoed over the hills."

Sifford had dropped the putt.

Sifford stood there on the 15th green, raised his putter, doffed his cap, and smiled broadly. Before he knew it, Maggie Hathaway had rushed onto the green ahead of everyone else, and embraced and kissed him. She had fought for Sifford and other black golfers since 1955, written about them when no one else would, picketed Southern California golf courses, pointed a finger at Bing Crosby for not inviting Sifford, and called, written, and telegrammed Bobby Jones, chairman of the Masters Tournament. (Hathaway said many asked her why she kissed Sifford. "Everybody asked except Charlie Sifford and Mrs. Charlie Sifford. Why? Because they know why.") Dodger pitcher Don Newcombe ran out and grabbed his hand, and other friends and fans enveloped him on the green.

As darkness descended on Rancho Park, Charlie accepted the winner's check for $20,000. It was a memorable moment for Charlie, winning in his adopted hometown.

It was a memorable moment for the game.

Sifford had proved something to himself and to golf. He had fulfilled the promise to boyhood friend Walter Ferguson that they could make a living at the game. He wanted to be known as an accomplished professional golfer who could make a living on the Tour.

He never could be accused of oozing warmth; he was usually a silent, colorless personality on the course. At worst, he could be a forbidding figure, with slightly hooded eyes, a cigar as big as his forearm stuffed in the side of his mouth.

But at long last, in the unseasonable cold of a Southern California dusk, Charlie shed his somber mien, took off his hat, and did what he rarely did—he smiled, smiled often, smiled broadly.

He was, all of a sudden, the unlikeliest of heroes. At age forty-six, Sifford was ten years past his prime, still grinding when other playing pros had semiretired to cushy jobs in the Sun Belt. He was a winner, not just respectably in the money, even though he was no longer the best Negro golfer. Pete Brown possessed the more powerful game and Lee Elder displayed a magical touch that was just too consistent to be lucky. But for this long weekend, only one other golfer had hit more fairways than he did; only three others had hit more greens in regulation. With Rose and his two kids, twenty-one-year-old Charlie junior and two-year-old Craig, around him on the 18th green, Sifford accepted the $20,000 winner's check.

And then he talked about how, with seven or eight other blacks playing in professional tournaments, he was no longer alone on the Tour. Five others had played in the L.A. Open—Pete Brown, Lee Elder, Junior Walker, Rafe Botts, and Curtis Sifford, Charlie's nephew.

"I got one real thought about this. The Lord gave me some courage to stay in there when it got close. I don't know whether I proved that the black man can play golf, but I proved that Charlie Sifford can."

Henning was gracious about Sifford's win but moved quickly to catch a flight after the tournament. He would not have been allowed to play in the same tournament with a black man in his own country, South Africa. Maggie Hathaway pressed him for a promise that Sifford would be invited to play with him in his home country.

"I am not a politician, Madame," he told her. He smiled, turned, and quickly answered questions of other reporters.

"I am a golfer and not a politician. Charlie is a wonderful player. I have played with him before and it is always a pleasure."

The celebration started that night at the Center Field Lounge on South Crenshaw Boulevard, owned by the Dodgers' Willie Davis. Pete Brown was there. Rafe Botts, too. Junior Walker and Lee Elder were there. And Charlie's nephew, Curtis Sifford, was also there, as was Joe Roach, the amateur UGA champion from Miami. They talked about Charlie, but they also talked about the event that would lead sports sections across the country, the stunning upset of the Colts by the New York Jets and their cocky quarterback, Joe Namath. Willie Davis brought another guest over to Charlie's table. Bill Spiller, now fifty-five, had watched the tournament on TV at the Western Avenue Golf Course.

It didn't end at the Center Field, because Los Angeles had just begun to embrace Sifford's win.

By late that week, the sports editor of the *Sentinel* was likening the victory to Dr. King's march on Washington and the desegregation of Central High in Little Rock. "Sifford's great sudden-death win did more for black golfers and his race than any other athlete since Jackie Robinson broke the color line in baseball," gushed Brad Pye, Jr., of the *Sentinel.*

Los Angeles mayor Sam Yorty declared February 3 Charlie Sifford Day. And Sifford would get his own parade through Watts, starting at 108th and Central and running up Central—dubbed Charcoal Alley during the Watts riots three years earlier.

After his parade, Charlie was feted at the Black Fox nightclub and showered with gifts, commendations, telegrams. As he hugged his wife, Rose, Sifford thanked all the people who came to honor him. "It's just so wonderful to think a black man can take a golf club and become so famous. I would like to say to all the young people in America today, all you have to do is be ready and produce. I just wish I could call back about 10 years. I really believe I could really play golf."

Hundreds of telegrams poured in, from friends and celebrities. Box loads of mail came addressed to Charlie, some from kids who were no longer content to be caddies; they wanted to be golfers.

All things seemed possible now. Wouldn't the endorsements, the invitations, the respect, now follow? He could even laugh now about the L.A. Open queen, who kissed all of the tournament's winners, but who wasn't around that Sunday evening at Rancho. "I think we ALL understand," Maggie Hathaway later wrote.

While Charlie was so weak, he had to drop out of the Bing Crosby, his win at Los Angeles made him the Tour's leading money winner, though the season was only a few weeks old. It got him an invitation to the Tournament of Champions, earned by virtue of winning one of the tour tournaments during the year. In a few weeks, Charlie's own signature golf clubs would be on the market.

As Charlie rode in his own parade up Central Avenue that February afternoon, a fan yelled to him.

"Next stop, the Masters!"

Sifford smiled and said, "I hope you're right."

The Masters was an invitational, which historically had often meant to blacks that we'll-invite-anybody-but-you. The Masters had its own set of rules about who could play and who couldn't, and often there was confusion about what those rules were.

It was held at the exclusive Augusta National Golf Club, built in the thirties by America's first true golf hero, Bobby Jones, and a group of investors, headed by Clifford Roberts, Jr. With the help of Scottish golf course architect Alister MacKenzie, they built a golf course on the grounds of an old horticultural nursery that would become widely admired for its natural beauty and for its challenge—thanks, in part, to Jones himself, who during construction would roam the layout hitting balls from various spots. Jones, a Georgia gentleman who earned a ticker-tape parade down Broadway after he won golf's Grand Slam in 1930, was president of Augusta National and embodied the courtly southern image of the Masters. Clifford Roberts, who'd made his fortune on Wall Street and cultivated a friendship with Jones and later President Dwight D. Eisenhower, became chairman of Augusta National and served as its autocrat, overseeing every detail.

The Masters was played each year in April when the magnolias were blooming at Augusta National, about 150 miles east of Atlanta. The first tournament at Augusta National was played in 1934, in the depths of the Depression. (Bobby Jones came out of retirement to play, but Horton Smith won it.) As time passed, the tournament invented its own rituals and traditions, including a presentation of a green blazer to the winner and a champion's dinner on the eve of each tournament. In America, where tradition is sometimes bought, sometimes invented, and sometimes earned, the Masters made itself one of the four major golf tournaments—in addition to the U.S. and British Opens and the PGA Championship. For all those reasons, it could not be ignored.

No black had ever qualified for the Masters by the time Charlie Sifford won in Los Angeles. When Pete Brown won the Waco Turner Open in 1964, he was invited to the Tournament of Champions, but not to the Masters. When Sifford won the Hartford Open in 1967, he got no invitation. It's not that the Masters had a Caucasians-only clause; its arcane rules were not overtly racist. But one didn't need too much imagination to understand the

Masters reflected many of the values of its geography, its sport, and its benefactors. This was one of the most exclusive country clubs in the world, and it was located in Dixie.

And Cliff Roberts, though a successful businessman from New York with an obsession for creating and controlling his surroundings, found his views on race dovetailed with those who were attracted to Augusta National.

When an old friend and member of Augusta died, his widow put a Christmas wreath around the neck of his favorite servant, a black man named Claud de Tillman, attached a note, and sent him to Roberts, who gave the man a job in the kitchen. And Augusta always had a place for Negroes, in classical Deep South tradition, as caddies, waiters, locker-room attendants—just not as golfers.

The members, as legend had it, had another use for their employees in the forties and fifties. For the pleasure of those in attendance, they would have a couple of the black workers come up to the lawn outside the clubhouse and fight until one of the combatants got knocked out. Mr. Roberts, it was well known, was a big fight fan himself.

There remains an ambivalent feeling about the Masters, among even the most open-minded golfers. "The Augusta National membership is, without question, the most out-of-touch-with-reality group of semi-rich, lily-white provincials ever assembled on one sagging veranda," said writer Thomas Boswell, in 1993. "And have they got a beautiful golf course to lord over you!"

But now that Charlie had won the L.A. Open, he thought the golf world could hardly ignore him, including the Masters. He had let his feelings be known about the Masters in no uncertain terms in the past, insisting that the tournament had changed its rules just to keep him out. For example, Sifford said that in 1962, a call came to the clubhouse at the Canadian Open right after he shot a second-round 67 to take the lead, and its message was posted on the bulletin board: "The Masters golf tournament has announced that it will not offer an automatic invitation to the winner of this year's Canadian Open." Purely a coincidence? "I don't think so," Sifford wrote in his autobiography.

Leaving Rancho Park in Los Angeles that Sunday night, Charlie initially deflected questions about the Masters. But friends and supporters had already taken up the fight on his behalf. Columnists for black newspapers throughout the country said the time had come for a black to be invited to the Masters; the time was now.

The Masters, by including Sifford, could take the pressure off white organized golf, wrote Frank Lett, Sr., former president of the UGA and a golf columnist for the *Michigan Chronicle*. "Certainly the barrier in all other sports, which was based on the color of one's skin, has long been dispelled and the popularity that these sports have gained by opening the door is unbelievable." By late March, Augusta was receiving hundreds of telegrams, mostly from blacks, urging the tournament to invite Sifford.

At least Sifford's win had flushed out the Masters' requirements for inviting American professionals. Lett himself got a copy of the more than dozen different ways one could get invited: finish among the top sixteen in the previous year's U.S. Open; finish among the top eight slots in the previous PGA Championship; win the previous British Open; become a member of the Ryder Cup team; finish among the top twenty-four in the previous Masters. Also, six other pros with the best finish on the Tour over the last year would be invited.

The process to select foreign players had never been revealed, but as Jim Murray said, it seemed easier to get an invitation from the Masters if you were from Formosa than from North Carolina.

Some blacks expressed little desire to play at Augusta, deep in the heart of Dixie. At Greensboro only a few years earlier, Charlie had gotten a taste of how open hostility to blacks was tolerated. Some black golfers felt that playing at any PGA tournament in the South, even at the great and glorious Masters, wasn't a priority.

"I didn't want to play it—period," said Pete Brown, who grew up in Mississippi, years later. "Because nobody wants you down there. Why would I want to go somewhere where they don't want me?" Those rules the Masters insisted were so sacrosanct were changed in 1972 to allow all the previous year's PGA tournament winners to qualify. It came too late for Brown, who won the Andy Williams Tournament in 1970.

By then, Cliff Roberts was praying for anyone but Charlie, according to Brown. "I was so close [to qualifying for an invitation] once, Cliff Roberts followed me for three days in Florida," said Brown. "He wanted me to play before Charlie, anybody before Charlie; he didn't care who it was. He hated Charlie's guts. . . . He wanted to invite me, but he knew I wouldn't accept—not an invitation, not without earning it."

The Masters insisted it had its rules, and no amount of pressure, publicity, or protesting would change the way to get into the tournament. In effect, it said, you had to earn it. Some suggested that the PGA pull out its pros to protest the Masters' discrimination. Even if there had been sympathy in the PGA for such a bold move—and there definitely was not—Masters officials would probably have shrugged their shoulders. "They would have played with amateurs," said Brown. "It's their tournament. It's private. They got their own rules committee, their own everything,"

Art Wall, the 1959 Masters champion and a friend of Sifford's, expressed a similar attitude. As a golfer, who was he to suggest that a venerable tournament change the way it was doing things? "It's not my business. They run their tournament. If you don't like it, it's too bad."

Sifford's last chance to qualify for the Masters came the week before the 1969 tournament, in Greensboro. He had to win it to gain enough points to qualify under the rule that allowed the top six other players to qualify. But he shot a 74 in the first round, basically taking himself out of the running. He turned to columnist Jim Murray and said bitterly: "Now they can keep their tournament down there lily-white."

There was one other way to get into the Masters, and that was by a vote of past champions. In 1969, the pressure built for Sifford to get that invitation, if all else failed, by the annual balloting of former champions. But the champions let him down.

Art Wall was the only champion to publicly acknowledge that he voted for Sifford.

"I don't know whether anybody else did or not," Wall said. "Charlie had had a good winter. I told Charlie, and that was the end of it. The rules were out there, and if you were eligible, I was sure they would welcome you with open arms like they would welcome anybody. I felt those people at Augusta, Georgia, ran a first-rate, fair tournament."

It begs the question why others didn't choose Sifford. Most of the former champions, instead, voted for Bob Murphy, who had also had a fine year. Sadly for Sifford, Murphy would have gotten an invitation anyway, since he finished second in the Masters' point system.

"It was like sending money to Rockefeller or rice to China," said Murray. So the week of the Masters, Charlie was in Hattiesburg, Mississippi, playing in the Magnolia State Classic. (He tied for sixth and won $1,450.)

In fairness, the former champions were polled before the results of the point system were final. And Sifford, certainly, wouldn't have won a popularity contest on the Tour, even though he considered several white touring pros his friends.

One reason is for sure. Not enough of the former champions had seen firsthand what Sifford and other black golfers were up against. Perhaps if they had driven with Sifford from one tournament to the next, they might have thought a bit longer about what constitutes fairness, and lingered a bit longer over their ballots, and cast a vote for history rather than for technical achievement during a specific period of time.

Perhaps if they had taken the same journey with Sifford as Larry Mowry, a young pro at the time, had taken earlier in the sixties, they might have voted differently. It made such an indelible impression on Mowry that he wrote about it more than twenty years later in *Golf Digest*.

Mowry had finished his final round at the Doral Open in Miami and gladly accepted a ride from Sifford to the next tour stop in Wilmington, North Carolina.

"Do you know what you're getting into, driving with me?" Sifford asked him.

It never occurred to Mowry, from San Diego and in his twenties at the time, that it might be hazardous for a white man and a black man to ride in a car together in the Deep South. To him, it was a chance to pick up some tips from a veteran pro he admired.

During their stops along the way, Sifford stayed in the car while Mowry got the coffee. The young white golfer got some strange looks, but Mowry attributed that to his loud golf slacks and white shoes. When they pulled over for gas that night at a dimly lit truck-stop in south Georgia, Mowry got out to get a couple of Cokes while Sifford took care of the gas.

As he retrieved the drinks from a vending machine, two cops out of central casting—cigars, open shirts, hats tipped back—eyed Mowry with contempt. "You jes' don't care who you drive with, do you, son?" said one, who had a scar creasing one cheek, with an intimidating look.

The cops walked past Mowry and out to Sifford's car. Mowry returned to the car in time to overhear Scarface, as he called him, ask Sifford if the car was his.

"No-saa. Ah's drivin' for Mistah Larry," Sifford said in a falsetto. Scarface eyeballed the California plates on the new Buick Wildcat and added: "You better drive slow and steady out of this county, or I'll run you two in."

Sifford drove slowly, and the two men didn't speak until they had crossed the county line. "If he knew this was my car, we'd both be buried in a cotton field and never heard from again," Sifford said, breaking the silence. Mowry was speechless.

They drove through the night and into the next day, Mowry ducking into a restaurant to get food and returning to find Sifford under the dash, tired of the stares and the pointing, as though he were some animal. But there was no other way. Sifford would have had to go around back to the kitchen door, pay in advance, and wait, perhaps not getting anything in return and with no right to complain. Even when they arrived at Mowry's motel in Wilmington, the owner ignored Mowry and glared at Sifford until he was assured Charlie was staying elsewhere.

Mowry was no longer a naive young kid. "Charlie lived in a different country than I did." Mowry wrote.

Teddy Rhodes also lived in that other country.

But, unlike Charlie, who would stay on the road and keep grinding away in hopes of a breakthrough, Teddy would come home for good.

By the time he finally returned to Nashville, the native son had won, by a number of estimates, more than 150 golf tournaments. But, of course, no one kept any official statistics on the UGA tour. He had won the Ray Robinson Open in 1949, with a 62 and 68 in the final two rounds. He had won Joe Louis's invitational three straight years, and captured the National Negro Open four times, including a run of three straight in the late forties. After the first round of the 1947 L.A. Open, in which Rhodes was coleader with three others, the *Los Angeles Times* pronounced him "America's greatest Negro golfer." In 1949, he finished fourteenth at the Tam O'Shanter, then the highest finish by a black golfer in a PGA event.

When Teddy eventually returned to the city where he was born, he lived much of the time at the El Dorado Motel, a short walk from Cumberland Golf Course. He continued to play, when his health allowed, and he rarely tired of trying to help younger players. Under a tree on Twenty-sixth Avenue North, across from Cumberland, Rhodes would teach golf.

He would demonstrate his own swing, which had inspired such names as "Straight Arrow" and "Sweet Swinger." He would hit shot after shot, pinching the ball as if he were hitting a cue ball on a pool table. And his irons would land, oh so softly, on the green, like butterflies landing on cotton, his old friend Joe Hampton said.

"Young guys like me would come by just so they could sit beside him and listen to him talk about golf. He understood the game," said Jim Dent, who became a PGA tour and PGA senior tour player.

He turned fifty the year Pete Brown became the first black to win a seventy-two-hole, fully sanctioned PGA tournament, in 1964. He lived to hear about Charlie Sifford's breakthrough at Hartford in 1967, and then at Los Angeles in 1969.

And he watched as his protégé Lee Elder matured into a bona fide PGA threat. He had transformed Elder, who was orginally a cross-handed player like Howard Wheeler, through several of those under-the-tree ball-striking sessions in St. Louis, where Teddy lived for several years.

"But Ted's love of the game and those who played it never dimmed," wrote *Nashville Tennessean* columnist John Bibb. "If there was bitterness, I never heard him say it. He would help any man with a golfing problem and was particularly interested in seeing youngsters get a good start in the game."

He had developed heart and kidney problems—some said from the brandy he favored; others, from the long years on the road when you'd hold your water because you didn't want to stop and couldn't find a bathroom that allowed blacks if you did. Gradually he got weaker, barely able to finish four or five holes some days.

But his short game remained laser-sharp. There was an old tree by the 1st tee at Cumberland where Teddy could still demonstrate his "Helicopter Shot"—which went straight up, over the tree, and came down on the green, not more thirty feet away, long before the days of the specialized clubs that did everything but swing themselves.

In early July 1969, Rhodes went out and shot 33 on the nine-hole Cumberland course. Later on, back at the El Dorado, he and Joe Hampton gathered by the pool to discuss what they were going to do the next day. "We were going to play golf. We always had something going," said Hampton.

But the next day, the manager of the El Dorado called Hampton to deliver the news. "I believe Ted is dead," he said. Rhodes was walking out of his room on the Fourth of July and dropped dead of a heart attack. He was fifty-five.

Teddy's death was reported in three brief paragraphs on the obituary page of the *New York Times*. But many in golf recognized his talent and wondered what might have been. "No question, he would have been a winner," said Bob Rickey, the former MacGregor Equipment executive who knew most of the touring pros of the time. "He never got the opportunity."

Sifford, writing in his book years later, called him "the black Jack Nicklaus, but you've probably never heard of him because he was black and living at the wrong time. His story is one of the great tragedies of golf."

But Rhodes made the front page of black newspapers, which understood the significance of his life to their community and to golf. "So long, old pro," Maggie Hathaway wrote in the *Los Angeles Sentinel*. "Hope you enjoy the heavenly courses where all golfers are equal and can join the PGA."

18

"What Have I Done to You, Sir?"

In August 1969, while 400,000 kids were gathering peacefully for a music festival near Woodstock, New York, there was trouble brewing at, of all places, a golf tournament.

The PGA Championship was scheduled at the National Cash Register Golf Club in Dayton, Ohio, and officials expected problems. They went to the trouble of obtaining a court order against the local branch of the Southern Christian Leadership Conference, which was planning demonstrations against the PGA and the South African Gary Player.

For his part, Player anticipated trouble. He played a couple of practice rounds with Pete Brown, never straying far from him. "We were like twins walking down the fairway," said Brown, able to laugh about it years later.

On Thursday, the first day of the tournament, only a few pickets lined up outside the golf course. One of them held a sign that said: PROFESSIONAL GHETTO ASSOCIATION SPONSORED BY THE DAYTON CHAMBER OF COMMERCE. Inside the gates, record crowds swarmed over the course to watch golf, and none came to demonstrate. Just in case, however, the tournament had 125 Pinkerton guards protect the greens at night from vandals.

As a warm, pleasant day dawned Friday, another record crowd streamed through the gates. And Player began the day just two strokes behind a group of nine golfers bunched in the lead with 69s. He and Jack Nicklaus were paired together in what promised to be the day's marquee group.

But on the 4th tee, it began, without warning. Someone threw a program at Player as he was about to tee off.

At the 10th, things got more aggressive.

Walking to the tee, Player got a cupful of ice and soft drink tossed in his face and was called a racist. As the protestor was arrested, Player toweled off and asked:

"What have I done to you, sir?"

Then it got worse.

Nicklaus and Player walked onto the par-5 10th green and began lining up their putts, when a group of demonstrators rushed onto the green. A stunned Nicklaus held up his putter in self-defense, watching as one person picked up his ball and tossed it off the green. Player was jostled but not hurt. The surreal scene played out quickly, when police stormed the green and arrested seven people.

As the excitement died down, both Player and Nicklaus holed their birdie putts, but already a rumor had shot back to the press tent that Player had been knocked down in the scuffle. Finally, three holes later, Player endured the final disruption: a girl tossed a ball onto the green as he putted, and she was taken into custody.

As he and Nicklaus completed their round, some of the 20,000 fans applauded Player and Nicklaus at each hole. But the golfers, both known for their steely competitive nerves, had been shaken. Their civilized workplace had been violently disturbed, and now they felt vulnerable themselves.

Nicklaus, for his part, showed the strain. A triple bogey 7 on the last hole effectively dropped him out of contention. "My hands were quivering. I didn't know what the hell to think. I just wanted off the golf course. It took me a little longer than I would have preferred."

For Player, it was the toughest round of golf he'd ever played.

"I honestly thought I might get shot because of South Africa. It was unbelievably difficult to concentrate out there," Player said. "I'm no racist. I want everybody to understand that. I love all people— white, black, yellow."

"I think the majority of people today were so nice I don't think you should let lousy things be publicized," Player told reporters after the round. When one of them asked him whether he considered quitting during the round, Player responded:

"Never. If all those thousands of persons out there are so nice, you can't let five others drive you in. That's just letting them have their way."

Security was beefed up for the next day. Wherever he went, Player had a deputy sheriff shadowing him.

"Does it look bad out?" Player asked people in the clubhouse before he walked to the practice tee.

"Yes, it's cloudy; it may rain," someone told him.

"Rain is my last worry," Player said, smiling.

On the final day, Player and his playing partner, Raymond Floyd, were told not to leave any green without a police escort. As many as eight officers waited at each tee and green. But Player seemed buoyed by the constant applause, tipping his hat throughout the day. No demonstrators spoiled the day, and he ended the tournament in second place, just a stroke behind Floyd. But he never forgot the effect it had on his game.

"I will go to my grave knowing that I really won that PGA," Player would say years later.

Privately, Player worried about the harassment and the death threats by phone. Though the tournament had ended, he decided to make contact with a group of Dayton protestors and meet some of its members. He had become accustomed to people associating the policies of his country with him personally, but, Player said, he talked about how he had been raised, and they seemed to understand him a bit better.

"I just explained to them that my father brought me up to love all people and treat them with respect," he said. ". . . They were very nice and I never had any trouble after that."

But, in fact, the trouble had not ended.

A wave of public criticism about South Africa's policies gathered momentum, and when Player returned to the United States the next year, he was accompanied by security at virtually every tournament.

He had been forewarned to expect protests.

Black activist Harry Edwards—the political guru to the American track athletes who had raised gloved fists in black power salutes at the Mexico City Olympics in 1968—warned that Player's life on the Tour would not be pleasant. Player's black caddie, Ernest "Nippy" Nipper, received a warning that there would be trouble if he worked for Player at the Monsanto Open in Pensacola, Florida. And Player was now routinely telling reporters: "Look, I'm not a racist."

It didn't help that Arthur Ashe had been denied a visa to play in a tournament in South Africa—a decision, the South African government said, that was based on his politics, not on his race. But it raised the logical question why Player, a white man, could come to the United States and make lots of money playing golf, when Ashe, a black man, could not gain entrance to South Africa.

The heat was turned up in the black press. Maggie Hathaway of the *Los Angeles Sentinel* used her column to excoriate Player. For years now, she had been asking him pointed questions whenever she attended a pro tournament; in 1963, she took the bus from Los Angeles to the Bing Crosby tournament in Carmel to ask Player how he felt about playing in the same tournament with Charlie Sifford. Seven years later, Hathaway was still on the Player beat.

"Here we are again ready to watch a segregated Masters," she wrote in an April 1970 column. "Player is a Master and last year did not vote for Charles Sifford. This year he did not vote for Pete Brown or Sifford. I believe the PGA is allowing this segregation or it would not stand for any kind of segregating tournaments to be booked. Did not America expel South Africa last month because of Arthur Ashe? Then what do you think the PGA is waiting for? The Beverly Hills–Hollywood NAACP (which I am the founder of) is going to declare war on PGA if they don't handle Player, [South African golfer Harold] Henning, and The Masters."

Hathaway even included in her column a letter from a man who vowed that "I personally will run Player off the next golf course in this state."

Player had been thrust into a situation that most athletes abhor— talking politics. Most pro golfers tend to be political conservatives, if political at all. But the events of the past several months had coalesced into a critical mass that made Player's situation virtually untenable. Politics do affect sport, and countries around the world had taken action to bar South Africa's athletes from international competition because of apartheid. South Africa had been barred from participation in the 1968 Olympics. It had been barred from Davis Cup competition. And its cricket and rugby teams had been turned away from international competitions.

Gary Player remained his country's most high-profile international sportsman, playing golf around the world. When he first set foot in the United States in 1970, he issued a written statement saying he wished sports could be above politics, but that he deplored Ashe's ban. He also said he was willing to play a series of exhibition matches with Lee Elder, Charlie Sifford, and Pete Brown, with the proceeds to go to the United Negro College Fund. But he steadfastly refused to criticize his home country.

He did himself no favors when later in the year he was quoted as saying South Africans appreciated their own blacks more than Americans did theirs. "What's more, I think we have a greater love for and understanding of the non-white people in this country than they have in America for their Negroes," he said. Thirty years later, Player stood by the statement and pointed to America as having repressed blacks since the Civil War. "My grandchildren will look back and say the leaders in America and the leaders in South Africa must have been almost barbaric to allow those laws to take place. Thank goodness that it's finished in America and finished in South Africa and we can move ahead," he said.

Whatever his public statements and private convictions, Player's appearance in American tournaments was kindling to the fire. His success on the Tour just made matters worse.

In 1971, Player came to suburban Philadelphia again, this time to the Merion Golf Club, not more than five miles from the scene of his 1962 PGA win at Aronimink, the site of the tournament after Stanley Mosk's threats. This time, the United States Open championship was at stake, and South Africa was squarely in the news.

During the first round, Player was paired with Art Wall and Bob Goalby, two American pros who had befriended black golfers. But on the 16th and 17th holes, Player was heckled by two black spectators. At the 17th tee, they yelled, "Arthur Ashe, Sharpsville!" It was a reference to the black American tennis star's difficulty getting a visa to compete in South Africa. The two spectators were escorted off the course, and Player later tried to downplay the incident. "It was nothing, absolutely nothing. I'm not getting involved in politics at all."

During the second round, he was accompanied by a uniformed policeman. During the third round, four security officers, two of them armed, followed Player around Merion's 6,544-yard layout.

"This is a heck of a way to have to play," he said to one of them.

Whether it affected his golf, Player wouldn't say. But he finished out of the running, nine strokes behind Nicklaus and Lee Trevino.

By then, Player was a different man, at least by his public actions. When he first came to the United States to play, he was reticent about his country's politics, saying he was an athlete, not a politician. By now, in 1971, Player had gained a reputation among black players as someone who would help them. In a bold public move, he invited Lee Elder to South Africa to play in a tournament.

It was a move that branded Player as a traitor even among some of his own people, and blacks in America were wary of the trip. Elder, too, was cautious at first. Was he being used, somehow?

Hathaway expressed that ambivalence in her column. "We do hope Lee Elder is not making a mistake going to South Africa to play to prove that Gary Player loves blacks in America."

It's unclear whether Player had gradually changed over the years, had been transformed by the protests, or had merely decided to reveal himself over time. But his support for black American golfers, often quietly expressed, had endeared him to many of them. Even years later, Player would make time to help black golfers by playing exhibitions or giving clinics to benefit their local causes.

"You couldn't ask for a finer man than Gary Player," Sifford said in 1971. "He's helped me so many times I've stopped counting." One of those times was earlier in the year when Player sought out Sifford during the annual public speculation about Sifford and a possible Masters invitation. "If it'll help you get into the Masters, you've got my vote, Charlie," Player told Sifford.

During the Elders' three-week trip, they visited Kenya, Uganda, and Nigeria, where Lee won that country's open championship. In South Africa, however, Elder made his biggest impression. His visit was trumpeted as one that, temporarily at least, broke down racial barriers at hotels, golf courses, and even a movie theater. As Elder and Player teed off together, more than 5,000 people watched, some blacks and whites mixing at a sporting event for the first time. The following day, the gallery doubled in size.

Player credits Elder with helping break down segregated sport in South Africa, while both men withstood enormous pressure to pull it off. "We did what we believed was right and it turned out it was right," Player said.

You could gauge the trip's impact merely by reading Maggie Hathaway. She could hardly contain her enthusiasm. In fact, she had been invited on the trip herself. "At this point we must admit cowardice. . . . Player invited us to come to South Africa and we chickened out. Our mistake."

It was a radical change of heart about the man she had hounded for so many years, and to whom she would eventually offer a handshake and a heartfelt apology.

19

The "Garbage Tour"

By the early 1970s, the black tour was losing steam. While many of the tournaments still provided opportunities for blacks to gain valuable competitive experience, the best blacks now had opportunities on the PGA Tour that didn't exist a decade earlier.

The black tour had always had a bit of a ragtag, make-it-up-as-you-go-along quality, even in the so-called golden years when Wheeler, Rhodes, Spiller, and Sifford played. Even then, it was called a lot of things, few of them flattering: the Peanuts Circuit, the Chitlins Circuit, the Neck Bone Tour, and so forth.

Even the UGA National, considered the most important black tournament of the year, had been the source of occasional bitching by the pros, with its paltry purses and overcrowded fields.

But now the competitive gap between the PGA Tour and the black tour had become larger, if only slightly, because the best blacks could afford to miss more and more tournaments on the UGA circuit. In addition, the loose-knit quality of the black tour led to more disorganization and administrative bickering. The individual tournaments, always their own fiefdoms, answered to no one, unlike the PGA tour events, which fell under the organization's umbrella.

It was no coincidence that some disgruntled players and tournaments had already begun to consider starting an alternate tour. Thomas "Smitty" Smith, a pro in Atlanta, and others grandiloquently named their endeavor the North American Golf Tour, although it was actually a regional tour of a dozen or so tournaments mostly situated in the Carolinas, Georgia, and Florida. Still, it was a start, an effort to reinvigorate the black tour.

So it was bound to happen. The complaining gained an edge, and somewhere along the line somebody coined the term "Garbage Tour" for the black circuit.

It may have come from Willie "Barracuda" Jefferson, who played golf on the black circuit and turned heads at the L.A. Open one year, not with his golf, but with an entourage of seductively dressed women who followed him. Few people had seen such fans at a PGA event, women whose dress more closely resembled the Dallas Cowboy Cheerleaders' than the average golf fan's Bermuda shorts, golf shirt, sneakers, and visor. But Jefferson's comments rang true for some players.

"We play 'garbage courses' where the greens are so bad you would rather chip than putt. To play the 'garbage tour' you have to love the game. It's all we got. It's like the old story of the crooked dice game— you know it's crooked but it's the only game in town, so you play."

And even if you wanted to play, he added, it was difficult finding out about the tournament schedule. "It's easier to get a copy of the Pentagon Papers than information on the black tour."

Not only were Sifford, Pete Brown, and Elder doing well on the PGA Tour, but another group of golfers had set their sights on the Tour's pot of gold—players like James "Junior" Walker, Nate Starks, George Johnson, Rafe Botts, Jim Dent, Cliff Brown, Howard Brown, Curtis Sifford, and the Thorpe brothers, Chuck and Jim.

George Johnson, whom everyone knew as G.G., was a case in point. He had a game that occasionally thrust his name high on the leader board. In 1971, he made noises like he might beat Charlie, Pete, and Lee to the Masters. He flirted with the Kaiser Open in Napa, California, finishing four shots off the lead. In December, he won the Azalea Open in Wilmington, North Carolina, but by then, the Masters considered it a satellite event and its winner not worthy of an invitation. Many pros had tagged Johnson as the next black likely to win a major PGA tournament.

Jim Dent was another golfer who showed great promise. He'd won the UGA National in 1969 and was making a name for himself as the longest driver in the game. "This guy makes me feel inadequate," said Jack Nicklaus, the Tour's biggest hitter for years.

Known to some as Big Boy, Dent was six feet two and 220 pounds and a former all-state high school football player from Augusta, Georgia, where he had worked as a caddie at Augusta National. Soft-spoken and shy, he knew why he was trying to make it on the PGA Tour. "They're giving away $8 million. That's why."

Perhaps it was coincidental, but 1971 also marked the first time since the UGA's inception in 1926 that its championship was won by a white man. In it, Jack Price edged Nate Starks to capture the championship at Pittsburgh's North Park Golf Course.

A local club professional, Price was among the few whites in the tournament, but he recalled a friendly atmosphere in which he was treated just the same as everyone else, especially by the gamblers. On the par-5s, Price drew heavy action for his ability to reach the green in two shots.

"You just won me twenty bucks," one fan told Price as he walked up the fairway.

"How's that?"

"You just hit the ball up there in two."

You would be hard-pressed to cite a U.S. Open in which a bettor sidled up to Nicklaus or Watson to thank them for saving par with a bunker shot or for sinking a long eagle putt.

Price was also the target of a bit of gamesmanship. During the third round, one of the other players sent a kid over to disrupt his concentration with an old hustler's trick: get the other guy thinking too much.

"What are you thinking about when you swing?" the kid asked him.

"I'll tell you later," Price said. "Right now, I'm just thinking about hitting it on the green."

Trailing Starks during the third round, Price played the last four holes in three under par. His wedge to the 18th green lipped the cup, leaving him an easy birdie and a slim lead he would not relinquish the next day.

The UGA was rightly proud that its tournaments never excluded anyone who qualified to play, and thus it welcomed anyone of any race, and occasionally white golfers competed in its events, including Al Besselink and 1968 U.S. Open champion Orville Moody. Even that rubbed against the conventions of the day, which in some areas of the country forbade blacks and whites to compete against each other in organized competition. In 1962, for example, the UGA took the National to Fuller Park in Memphis, where it attracted white entrants in its junior championship. Even then, mixing was forbidden, but the sportswriters looked the other way. "Nobody took any action against us," said UGA president Maxwell Stanford. "We had no problems."

But playing the circuit was always a struggle. Most of the tournaments had small galleries—sometimes with as many white fans as black—and were played on courses that sometimes lacked much grass; often you were hitting off hard pan, on the tees and in the fairways. And the greens were bumpy from so much play and so little grooming. Elder, who became known as a putter who could negotiate his putts on those bumpy greens, had a difficult adjustment on those billiard-table PGA tournament greens.

"All these guys, they were scuffling," said Smitty, speaking softly in his golf shop outside Atlanta. "We would help each other, then we'd laugh about it. We'd eat baloney and cheese and soda crackers. And enjoy it, and go about our business. Well, I don't know, it was just something that we loved about the golf. I've let many guys come in, and sleep on the floor," he said, motioning to the hard floor in the golf shop.

Small favors were never forgotten. Smitty still remembered one from more than thirty years ago when he'd taken the train up to Baltimore for a tournament but had no place to stay that night. Harold Dunovant was at the YMCA and offered to share; so the reed-thin Smitty and the huge Dunovant squeezed onto a single bed that night.

"It was a scramble, you know," Smitty said. "But when you look back over it, I always say the Lord took care of us. We drove all these miles and didn't have accidents and never got into any real trouble at the golf course, like fighting and all this kind of stuff.

"We kind of stuck together, helped one another to get over."

In 1971, the crown jewel of black golf went unnoticed by the most prominent black newspapers around the country—by the *Afro-American* in Baltimore, the *Defender* in Chicago, the *Sentinel* in Los Angeles, the *Michigan Chronicle* in Detroit.

There were good reasons. For one, the UGA National had become an anachronism in increasingly integrated American sports, even in the atavistic realm of golf. During the forties and fifties, before sports were widely integrated, black-run championships and the fight to integrate were big news. Now, sports pages were devoted to either local sports heroes or the exploits of blacks in big-time sports, where they now played a major, sometimes dominant, role. Somewhere along the line, the UGA National slipped through the cracks of the blacks' success in sports.

Even in the city that hosted the tournament, where the local black press routinely lavished attention on the National, the *Pittsburgh New Courier* made no mention that year of the championship.

The UGA circuit would continue to feature fine players, but it was no longer the staging ground it had once been. Sadly, the glory days of the UGA had ended, and no one had bothered to write its obituary.

Pete Brown had at least one more comeback in him. He'd experienced them in life and in golf, and now in 1970, he was trying to break the long drought that had followed his win at the Waco Turner Open in 1964.

He began the last day of the Andy Williams–San Diego Open seven strokes behind the leader—and that leader was Jack Nicklaus. But Brown's 65 forced a playoff with England's Tony Jacklin, while Nicklaus's missed four-foot putt on the 18th kept him out of the playoff.

The playoff lasted only one hole. Brown made an easy par-4 at the 15th and Jacklin could only manage a bogey after his second shot hit a tree branch. It was good for a $30,000 payday—nearly half his career earnings on the Tour—an embrace from Margaret, and a song from Andy Williams. Pete's thirty-fifth birthday was the next day, and by then, the celebration was still going.

With his game, some wondered, why hadn't there been more wins, more celebrations?

He was one of the biggest hitters in the game, able to reach many par-5s in two when other golfers could not. Jack Tuthill, the Tour's tournament director for many years, remembered an extraordinary sound at one California tournament. Tuthill had little time to actually *see* the golf as he attended to whatever problems popped up. He often followed a tournament simply by listening. "I heard somebody hit the tee shot like a rifle shot. 'I've got to see who hit that shot.'" It was Pete. His swing was widely admired by other pros, including Hogan, as one of the finest on the Tour. Hogan took Pete aside in 1964 and told him so, a rare compliment from the game's master technician of the swing.

Now that Pete had won two PGA tournaments—Charlie was the only other black golfer with a PGA win, having captured Hartford in 1967 and Los Angeles in 1969—why weren't there more? Was there a disadvantage to his amiable personality; perhaps Pete was too nice, too deferential, even too timid at times, and didn't exhibit the killer instinct enough? Some pros, both black and white, thought so.

But it was precisely that easygoing manner that had gotten him here, just as Charlie's fierce single-mindedness had gotten him through the tough years. They were two sides of the same coin, men who prevailed in their own distinct ways.

It was his moderating influence, for example, that Rose Elder was grateful for during a tournament in the South, when Pete skillfully steered her away from a hotel clerk—and an explosive confrontation she could never win—who denied her a room, despite her reservation.

Brown had been an ambassador for golf under the most trying of circumstances. He was the black player paired with other golfers who didn't want to play with blacks. He was the player the PGA asked to play exhibitions in places no other blacks would go. One year, he traveled to a resort in a part of Florida where the KKK was still active, and chose to sleep in his car rather than his

$150-a-night room, for fear he would be a sitting duck for some nutcase with mayhem on his mind.

Of course, he had to endure all the usual indignities, even in the so-called liberal North. Between holes during the 1964 PGA Championship in Columbus, Ohio, he ducked under the ropes to get a hot dog but was blocked from rejoining his group because a security officer didn't believe he was a contestant.

"I'm playing," Pete told him.

"Oh, yeah, you bet," the guy told him.

Only after his playing partner, Bobby Nichols, vouched for him could he get to the tee and resume the round. At the same tournament, he walked out to the parking lot and found some kids disconnecting the driveshaft from his car. "It was just laying down on the ground," Brown said.

And there was his health. He had conquered polio years before, but his muscles in his back and legs often wouldn't allow him to play more than two or three tournaments in a row. Sometimes, his back would lock up in the middle of a round, and he'd be done for that week, and often longer.

In the afterglow of his win in San Diego, Pete returned to Mississippi for Pete Brown Day in Jackson. At city hall, he was greeted by the mayor and presented with a resolution and some gifts, including a fishing boat and trailer. During the ceremony, Pete recalled his days as a boy in Jackson, when he first set eyes on the old municipal golf course, where he worked as a caddie but wasn't allowed to play a round of golf.

"When I saw people out on the greens, I had no idea what they were doing," he said. Now, more than three decades later, no one knew better what they were doing on a golf course than Pete himself.

20

Black Orchid

On a Monday morning in April 1974, Americans opened their sports pages to a picture of a black man weeping into a towel. In a voice choked with emotion, he was telling his wife over the telephone: "Baby, we did it! We finally did it, baby. We finally won."

Lee Elder had won the Monsanto Open in Pensacola, Florida, and thereby earned himself an invitation to the Masters golf tournament. He would become the first black man who wasn't carrying someone else's golf bag to walk down the fairways at Augusta National Golf Club. As one writer said, "The grass will still be green at Augusta, but all the American-born players won't be white."

Elder would be the first. Not gruff old Charlie Sifford. Not amiable, talented, but injury-riddled Pete Brown. Not a handful of other black players who had come close. It would be Robert Lee Elder, the man who millions of white Americans thought was a dead ringer for comedian Flip Wilson.

And to think Elder had almost passed up the Monsanto, just like some of the games' big names—Nicklaus, Player, Trevino, Miller, Casper, Palmer, and Weiskopf. Not only was it scheduled on a week between the Masters and the Tournament of Champions, but talk that the tournament might lose Monsanto as its sponsor had also thrown its future into doubt.

Years earlier, Pensacola had gained a reputation among black players. Weiskopf remembered a tournament there in the mid-1960s when country club officials wouldn't let Sifford into the locker room. Some of the white golfers chipped in to buy a nominal club membership that allowed them to take Sifford in as a guest.

Elder had apparently learned for himself about Pensacola. In 1969, just his second full year on the Tour, Elder was quoted in an Associated Press story as saying Pensacola's galleries were well known for race baiting, and that he would no longer play there. (A few days later, he denied making the remarks and said he intended to return to the Monsanto tournament.)

In the intervening years, Monsanto tournament officials had treated Lee well, and so in 1974, he decided to play. And this time, he found a gallery that was pulling for him.

In western Florida, at the tight Pensacola Country Club layout that winds in and out of dense growths of pine, Elder stayed within sight of the leaders all four days. Heading into Sunday, he was paired with the leader, Peter Oosterhuis, a tall, likeable Briton. Oosterhuis started the day two shots ahead of Elder at 205, and one ahead of Al Geiberger, at 206. Though young, and playing only his third tournament in America that year, Oosterhuis had won sixteen international titles already. He had fired a torrid 63 on Friday to take a three-shot lead, only to drop off Saturday with a 72.

And throughout the day, he had held off Elder, holding a two-stroke lead with two holes left on Sunday. To have any hope, Elder needed two birdies. And he got them, with a three-foot birdie on the 17th and a five-foot birdie on the 18th (after a miraculous low second shot from behind two huge pines).

A playoff.

His win-loss record in playoffs was not good. He had lost to Trevino in Hartford two years earlier. And, of course, he succumbed to Nicklaus after a five-hole playoff at Firestone in 1968. But the fates were with him this time around, as Oosterhuis missed short birdie putts on the first two holes, as Elder scrambled to pick up one-putt pars. On the fourth extra hole, Elder sunk a putt, and suddenly, the door swung open to the Masters.

Curiously, Elder, at first, was coy about accepting an invitation to the Masters. "It's a year away. I'll have to weigh that somewhat. I really don't want to be put on the spot as to yea or nay right now. I'll have to weigh it carefully."

Whom was he kidding? Reporters couldn't believe it; this was something Elder had talked about for years, becoming the first black to play in the Masters, being the first black to earn an invitation.

But the suspense was soon over. Clifford Roberts issued a statement saying Elder would definitely be extended an invitation to the 1975 tournament. "He has automatically earned his invitation . . . and we are very delighted he has done so," Roberts said.

"That's fine," Elder said with a smile. "Tell Mr. Roberts I'll see him at the Masters."

And from the moment Elder sank the final putt in Pensacola and broke down into tears when he called his wife, Rose, and said, simply, "Baby, we did it! We finally did it, baby. We finally won," Elder's own journey to the Masters would be unforgettable, and not entirely pleasant.

Elder would be sealed in a bubble from which he could not escape at least until he played in the Masters, fifty-one weeks later. It would be the longest year, the year that Lee Elder, the journeyman golfer, would become Lee Elder, the national celebrity.

He was the recipient of an outpouring of good wishes—hundreds of letters and hundreds of telegrams. So many people gathered outside his three-story brick house in northwest Washington, the D.C. cops had to assign an officer there to direct traffic. President Gerald Ford wanted to play golf with him. Sammy Davis, Jr., wanted him to model a line of clothes. Publishers clamored for his autobiography. His hometown newspaper, the *Washington Post*, congratulated him on its editorial page. Mayor Walter Washington gave him the key to the city, proclaimed Lee Elder Day, and said: "He is ours; he belongs to us." And the president was among 1,200 people who had turned out at a fifty-dollar-a-plate testimonial at the Washington Hilton to raise money for Elder's new scholarship fund.

His journey had also become a parable, with lessons for whites and blacks alike. Elder had earned his way to the tournament, not been handed a pass because of public pressure or white guilt. To some blacks, Elder was an example of how you had to prepare to be successful and had to be ready to take the steepest, rockiest, most precarious path "'cause it ain't gonna get handed to you."

For whites, Elder's victory at Monsanto was a different proposition altogether. You could take his victory as a threat to the traditions of the game—the white-dominated pastures of prestige—or as an affirmation of true equality in sport and, therefore, in life. Give blacks an equal shot, and they will succeed. One need only look at other sports—basketball, football, baseball. And also, understand that to many blacks and whites, Elder and other black golfers had succeeded in a game that embodied all the class and race barriers that existed in America.

Like it or not, Elder had become a symbol. Everywhere he went, reporters and cameramen showed up, wanting to know how he felt, how he felt, how he felt.

Frankly, at times, he felt lousy. And at times, he was wistful for those days of obscurity.

His phone didn't stop ringing. "I appreciate the columnists and the other people calling, but it's not helping my golf game any," he said. And Rose, as business manager, was besieged with requests for tickets to the Masters—not only from relatives and friends, but from people she didn't know. Even some reporters called her asking for help to get press credentials to cover the tournament.

So as 1974 turned into 1975, Elder was not playing good golf. He tied for thirty-sixth at Tucson, withdrew from the Crosby after three rounds, and then missed the cut in four straight tournaments—the Hawaiian Open, the Bob Hope Desert Classic, the Andy Williams–San Diego Open, and the Los Angeles Open.

His back was giving him trouble, he was wearing a brace on his right knee, and he had put an extra ten pounds on his small frame. Sometimes he wasn't that same affable fellow who shrugged and smiled when someone asked him about pressure. Besides, so much business had piled up that Rose had to stay home and attend to it. Accustomed to having her with him on the road to take care of all the distractions, Lee was alone on the Tour, trying to juggle interviews, appointments, dinner dates, and, oh, yes, golf. Most days, he was on the phone three times a day with her, but he couldn't keep up with the details.

That was left to Rose Lorraine Harper Elder, one of the few black wives who went on the road with their husbands and managed their careers. His career had been her career since they married, a year after they met at the driving range at Langston Golf Course in Washington. They were truly a pair, in marriage and in business. The commissioner of the PGA Tour, Deane Beman, said as much during one of the events to honor Lee, when he paid tribute to Rose, "who worked as hard as Lee." They had come together but from worlds apart.

At an early age, Elder had lost his parents and had been moved around among relatives, and then he moved around on his own, trying to make his way, taking care of himself the best way he could, living on the edge at times, doing what he had to do, and not always the right thing. He'd been a hustler and had been married at least once before—Rose later found out that Lee's previous marriage hadn't been legally ended. And he had left some enemies and debtors in his wake.

"His background is one that you know he did a lot of things to survive," said Rose. "My background is one that I was very protected. I didn't have to do anything to survive, because my parents protected me."

She was raised in a middle-class Washington, D.C., family, one of seven kids born to a career military man. Before she was twenty-one, she had gained more business sense than most women twice her age. Working in the office of an electrical contractor near Twelfth and E Streets, she came to do the banking, contracts, collections, and payroll. She'd tried Howard University for a few months but realized that she needed to work and was gaining another kind of education that had more value to her. She was also a model, popping out of a huge Ballantine beer can, dressed in a two-piece gold lamé bathing suit, at one of her gigs. And she took up golf and refused to give it up for a man who had her fitted for an engagement ring at Tiffany's.

Then she met Lee and entered another world.

His was a life on the road, driving from one tournament to another.

Soon after they were married, she went along with Lee and a friend, Jimmy MacMillan, to a tournament in Georgia. After driving farther and farther south, passing up restaurant after restaurant, they finally had to stop for gas.

When Rose asked for the key to the locked bathroom, the attendant looked at her and said, "We don't have a bathroom."

"There's a bathroom right there, and I want the key."

When she and Jimmy began arguing with the attendant, Lee quickly sized up the situation and ordered them both into the car.

"This was the first time in my life I had ever seen anybody with a real gun," Rose said. "It was a rifle, a shotgun; it was a long gun. He came out with this thing, [saying] 'Well, I don't have a bathroom.' Oh, we got in that car and Lee took off."

But she also learned that sometimes it didn't matter where you were. At the Bob Hope Desert Classic, she went into the clubhouse looking for a rest room at the El Dorado Country Club. A black employee asked her to leave, saying she wasn't a member. Rose pointed to several other wives of touring pros, all of them white, sitting nearby. Not one of them spoke up, she said, and she didn't return to the El Dorado for years.

As vice president and chief operating officer of Lee and Rose Elder, Inc., Rose managed Lee's business affairs, including the exhibitions, endorsements, and tournaments. After the Monsanto Open, that meant she was the one who had to say what he couldn't: "No."

Elder felt an obligation to people who had been nice to him along the way. But Rose could say no and often did. She was the one trying to negotiate long-term contracts with national sponsors, most of whom offered one-year deals rather than three- or four-year agreements. The Elders also waited on that affiliation with a country club that provides most tour golfers with some security, but Elder had yet to be asked. "Without Rose, it would be a lost cause," Elder admitted. "When she's around, I know she can take care of everything, and I can concentrate on playing golf. When she goes, there goes my golf."

"The Masters is coming at me fast, like a mountain. I won't say I'm feeling the pressure of the tournament. It's just that it's on my mind all the time. People won't let me forget and the galleries have grown since I've had the Masters invitation. I'm having a lousy year but have reached the point where I know things can't get any worse."

His golf had improved somewhat in the few weeks before the Masters. He tied for seventeenth at Jacksonville, Florida, and took home $1,808, which didn't seem like much but was more than he had earned at a tour event in seven months. And at Greensboro, the warm-up event before Augusta, Elder fired a 69 on Sunday to finish twelfth.

Despite the advice of some friends, Elder had no intention of boycotting the tournament. He felt he could do more good by being there than he could by staying away. He had spent so much time trying to get there, what was the point of staying away? Besides, he had seen the course and loved it. The previous October, he played a round with Coca-Cola president J. Paul Austin and shot a 74. The course was everything they said it was—picturesque and demanding. He would be there.

He would be there, and so would a sizable entourage—fifty-five people at last count, who would require two large rental houses and four motel rooms. It had been the longest wait since the invitation—fifty-one weeks. But finally, among the white azaleas, the white magnolias, and the white dogwoods, there would be a black orchid.

When many pros talk about driving up Magnolia Lane at Augusta National, they speak in reverential tones, and some even choke up. All that tradition, those magnificent surroundings, and the golf course. Augusta was, Jack Nicklaus once said, "a monument to everything great in golf."

There was a certain amount of tension as reporters, photographers, fans, and Augusta officials waited for Elder to drive up Magnolia Lane on Monday. Asked when Elder would arrive, a green-jacketed Augusta official snapped back, "I don't know. You newspapermen will be making a lot out of it, but to me, he is just another golfer."

In fact, Elder was due at noon, but his car didn't arrive until two hours later. Waiting for him was a larger group of reporters and photographers. Elder emerged from the car with Rose and long-time friend Dr. Philip Smith, medical director of the Martin Luther King Hospital in Los Angeles. "All you could see was flashes and clicking, flashes and clicking," recalled Rose.

"I'm not talking," said Elder, walking past them. "Every time I talk, I get into trouble." Instead, Rose scheduled a press conference for the following day to accommodate everyone at once.

One reporter summed it up for his readers the next day: "History came to Augusta today, but History wasn't talking."

Elder went into headquarters, registered, and then was taken to the locker room, where he was assigned his locker. He also met with his caddie, Henry Brown, a veteran of the Masters. A taxi driver most of the year, Brown had carried for Argentinian Roberto De Vicenzo, who in 1968 had tied for the lead on Sunday, only to learn that he had signed an erroneous scorecard and was forced to take the higher score, which dropped him to second. Brown had also been Cliff Roberts's caddie and a one-handicap golfer himself. But he was a better-than-par companion of the press that week.

"All he has to do is stay cool and relax," the thirty-six-year-old caddie told reporters that Monday. "I have been caddying here since 1952. I can walk this course backwards. I know every blade of grass on it. I am No. 1."

The next day, Elder's first day on the golf course, he three-putted the 18th, but still shot a respectable 71. He went immediately to the press tent, where he explained that he hoped to answer every-body's questions then and there and avoid the hundreds of individual interviews that would drag him away from golf. "I hope you understand. I've waited a lifetime to get into this tournament. Now that I'm here, I want to give it my best effort."

Facing 100 reporters and rows of cameras and microphones, sipping a beer and drawing on a cigarette, Elder said he didn't feel like a racial pioneer, just a golfer trying to win for himself and Rose. Then a reporter asked a question that had Elder laughing for the first time that afternoon: Why aren't there more black pros?

"It's a little tougher to hit a two-iron off the roof of some apartment house in the ghetto than it is to hit off the fairway at some plush country club," he said.

There were nerves, to be sure, both on the part of Elder and the people who ran the tournament. There was talk of extra security, of avoiding some kind of incident involving Elder that would embarrass Augusta. Cliff Roberts would not have it.

And for all his protesting that he was playing merely for Lee and Rose Elder, many blacks disagreed with him—most prominently, a singer with his own radio station and a minister with a pulpit.

In the journal he kept with sportswriter Phil Musick that week, Elder remembered hearing soul singer James Brown, who owned a radio station in Augusta, go on the air and insist that Elder was wrong, that he was playing for all blacks.

At the Greater Mount Canaan Baptist Church on Wednesday night, the eve of the tournament, Rose and Lee Elder listened as the preacher prayed:

"It's been a long time coming, Lord. A *long* time. Now this man, Lee Elder, is here to play in the Masters. Tomorrow, a black man will walk on that country club . . . course right here in Augusta.

Lord Jesus, be in his arms and his hands and in his feet and in his heart. Lord give that little white ball eyes so that it might see its way."

"Amen."

As Lee Elder arrived at the 1st tee Thursday morning, his playing partner Gene Littler put an arm on his shoulder and wished him luck. As he stepped on the tee, he was greeted with polite applause from a gallery of hundreds. He was unaccustomed to such attention; normally he teed off at 8:00 A.M. with only his wife and his playing partners as spectators.

This day, he wore an ensemble of greens—different shades of green pants, shirt, and sweater—hoping it would be good luck for a tournament that honored its winners with a green blazer. "Green has always been one of my favorite colors," he said. "I thought I would wear it today, rather than waiting until Sunday. I figured you fellows would like to see me in green." In truth, he and Hubie Green wore green all the time, assuming that green would attract green—cash, and in this case, a green blazer.

In a drawl, a tournament official announced Elder. "Now on the tee, Mr. Lee Elder. Fore, please."

It was a moment in sports that many in attendance would remember—a black man teeing off for the first time in the Masters.

Maggie Hathaway, for example, and football great Jim Brown had somehow gotten badges to get inside and made it to the 1st tee. Elder had received twenty-five badges, many more than the usual allotment to a first-time competitor, but far too few to accommodate his request for sixty-nine passes. But the Masters had no public sale of tickets; the list of patrons was virtually unchanged from year to year, and never had there been much demand from blacks to see the tournament.

Hathaway had been sick for days but was determined not to miss this moment. Even on the plane to Atlanta, with Brown, she got violently ill. But she made it and used her press pass to get a badge, while Brown had to give $100 and an autograph to an Augusta employee to get his.

And suddenly, it was time for Lee to tee off. She remembered a little boy on the tee praying out loud, forcing Elder to pause before hitting. "He walked up and hit his ball. It went a mile. It was beautiful! And all of a sudden I fainted. Stopped the whole tournament. They thought I had dropped dead. And they rushed me to the hospital on the 9th hole." She had peritonitis. Later, someone else sought help at the Masters medical facility: her nemesis, Gary Player.

For the caddies, the waiters, and the other black employees of Augusta, the moment was a proud one. For one former Augusta caddie, in particular, the moment was overwhelming. Brad Pye, Jr., a newspaper editor and columnist, could almost hear his old friends from the caddie shack: "Never thought I'd see the day." As he watched Elder tee off, Pye could barely hide the tears welling up in his eyes. It was a moment of pride to him that nearly rivaled Dr. King's speech near the reflecting pool in Washington.

Rose Elder never heard the commotion on the 1st tee. She was too intent on following Lee's drive up the fairway to make sure nothing funny happened to the ball once it landed.

This had become a ritual for her, whenever she attended a tournament—station herself up the fairway to watch his ball, get close to it, and protect it. Lots could happen to it—more precisely, people could do lots of things to hurt Lee. They could merely step on it and force Lee to play a tough shot or, worse, to take a stroke penalty for unplayable lie. They could kick it behind a tree. They could put it in their pocket. They could throw it over a fence. All these things could result in a penalty. Rose knew; it had happened lots of times before. Lee had hit a ball right down the middle of the fairway, walked up to where it was supposed to have landed, and discover that the ball had disappeared, and not a gopher hole in sight. Rose didn't really expect that to happen at the Masters, where the galleries were said to be among the best behaved and knowledgeable in the game. And the Elders had been treated quite well all week. But no black man had ever invaded this last white sanctuary of professional golf, either.

Elder himself had actually held his breath as he let it fly on that first drive and then saw it drop to the fairway 260 yards away. And before he walked down the fairway, he looked around for his friend, the comedian Flip Wilson. Flip had told Rose he was going to show up dressed as one of his famous characters, Geraldine. He was a no-show, but Jim Brown and Leroy Kelly were there.

Elder rimmed out an eight-footer for a birdie on the 1st and then holed out a fifteen-footer on the 2nd. Elder now believed with one more birdie, he would be on the leader board of the Masters. Among the more than a few hundred blacks in the gallery following him, some of them wearing GOOD LUCK, LEE buttons, there were those who allowed themselves to think about the first black in the Masters also being the leader of the Masters. But his ragged putting tempered their optimism as he bogeyed the 4th and the 6th.

On the back side, he went out with five straight pars. When he reached the 15th, Elder faced a decision that all golfers have when they come to that historic hole. The 520-yard par-5 hole had been immortalized by Gene Sarazen, forty years earlier. He had come into the 15th trailing leader Craig Wood by three shots. With Bobby Jones watching from the green and playing partner Walter Hagen eager to finish his miserable round, Sarazen hit his spoon (three-wood) 230 yards, the ball flying over the pond fronting the green and into the hole for a 2—a double eagle. With one dramatic shot, he had tied Wood for the lead and gained the momentum to win a playoff the next day.

In 1975, with better equipment and stronger players, the decision to shoot for the green was easier. Still, Elder looked at the pond that guarded the green and, as he said later, it looked like the Indian Ocean.

He laid up in front of the pond, needing only an easy wedge to the green. But he struck it weakly, the ball hitting the embankment and nearly rolling back into the water. He pitched within eight feet but missed the putt. A bogey. Players look to the par-5s for their best chances for birdies.

On the 16th, he took a bogey again with three putts, and, according to one reporter, it was the only time all day that there was anything worse than polite applause, when a few rednecks on the bank of the green whooped and applauded when he missed the putt. But there was no indication Elder was bothered by it; he never mentioned it later when he recalled the round. With a birdie on the 17th, and a tricky little par-saving putt on the 18th, Elder came into the clubhouse with a two-over 74.

Sure, he'd made mistakes in judgment and by underclubbing himself much of the day. His putting was erratic. But there was hope for tomorrow. There was hope he would play into the weekend. Bobby Nichols led the tournament after one day with a 67. Jack Nicklaus lurked one behind at 68 and Arnold Palmer, Tom Weiskopf, and J. C. Snead were bunched at 69.

"Knock a stroke off that 74 tomorrow and Old History will make the cut," Elder wrote later. "I didn't come down here to miss the cut. Maybe not to win. That's dreaming. But not to miss the cut."

But too many things worked against Elder that late April. The pressure, the distractions, the golf course, his golf game, even Henry, his caddie. Although Elder never used it as an excuse, his game didn't set up real well for Augusta, which required high-arcing iron shots and a draw—right-to-left action—for many shots. He hit low shots and favored a fade—left to right. With the wind picking up a bit, making tough shots slightly tougher, Elder needed a strong start. Instead, he bogeyed the 2nd and 3rd holes. He was four over par on the front nine, spraying his shots all over the course. He came back in with a 38 for a 78, and missed the cut by four shots.

"I felt I could do almost anything and shoot par," he told reporters. "But all I did seemed to be incorrect. The distances were incorrect. . . . It looked like we were just a bunch of choppers, Henry and me."

He would be going home, not Sunday night, but today. He wouldn't hang around to watch Nicklaus hold off a furious rush by Johnny Miller—65 and 66 on Saturday and Sunday—to win his fifth Masters, his fifteenth major tournament. Even the crowds sensed Elder would have an early exit; they peeled off as the round went on. On the back nine Friday, Rose walked alone.

He would leave, having been abandoned by his putter and let down by his caddie. Despite his talk, Henry Brown had let Elder down, constantly underclubbing him. In his journal published a few months later, Elder criticized Brown reluctantly, having been a caddie himself for many years. Elder said he should have fired Brown after the first round, because he constantly got the distances wrong at Augusta. But he was talked out of it.

"That to me was the difference in Lee playing well and making the cut," Rose recalled, more than two decades later. "Because this guy they put on his bag, he was not concentrating at all on what he was doing. He was more into the press and the media."

After they left Augusta, Lee and Rose retreated to Washington and spent Sunday talking about what went wrong. They resolved that he should have spent more time at Augusta, practiced more to sharpen his game, looked more carefully for a caddie. Perhaps he should have handled the press differently giving his news conference the week before, at Greensboro.

But first, before he left, Elder walked into the press tent on Friday for his valedictory interview session—unusual for a player who trailed the leaders by seventeen shots—and patiently answered questions.

Yes, he saw more of Augusta's beauty than he cared to. Yes, it was worth the effort getting to the Masters. And, yes, he hoped to come back again. "Thanks," he said with a smile as the interview ended, "and see you down the road."

The road didn't lead back to Augusta for another two years. It was a tough time for Elder, wondering about his game, about his goals, about the Masters. He wondered whether he had peaked with his appearance in 1975. He did not want the tournament to define him (First Black to Qualify for Masters). He also had long since tired of being called golf's best *black* golfer; he wanted to be

judged as an athlete. Henry Aaron was not called the most pro-
digious *black* slugger and Jim Brown was not the best *black* running back. But it was destined to be that way, so long as so few
blacks filtered into the pro ranks.

It can be a simple thing to change around a golf game. In Elder's
case, it seemed to be a tip from another touring pro, Dale Doug-
lass, at the Hawaiian Open, at the start of 1976, about setting up
too far in front of the ball. It was something he practiced for hours
on the practice tee. At the Bob Hope Classic, Elder finished twelve
under par. He was two under at Los Angeles, ten under at the
Tournament Players Championship, four under at Greensboro,
ten under at New Orleans, eight under at Phoenix. And then came
Houston.

Play at the Woodlands Country Club, a resort north of Houston,
was due to begin Thursday, but torrents of rain postponed play
until Friday, with golfers compressing four days' play into three.
That meant they would play two rounds, thirty-six holes, on
Sunday—a grueling regimen that the U.S. Open and other tournaments had abandoned. Players began teeing off at 7:00 A.M. on
the 1st and the 10th for the first round Sunday.

But the course played easy, with the rains softening the greens,
and more than half the field equaled par and better. Four players
were bunched in first with 67s; Elder shot 70. On Saturday, the
wind blew away the clouds, but the breezes made club selection
difficult. When Elder fired an even-par 72, for 142 total, he had
dropped six strokes back and faced a long day on Sunday.

Before the day began, Elder had two other handicaps. The first
was Rose's admonition to stay away from the cigarettes as long as
possible. With thirty-six holes to walk, he needed his legs under

him, and his pack-a-round habit wouldn't help the circulation problem he had in his left leg.

The second was he was so far behind the leaders that he, Charles Coody, and John Mahaffey drew the first tee time: 7:00 A.M. "I guess we had a gallery of about 10," Elder said. "There was Mahaffey's wife and his former sponsor, and a couple of brothers. I spotted the brothers right away. They sort of stood out." But the early hours suited Elder and Coody. They both shot the lowest scores of the third round, five-under-par 67 on Sunday, just one stroke behind of the leaders, George Burns and Wally Armstrong.

That afternoon, Elder started his second round of the day on the back nine and grabbed the lead with birdies at the 10th, the 13th, and the 15th, a 178-yard par-3 where he put his tee shot one and a half feet from the cup. At that point, the cigarettes came out. "By now, I was feeling the pressure. I guess I puffed the rest of the way in."

But he then hit a patch of holes where the putts wouldn't drop. He missed a three-foot birdie putt on the 2nd, and then an eight-footer at the 3rd. (Meanwhile, Rose was watching a basketball game on TV in Washington, when the announcer said the Houston Open would follow and that "Lee Elder is leading after 67 holes." The phone began to ring and people started dropping by.)

At the 6th, Elder's bogey-free round ended when he blasted out of the bunker to within six feet and missed the putt. At the 9th tee, his last hole, he looked at the leader board and saw that Burns was ten under, a stroke ahead. He thought he had lost it and knew if he had any chance, he needed a birdie now. He lasered a driver and started walking up the fairway. "Go get 'em, Lee," the gallery was yelling.

He lofted a nine-iron to within four feet, and had anyone looked closely enough, they would have seen he was shaking slightly and had lit a cigarette to calm himself.

But the putt caught a corner of the cup and dropped for a birdie, and he had finished ten under par. All Elder could do was wait. Burns, a twenty-six-year-old tour rookie, had eight holes to play.

In the pressroom, Elder talked about taking an early flight home, but a reporter told him he might want to stick around in case of a playoff. At that moment, Burns bogeyed the 12th, to fall into a tie with Elder.

"Okay," Elder said, softly.

As Lee talked on the phone with Rose, Burns took another bogey, dropping a stroke behind Elder. At the par-3 15th hole, Burns had taken three putts. His putting had deserted him entirely, he knew, when he missed a three-foot birdie to jump back into a tie. And when he missed a tricky four-footer on the 17th, Burns dropped two back and out of contention. The fatigue and pressure of his first tournament in contention had worn him down. "I'm going to take this as a learning experience," a dejected Burns told reporters. "I missed a few putts in the clutch, and that's part of the learning experience. Toward the end I was weary and wasn't thinking. That's part of the learning, too."

Elder had no such learning to do.

"I called home while I was waiting and I could hear the noise in the background. It sounded like the house had fallen in. Then, when I won, I called Rose again and this time I was sure the house had fallen in."

Elder had won a silver plate for his trophy room and a $40,000 check.

His plane wouldn't arrive in Washington until late, but about forty friends and family waited for Lee at the airport, including his eighty-five-year-old grandmother, Dora Head. On the plane, Lee realized that he was back. And he realized that despite all the pressure, the distractions, his inconsistent play, people had not forgotten, had not stopped believing in him. If Burns was a rookie and just learning about the Tour, Elder had completed his postgraduate work, a forty-two-year-old black man allowed to play on the Tour relatively late in his career. Other tournament victories were possible. The Ryder Cup team was on the horizon. And, of course, he was no flashing comet, illuminating the sky briefly, only to disappear from sight and from people's memories. He had won two PGA tournaments, and now he had earned a second invitation to the Masters.

The captain of the jetliner from Houston to Washington, D.C., announced that Lee Elder, who had just won the Houston Open, was on the plane. People cheered as though he'd just rolled in that final birdie putt. The stewardesses passed around glasses of champagne. And then an amazing thing happened: the passengers started singing "For He's a Jolly Good Fellow." Tears welled in his eyes. Elder felt, at last, he had paid back a few people whom he'd let down in Augusta, Georgia.

21
Implacable, Impeccable

Two A.M., and he'd be on the softball field at Sunrise Park in Fort Lauderdale, hitting ball after ball. (Five-iron. *Whhuutt!*) He'd wake up in the middle of the night, thinking about some hitch in his swing, and try to get back to sleep. Finally, he'd get dressed and drive over to the ball field, where they forgot to flip off the lights. The neighbors would call the police sometimes, but cops would come and discover he was just hitting golf balls. "They'd sit there in their patrol car, and sit and watch me hit balls. 'Nice five-iron, Calvin,'" he said. They'd finally leave, because Calvin Peete would hit and hit and hit until dawn, go home for breakfast, and come back and hit some more. All alone. No distractions. Quiet, except for the sound of his club hitting the grass and the ball.

Five-iron—*whhuutt!* Five-iron—*whhuttt!* Five-iron—*whhuutt!*

At first, he would wave off his friends when they asked him to go out to the golf course, but they finally lured him out there once, and, well, there was something to it, after you got used to it. There was something about hitting that ball, sending it into an arc, trying to see how far you could actually hit it. And it wasn't long before the game got a grip on him. And he began to work at it the way he worked at other things—tirelessly, relentlessly.

Five-iron—*whhuutt!* Five-iron—*whhuutt!* Five-iron—*whuutt!*

He'd been used to hard work since he was a child. As one of the youngest of eight kids, growing up in Detroit, he hadn't had much responsibility. But when his folks split up, he went to live with his grandmother in Missouri, then finally reunited with his dad, Dennis, and his new family in Pahokee, Florida, on the shore of Lake Okeechobee, in hot, flat, fertile land near the Everglades. Now he was the oldest of ten kids and found himself with a lot of responsibility, helping out. He had to grow up fast, and after the eighth grade, he had no time for school. He was up at 5:30 every morning to get out to the cornfields, where his dad was picking, to assemble cardboard boxes—at a penny apiece—for the women who packed the corn. It was demeaning work, about as low as you could get, and he resolved never to have a vegetable garden of his own. Under that hot central Florida sun, he noticed the peddlers from Miami, who came to sell cheap clothes to the field hands, leaving with thick wads of cash. At seventeen, he bought a 1956 Plymouth station wagon and started selling clothes and jewelry to Jamaican and Bahamian cane workers at the migrant labor camps. They needed clothes and jewelry like anybody else, and they often lived in camps that were miles from any town. So for the next eight years, he went on the road, calling home wherever he ended up that night, following the laborers who followed the crops up the eastern seaboard, through Virginia, Maryland, Delaware, New Jersey, and New York. It was hard and lonely work, but he had no family of his own, no home of his own. And he made a living out of it, as much as $200 a week. And to advertise some of the jewelry he had to sell, he convinced a dentist to inset a couple of diamonds in his upper two front teeth. Became known as the Diamond Man, with a smile that literally sparkled in the sun.

It was 1966, and he was twenty-three, when he first set foot on the golf course, tricked into playing by a group of friends in Rochester, New York. They picked him up at his motel and told him they were going to a clambake, but drove to Genesee Valley

Golf Course instead. Either play or wait in the car until we're done, they told him. He hadn't thought much of the game; it wasn't a man's game, like football or basketball. And he hadn't ever heard of Teddy Rhodes or Charlie Sifford or Pete Brown or Bill Spiller. He'd never been a caddie, the way most blacks learned about the game. No one figured he'd have much success at it. He was eleven when he'd fallen out of a tree and broken his left elbow in three places, never again able to straighten the arm more than a thirty-degree angle. So when he swung a golf club, it was with a crooked arm and a short backswing, and the results were predictable: no distance. But that night, after his first time out, he found a driving range and hit a bucket of balls. And then another. "It was the individuality of the game," he said. "It's all about you. I saw myself in golf, even at that moment. It was a vision of myself doing well in golf. I guess that was my gift that my father and mother told me I had. I had a blessing. It was like a light was shining. Calvin, this was it, this was what you were meant to do."

Five-iron—*whhuutt!* Five-iron—*whhuutt!*

His first round of eighteen holes, he shot an 87. Within two years, he became a scratch golfer. Never took a lesson, just pounded out bucket after bucket of balls. He read instructional books and even rigged a camera to take pictures of his swing. It's an old cliché, but it was true for him: he practiced until his hands bled. By then, he'd gotten off the peddling trail and was managing apartments in Fort Lauderdale. He would practice whenever and wherever he could. On the softball field. By the gymnasium with the floodlights, practicing short shots. He would hit hundreds of balls a day, sometimes with just one club. Because of his crooked left arm, he had to experiment. And while he thought he could make this his job someday, he'd never watched a golf tournament on television before—until he got rained out one day in August 1968. "That's why I was in the clubhouse," he said, and there on television were Jack Nicklaus and Lee Elder, a black man, locked up in an epic five-hole sudden-death playoff at the Firestone. "I was so impressed with Lee. That was the first black man I had seen play. That's the first time I ever heard of Lee Elder. Like a kid watching somebody on TV: if he could do it, no reason I couldn't do it."

It was one of the few times he'd ever sat through golf on TV; he was too busy on the weekends playing. When he did sit down in front of the TV to watch, he couldn't sit still for long. His thoughts would drift off to his own game, and he'd be gone to hit more balls. "I still get antsy watching it on TV." Time was short. He had started late and had lots of catching up to do. Five years after he first picked up a golf club, he turned professional. He tried to qualify for the PGA Tour but failed. He tried again and failed. But in 1974, he married Christine, a schoolteacher from Pahokee, and he played in mini-tour events and black tournaments, trying to make some money. Finally, he got his player's card in late 1975 and became the Tour's oldest rookie at thirty-two. At the qualifying school, one of the speakers who told you how to handle this or handle that on the Tour asked each golfer what made him unique. They probably expected Calvin to say something about being a black golfer. Instead, he drew a couple of looks, arched some eyebrows. "What makes me unique is I want to be the best golfer in the world."

Success was not easy. In seven tournaments, his total earnings were zero. Over the next three years, he averaged little over $20,000, barely enough to cover his expenses, driving an old Cadillac, sharing motel rooms with his caddie. He had given it his best shot; maybe he just didn't have the game. Or maybe he didn't belong. For one, he hadn't come up in a college program like most of the players.

He hadn't even gone to college. Later on in his career, when he learned the Ryder Cup team would not take players who hadn't graduated from high school, Christine tutored him so that he could get his high school equivalency diploma. The other players were nice enough to him, but the pro tour could be a lonely life, under the best of circumstances. Maybe God didn't intend it. "It's not God, Calvin," Christine told him. "You're letting yourself down." And he also remembered what his grandmother had told him: "You can give out, but don't give up."

Five-iron—*whhuutt!* Five-iron—*whhuutt!* Five-iron—*whhuutt!*

He dedicated himself once again to hours and hours and hours of time on the range, on the putting green, on the golf course. He was five feet ten, only 165 pounds, with a short, compact swing; so he wasn't going to outhit anybody. He had to do it his way, consistently, methodically. And when he went back out there, he became the straightest driver and the most accurate irons player in the whole game. In 1979, he had his breakthrough. First he finished eleventh in the U.S. Open, which, among other things, qualified him for the next year's Masters—an accomplishment that five years earlier would have been big news but was now barely noticed. Then he won his first tour event, the Greater Milwaukee Open, by five strokes, after he put together four straight rounds in the 60s, including a 65 on Sunday. "The hole kept getting in the way of the ball," he said. As if to show it wasn't a fluke, he finished second the next week in the Quad Cities. He had seven top-ten finishes and won $122,481. And just like that, he had won more money on the Tour in one season than any other black golfer before him. Maybe he did belong.

Three years later, in 1982, he won the same tournament again. That same year, he won four tournaments, tying Craig Stadler with the most wins that year. From 1982 through 1985, no one won more tournaments—nine. In 1984, he won the Vardon Trophy, for having the lowest scoring average on the Tour. The hard work had paid off. "Calvin has a tremendous talent for hard work," said Jack Nicklaus.

Five-iron—*whhuutt!* Five-iron—*whhuutt!* Five-iron—*whhuutt!*

He was implacable under that Ben Hogan cap or that visor. He had the diamonds removed from his teeth after a few years on the Tour and thus became as conservative as his game. Ironically, the most successful black man ever to play professional golf had not made his mark as a flashy dresser, a demonstrative competitor, a big hitter, a colorful personality. He wore dark glasses and occasionally a Fu Manchu mustache. On the road, he preferred to play, practice, or, except for an occasional game of pool with some of the caddies on tour, stay in his room with the TV on, mentally playing each shot on each hole. At the Doral-Eastern Open in Miami, a reporter once asked him the last time Peete had broken par on the Blue Monster. "About eleven-thirty last night," he said. "In my room." To Peete, it was about fairways and greens, fairways and greens, fairways and greens. Take the sure shot. Play within your abilities. Control what you can control. Be patient. The wins will come. And they did. In the eighties, only one man collected more tour victories than Calvin Peete, who won eleven tournaments, and that was Tom Kite, with twelve. "Let's face it," said Tom Watson. "Calvin is the most accurate striker of the ball in golf." And he had fulfilled his vow at the qualifying school in 1975. "I became the best golfer in the world from 1982 through 1986," he said.

Whhuutt! Whhuutt! Whhuutt!

Spiller's health had been deteriorating for years. Even in the late sixties, other golfers razzed him because of the number of medicines he was on.

First was the operation on his eye—the family believed that working with the flour at the doughnut shop had somehow aggravated it and forced an operation. He hadn't been the same since, and ultimately he stopped playing the game. More serious problems, however, were ahead—at least one stroke that weakened him. And his mind wasn't what it was. His middle-of-the-night rages frightened Goldie and forced Bill junior to find his dad's three guns and take them away.

Otherwise, he would awaken, grab his .32-caliber revolver, walk down the hallway into the living room, and swear revenge on some unseen tormentors.

"I'll get them for this! You wait and see!"

Finally, when he fell in the bathtub and couldn't get up, the family found a convalescent home in Torrance, where he could get the twenty-four-hour care he needed.

Bill junior went on to college, as did his younger brother and sister. And he began to understand his father, visit him often, and make some sort of peace with him. He came to understand the fight his father had tried to fight, and was proud of that. Although Bill junior had become a lawyer, his father never attended his graduation, perhaps out of a disappointment that his son had not chosen to carry on his fight or even adopt the game of golf.

For Bill junior, golf was always tied, inextricably, to his complicated relationship with his father. He had wanted to play football (his father wanted him to play basketball, as well as golf). Nevertheless, he had become an accomplished golfer by his late teens.

"But I didn't consider it an accomplishment. I figured that's what I was supposed to do, but it was because of him. I was a one handicap when I stopped playing. I was nineteen. I haven't played since. I haven't picked up a club since. No interest whatsoever."

Toward the end, his father would drift in and out but usually recognize his visitors. Turning to his oldest son, he'd say: "Have you made anything of yourself?"

As Bill junior would say about his father some years later: "Two chips. Both shoulders."

Bill senior would have moments to reminisce with friends who'd made the trip to visit him. He remembered first arriving in Los Angeles and getting a set of golf clubs. He recalled firing a 68 during the first round of the L.A. Open in 1948, matching Ben Hogan. And he'd ask his friend Frank Snow, who'd played golf with him for thirty years, whether he had outlived the men in the PGA who'd kept him out of the game.

"All those guys," Snow assured him.

Bill Spiller died in 1988 at the age of seventy-five. His remains were cremated; only a handful even knew about the memorial service. Bill junior called the newspapers and wire services, but no one seemed interested.

Who was Bill Spiller, anyway? He hadn't won a PGA tournament, hadn't even won the UGA National. He wasn't the first black to get his playing card; in fact, he hadn't gotten his playing card at all. He wasn't important enough to make the papers, to make the news, to make it on ESPN.

In sorting through his things, Goldie barely hesitated to banish the last symbol of the game whose unfairness ate away at her husband like a raging virus. The many years of bitterness, of anger, of frustration, were over. Bill senior's golf clubs were removed from the house on 122th Street and sold.

22

"You Are the Ones . . ."

As the nineties dawned, the barriers to African American golfers became more subtle, although on occasion the remarks of one prominent person reminded everyone that the game's exclusion had not been weeded out, only clipped to its most resistant and stubborn roots. In 1990, Hall Thompson, the founder of Shoal Creek Golf and Country Club in Alabama, where the PGA Championship was played, spoke his mind, and apparently the minds of many other country club members across America: "The country club is our home and we pick and choose who we want. . . . I think we've said we don't discriminate in every other area except for the blacks."

After the firestorm died down, Thompson's candor ultimately became an impetus to change, bringing the issue into the open once again and precipitating new membership rules for golf clubs that wanted to host PGA events. It also resulted in the appointment of the first African American, John Merchant, to the USGA's powerful executive board in 1992.

Sifford and Elder and Peete found rebirth and good money on the Senior PGA Tour, which also provided lucrative opportunities for other golfers who hadn't reached their potential on the regular tour. Jim Dent, for one, was the classic example, wowing galleries on the PGA Tour with his incredible length off the tee but failing to become a consistent enough player to play up to his potential. That all changed when he turned fifty and joined the Seniors. After nineteen winless years on the PGA Tour, Dent had won a dozen tournaments and $7 million on the seniors tour by 1997.

Charlie Owens was perhaps the unlikeliest member of the Seniors. He was playing on a fused left knee that was shattered during a nighttime jump as a paratrooper with the Eighty-second Airborne Division in 1953. His right knee constantly ached from several operations. His iritis occasionally caused temporary blindness in his right eye. He gripped the club cross-handed and used a fifty-two-inch long putter he helped develop to overcome his "yips." Still and all, he made some good money in the mid-eighties. And in the latter part of the nineties, Dent was joined by Bobby Stroble and Walter Morgan as successful regulars on the senior tour.

But on the regular tour, Jim Thorpe was the sole black scratching out a living. Thorpe's older brother Chuck preceded him to the PGA Tour after a string of victories on the UGA tour that rivaled Elder's run a few years earlier. Starting in 1971, he would win twenty-five of thirty-two events he would enter in the next two years. But Jim would make the bigger splash on the PGA Tour.

The son of a Roxboro, North Carolina, greenskeeper, Thorpe shot a 66 to lead the U.S. Open at Merion after the first round. He had grown up around golf—his family had a small house next to the 2nd green at Roxboro Country Club, where he sneaked out at night to putt by the light of his front porch. He caddied on weekends and after school to help out with the family; after all, he was the ninth of twelve children.

After playing running back at Morgan State in Baltimore, Thorpe gravitated to the black circuit, and then the PGA Tour in 1978, when he was comedalist at the qualifying school. The following year, he finished second in the Tucson Open and in 1980, sixth in the Pleasant Valley Classic and tenth at Hartford. His biggest year was 1985, when he won the Greater Milwaukee Open and the Seiko Tucson Match Play Championship, to finish fourth on the money list, with $379,091. The following year, he won the match play championship again, and earned $326,087 for the year. As the nineties drew to a close, Thorpe looked forward to joining the senior tour.

So, where, after the sacrifices of Spiller, Rhodes, Sifford, Brown, Elder, and others, was the cresting wave of young blacks in professional golf? Unlike other sports, golf persisted as a white-dominated activity.

The reasons are varied. For one, the caddie system—once a gateway for blacks into golf—was slowly becoming a relic on most golf courses and country clubs around the United States. When virtually every golf course moved to motorized or electric golf carts, the caddie became the victim.

The main staging ground for would-be professionals was now the colleges, the minor leagues that fed the PGA Tour and its satellite tours. Competition was fierce for golf scholarships, even at historically black universities and colleges, and some coaches recruited white golfers to infuse their programs. Eddie Payton, the late football great Walter Payton's brother and the golf coach at Jackson State University, was a lightning rod for criticism over his decision to recruit white golfers, while his team captured the predominantly black Southwest Athletic Conference's men's golf tournament. Were blacks being pushed aside, this time as coaches pursued a win-now philosophy over the long-term cultivation of blacks in competitive golf? Payton and other coaches said race should not be the overriding issue for scholarships, especially when they had trouble luring some of the best black golfers away from the bigger colleges and universities. Fielding the best team possible, they pointed out, was an argument that decades ago helped integrate major sports at predominantly white universities. The fierce competition for scholarships raised anew questions of fairness and merit—what was fair and who merited the scholarship?

To be sure, general interest in golf was increasing among African Americans. The numbers, according to the National Golf Foundation, indicated that 649,000 African Americans played golf on a regular basis in 1990, a significant increase over the 360,000 who played in 1986. Still, the numbers were low proportionately. While 10 percent of the white population enjoyed the game, only 2 percent of the nation's blacks were involved. Access was no longer perceived as the main obstacle; interest was.

Golf was mainly a middle-age pursuit, if you considered the average age of its participants, white and black, and jump-starting interest among minorities became the challenge of a number of programs around the country. On the whole, young African Americans were unaware of the black men—and women, such as UGA great Ann Gregory and LPGA pioneers Renee Powell and Althea Gibson—who had had an impact on the game. There was no black superstar in golf, someone who could plug into the dreams and aspirations of young boys and girls, to inspire them to invest the time, energy, and money on such a "minor" sport. Besides, basketball, football, baseball, even hockey, could be played in parks and streets with a minimum investment. Golf, as always, was different, struggling to shed its elitist image.

So as the profile of black pros declined, many in the game looked to one young golfer who had the *potential* to become the game's first black superstar.

Eldrick "Tiger" Woods had been groomed, almost from the cradle, to be a golfer. At every level, his promise blossomed into achievement. Junior golf. College golf. And the U.S. Amateur, which he first won at age eighteen, then again at nineteen, and once more at twenty. As he left Stanford University for the pros, would he be able to fulfill those pregnant hopes heaped upon him? The expectations were enormous.

By the beginning of 1997, Woods had been a professional for just a few months, but he already had won two of the eight PGA tour events he had entered. By the time he drove up Magnolia Lane at the Masters, he had also displayed to fellow pros a competitive fire that burned white-hot and a game of matchless power. In fact, Nicklaus himself announced that he and Palmer had conferred, like two gods on Olympus, and determined that Woods should win more Masters green jackets than their combined ten. The expectations just got greater.

Even so, what beautiful irony that Tiger Woods, whose ancestry was African American and Cherokee through his father and Thai and Chinese from his mother, won his first major tournament at Augusta National, which had the most ignominious history of racial relations in all of golf. He had won the tournament created and nurtured by Bobby Jones and Clifford Roberts, the former, American golf's first true hero but a traditional southerner, and the latter, a northerner whose autocratic style and views on blacks were no more progressive. But Jones, himself a golf prodigy, and even Roberts would have been awed by Woods's feat, had they lived to see it.

This brash but hugely talented golfer might have strung together the most impressive seventy-two holes in the history of major golf tournaments, and just eight months after turning professional. Certainly, he played the most astonishing three and a half rounds. On his first nine holes during the tournament's first day, he shot a four-over-par 40. Over the next sixty-three holes, he was twenty-two under.

Like some celestial phenomenon, Woods's win came within a few days of the fiftieth anniversary of Jackie Robinson's major-league debut. He became the first black to win one of the four major championships. He achieved a record-low score for the Masters, 270, and the widest margin of victory in a major tournament in the twentieth century, twelve strokes.

What's more, Woods looked back to the men who came before him, to the men who refused to be defined by white golf as nothing more than bothersome shadows, to the men who encountered the kinds of hurdles he would never know. Woods mentioned some of them by name—Rhodes, Sifford, and Elder. "I thank them. I was thinking about them and what they've done for me. I said a little prayer and said thanks to those guys. You are the ones who did it for me."

To those who had been denied, ignored, scorned, blackballed, cheated, those words were a gift of redemption, of affirmation. To many of them, the win and its afterglow were a measure of grace from the game they loved unconditionally. If they had any doubt, they now knew it was their game, too.

To Charlie Sifford, living outside Houston, Texas, watching on television. There was no doubting his feelings about Woods, who mentioned that Sifford was like a godfather to him. "What kind of question is that!" said the eternal curmudgeon Sifford. "Of course, I was proud of him!"

To Lee Elder, the first black man to play in the Masters, in 1975, who was now divorced from Rose, remarried, and playing on the seniors tour. He could not bear to watch the final day of the Masters from home in Florida; he had to be there, having known Tiger since the kid was fourteen, and witness the first black to *win* the Masters.

Elder caught a flight to Atlanta on Sunday morning and raced to Augusta. On the way, however, he was pulled over by a state police officer who had clocked him at 85 mph. "I told him, 'I'm hurrying to see Tiger Woods in the Masters.' He said, 'I don't know anything about golf.' Then he gave me a ticket." Elder made it and stood behind the clubhouse as Woods prepared to tee off, exchanging hugs and high-fives with a group of waiters from the clubhouse. He walked the final nine holes with Woods.

To Pete Brown, who lived in Dayton, Ohio, and played sporadically now, depending on his back and legs. That Sunday, he was at Madden Golf Course, where he was head pro. "I was happy he won; you got to pull for the guy to win," Brown said. The victory meant that a whole new generation of kids, including black kids, might be attracted to the game, Brown said. But he warned that it should not be billed as a panacea for the problems of exclusion—particularly at a vast number of country clubs across the country—that still persist.

To Maggie Hathaway, who had picketed golf tournaments, protested injustices, and even told caddies at the Masters that Bobby Jones was a "honky slave master," and who watched with great satisfaction from the bar at Chester Washington Golf Course (formerly Western Avenue) in Los Angeles. "I thought he was born to play golf. I was proud for him. I had been to the Masters. How he had deflated the Masters' ego, made them change the golf course!" About twenty blocks away, L.A. county officials would soon re-name a nine-hole golf course the Maggie Hathaway Golf Course, the first named for an African American woman.

But not necessarily to Bill Spiller, Jr., who didn't fly to Augusta or watch the Masters on TV. An L.A. lawyer, Spiller admired Woods's talent, hard work, and determination but wondered why the PGA now wrapped itself around Woods and had forgotten about its past. Bill junior walked away from the game twenty-five years ago because of the game's effect on his parents. There had been no apology from the PGA of America or the PGA Tour. "There's never been anything to recognize what happened in the past and 'We'd like to make amends for it.' And I'm not talking about monetary compensation necessarily, but a gesture when [they] were alive. Maybe that wouldn't have been enough to satisfy my mom or my dad, but it certainly would have gone a long way. As far as I'm concerned, the PGA doesn't exist."

To James Black, who had appeared as a promising rookie in 1964 and disappeared from the Tour less than two years later. As Woods triumphed, Black was recovering from open-heart surgery in his Charlotte, North Carolina, home, surrounded by his wife and two young children. He was now in partnership with the local police department in a program called Project ME (Motivation-Education), in which golf was used to promote discipline and education.

"I didn't look at it as a race thing or anything like that," Black said. "What I looked at was his accomplishments in the past, as a junior golfer all the way up, to become the kind of champion he was. That's the kind of thing I cherished. It was inspiring.

"I looked like I'd seen myself right there.

"Opportunities and time has its way, and that's something that we cannot bring back and something we can't regret."

Notes

1. Into the Light

p. 1   *"The next guy"*: Al Barkow, *Getting to the Dance Floor: An Oral History of American Golf* (New York: Atheneum, 1986), p. 228.

p. 2   *"If the white man is so evil"*: ibid., p. 235.

2. First a Job, Then a Game

p. 4   *"Yeah. We'd get down"*: Al Barkow, *Getting to the Dance Floor: An Oral History of American Golf* (New York: Atheneum, 1986), p. 197.

p. 4   *"I used to just walk"*: Bobby Mays, phone interview, June 22, 1998.

p. 6   *They had never heard of:* Arthur R. Ashe, Jr., *A Hard Road to Glory: A History of the African-American Athlete, 1919–1945* (New York: Warner Books, 1988), p. 65.

3. "We Will Play with You or Without You"

p. 8   *"The gay costumes"*: New York Times, July 19, 1896, p. 3.

p. 9   *"But the other golfers thought"*: Tuesday magazine, April 1969, pp. 17, 30.

p. 9   *"The account's specious"*: Golf Journal, June 1996, n.a.

p. 9   *"My father was a Negro"*: Eighty-sixth U.S. Open Annual, 1986, pp. 12–13.

p. 10   *"We will play with you"*: ibid.

p. 10   *Macdonald, angered at his play:* New York Times, July 19, 1986, p. 3.

p. 11   *"It was a little, easy par four"*: Tuesday magazine, April 1969, p. 17.

p. 11   *The* Chicago Tribune: ibid.

p. 11   *"He became"*: ibid.

p. 11   *After many years:* Larry Londino, *Golf Journal*, June 1996, n.a., and *A Place for Us: A Story of Shady Rest and America's First Golf Professional*, a documentary, 1994.

p. 12   *"You know, I wished a hundred times"*: Tuesday magazine, April 1969, p. 17.

4. Creating a World

p. 13   *"This is not for me"*: Al Barkow, *Getting to the Dance Floor: An Oral History of American Golf* (New York: Atheneum, 1986), p. 226.

p. 14   *"If a black person"*: Dr. James Farmer, phone interview, December 1998.

p. 14   *"Hello, Boswell"*: Hamilton Boswell, phone interview, January 1999.

p. 15   *The college was:* Boswell, phone interview.

p. 15   *At Wiley, sports:* Boswell, phone interview.

p. 16   *"You were going"*: Dr. Fred Lewis, phone interview, December 1998.

p. 16   *"I could do better":* Barkow, p. 225.

p. 16   *When he got to Los Angeles: Los Angeles Times,* February 27, 1997, p. S-1.

5. "Yep, It's All in How You Were Brought Up"

p. 18   *Very quickly, with lots of cash: Saturday Evening Post,* August 19, 1944, p. 20.

p. 19   *"He could do anything":* Dottie May Campbell, phone interview, January 1999.

p. 20   *"Let the colored boys win":* Eural Clark, phone interview, March 2, 1999.

p. 21   *"Show us some good golf":* Herbert Graffis, *PGA: Official History of the PGA of America* (New York: Thomas Y. Crowell Publishers, 1975), p. 236.

p. 22   *It was a 196-acre estate: Pittsburgh Courier,* February 2, 1952, p. 14.

p. 22   *"Well, like they say":* Joe Louis, *Joe Louis, My Life* (New York: Harcourt Brace, 1978), p. 210.

p. 23   *Despite the restrictions:* Arthur R. Ashe, Jr., *A Hard Road to Glory: A History of the African-American Athlete, 1919–1945* (New York: Warner Books, 1988), p. 65.

p. 23   *(Although the Depression . . .): Pittsburgh Courier,* February 2, 1952, p. 14.

p. 23   *The Negro National: Chicago Defender,* August 16, 1941, p. 23.

p. 23   *In 1938,* Time: "Negro Open," *Time* magazine, September 12, 1938, p. 35.

p. 24   *"After the first round":* ibid.

p. 25   *"To this day":* Calvin H. Sinnette, *Forbidden Fairways: African Americans and the Game of Golf* (Chelsea, Mich.: Sleeping Bear Press, 1998), pp. 32–33.

p. 25   *Joseph C. Dey, Jr.: Chicago Defender,* May 30 and June 6, 1942, n.a.

p. 26   *"I am fully aware that Negroes":* ibid.

p. 26   *"I can remember":* Campbell, phone interview.

p. 27   *But May saw:* Campbell, phone interview.

p. 27   *"I topped the ball":* Eural Clark, phone interview, February 23, 1999.

p. 28   *And as the: Chicago Tribune,* July 24, 1942, n.a.

p. 28   *"Late coming newspapermen": Saturday Evening Post,* August 19, 1944, p. 84.

p. 28   *"Jesus Christ, he could":* Bob Rickey, phone interview, January 29, 1999.

p. 28   *Like most black golfers:* Sinnette, pp. 92–93.

p. 29   *And he could put on a show: Michigan Chronicle,* May 25, 1968, n.a.

p. 29   *"He whacked it out there":* Bob Goalby, phone interview, 1998.

p. 29   *He often left course records: Philadelphia Evening Bulletin,* April 26, 1968, n.a.

p. 30   *Sifford had twenty dollars:* Charlie Sifford, *Just Let Me Play* (Latham, N.Y.: British-American, 1992), pp. 30–31.

p. 30   *It was no small compliment: Afro-American,* May 4, 1968, n.a.

p. 31   *"As Wheeler's drive whistled": New York Mirror,* January 19, 1952, n.a.

p. 31   *"Well how'd you do": Chicago Defender,* June 31, 1951, p. 18.

p. 34   *"Every tournament":* Will Grimsley, *Golf: Its History, People and Events* (Englewood Cliffs, N.J.: Prentice Hall, 1966), p. 91.

p. 34   *"Pvt. Searles was thus": Chicago Defender,* September 2, 1944, p. 7.

p. 34   *"And one year it rained":* Campbell, phone interview.

p. 35   *Leonard Reed: American Visions,* April 1991, p. 28.

p. 36   *Young wrote:* Ashe, pp. 67–68.

6. A Change in the Wind

p. 37   *Still segregated:* Doris Kearns Goodwin, *No Ordinary Time* (New York: Simon & Shuster, 1994), pp. 540, 626.

p. 38   *In 1947, the National: Golf World,* September 10, 1947, p. 13.

p. 39   *Those willing to take:* Shirley Povich column, *New York Post,* January 16, 1969, n.a.

p. 39   *"Hell, maybe it was":* Charlie Sifford, *Just Let Me Play* (Latham, N.Y.: British-American, 1992), p. 71.

p. 40   *"At a tournament":* ibid., p. 50.

p. 40   *"God, those guys":* Joe Louis, *Joe Louis, My Life* (New York: Harcourt Brace, 1978), p. 197.

p. 41   *"You can beat me":* Al Barkow, *Getting to the Dance Floor: An Oral History of American Golf* (New York: Atheneum, 1986), p. 226.

p. 41   *"What would I be doing":* ibid.

p. 41   *"and would get under":* ibid.

p. 42   *Sifford had come north: Norfolk Journal and Guide,* April 22, 1961, p. 2.

p. 42   *"I started playing": Time* magazine, February 14, 1969, p. 56.

p. 43   *But his problems off the golf course:* Sifford, pp. 22–23.

p. 44   *"Man, we can make us":* Walter Ferguson, interview, Philadelphia, February 1998.

p. 45   *Mr. B loved to play golf: Call and Post,* April 21, 1979, p. 19b.

p. 46   *"I remember": Nashville Tennessean,* July 9, 1969, p. 28.

p. 47   *"I gladly accepted": Golf* magazine, February 1961, p. 46.

p. 47   *"[Mangrum] put a bushel":* Joe Hampton, phone interview, May 21, 1999.

p. 47   *"I've seen many of 'em":* Robert Horton, phone interview, July 1999.

p. 47   *"This guy without a doubt":* Dottie May Campbell, phone interview, January 1999.

p. 47   *As if anyone: Los Angeles Times,* January 4, 1947, p. 6.

7. "Land of the Free and Home of the Brave"

p. 50   *"I've seen it both ways": Golf* magazine, February 1961, p. 50.

p. 51   *"Teddy was not a fighter":* Maggie Hathaway, interview, Los Angeles, June 1998.

p. 51   *In Phoenix years later: Golf* magazine, February 1961, pp. 18–19.

p. 51   *"It was embarrassing":* Hathaway, interview.

p. 52   *"He can't do this": San Francisco Examiner,* January 13, 1948, p. 18.

p. 53   *"So I said":* Al Barkow, *Getting to the Dance Floor: An Oral History of American Golf* (New York: Atheneum, 1986), p. 231.

p. 53   *"I heard Spiller": San Francisco Examiner,* January 13, 1948, p. 18.

p. 53   *"I do not have anything": San Francisco Chronicle,* January 14, 1948.

p. 54   *"The tournament is": Oakland Tribune,* January 13, 1948, p. 18.

p. 54   *"He said he would take":* Barkow, p. 231.

p. 54   *"He was a very":* Melvin Cohn, phone interview, June 3, 1999.

p. 55   *Rowell handed Watson: San Francisco Examiner,* January 18, 1948, p. 15.

p. 55   *"I'm going to build me": Oakland Tribune,* January 19, 1948, p. 25.

p. 56   *"This check looks":* San Francisco Examiner, January 19, 1948, p. 19.

p. 56   *"Blankety Blank":* ibid.

p. 57   *"They don't want the fellow":* Oakland Tribune, January 25, 1948, p. 27-A.

p. 57   *May said the:* San Francisco Chronicle, January 24, 1948, p. 1-H.

p. 57   *"We will never countenance":* San Francisco Chronicle, January 25, 1948, p. 4-H.

p. 58   *"The suits haven't":* ibid.

p. 58   *"Real progress is being made":* Golf World, January 28, 1948, p. 3.

p. 59   *"And then who would be":* ibid., p. 3.

p. 59   *"The PGA operates open":* ibid.

p. 59   *"I feel badly":* San Francisco Chronicle, January 18, 1948, p. 1-H.

p. 59   Oakland Tribune *columnist:* Oakland Tribune, January 13, 1948, p. 18.

p. 60   *"All citizens within":* letter from Jonathan Rowell to Thurgood Marshall, January 20, 1948, NAACP Legal File, Manuscript Division, Library of Congress.

p. 60   *"It is apparent":* letter from Rowell to Marshall.

p. 61   *About ten days:* letter from Dudley to Jonathan Rowell, January 29, 1948, NAACP Legal File, Manuscript Division, Library of Congress.

p. 61   *Rhodes's 67 was surpassed:* Los Angeles Times, June 8, 1948, p. 2-1.

p. 62   *And Rowell said:* New York Times, September 22, 1948, p. 45.

p. 63   *"Rowell comes down":* Barkow, p. 231.

p. 63   *"which must be met":* Professional Golfer (no month indicated), 1948, p. 16.

p. 64   *"That was a turning point":* Al Barkow, phone interview, January 12, 1999.

8. "We've Got Another Hitler to Get By"

p. 65   *"I want the people to know":* San Diego Union, January 14, 1952, p. b-3.

p. 66   *"I was swinging":* Joe Louis, Joe Louis, My Life (New York: Harcourt Brace, 1978), p. 78.

p. 66   *"I said to myself":* ibid., p. 85

p. 66   *"the blackest day":* Art Buchwald, "Capitol Punishment" column, Washington Post, April 19, 1981, n.a.

p. 66   *"Didn't train properly":* Louis, p. 90.

p. 67   *"It was a glorious":* Sam Daly, interview, Baltimore, August 24, 1998.

p. 67   *"He was that type":* Al Barkow, Getting to the Dance Floor: An Oral History of American Golf (New York: Atheneum, 1986), p. 198.

p. 68   *"Maybe I felt":* Louis, p. 101.

p. 68   *One summer, he lost:* Joe Louis Barrow, Jr., and Barbara Munder, Joe Louis: Fifty Years an American Hero (New York: McGraw-Hill Book Company, n.d.), p. 186.

p. 68   *Smiley Quick:* Golf Digest, April 1998, p. 188.

p. 69   *At Chicago's Wayside:* Barrow and Munder, p. 189.

p. 69   *"You start off playing":* Eural Clark, phone interview, February 23, 1999.

p. 69   *"I got it today":* Clark, phone interview.

p. 70   *"Well, the funny thing":* Louis, p. 221.

p. 70 *"Mr. And Mrs. North"*: Winchell radio scripts, January 13 and January 20, 1952, New York Public Library for the Performing Arts, the Billy Rose Theatre Collection.

p. 72 *"Don't think I'll fight"*: *San Diego Union*, January 14, 1952, p. b-3.

p. 72 *"I want to bring"*: ibid.

p. 73 *"We've got another Hitler"*: *New York Times*, January 15, 1952, p. 31.

p. 74 *"He had been"*: Herbert Graffis, *PGA: Official History of the PGA of America* (New York: Thomas Y. Crowell Publishers, 1975), p. 308.

p. 74 *"Generally speaking"*: *Sport* magazine, July 1952, p. 39.

p. 75 *"I do not know"*: United Press International, in the *New York Times*, January 15, 1952, p. 31.

p. 75 *"I didn't expect"*: Jack Murphy column, *San Diego Union*, January 15, 1952, p. b-3.

p. 76 *"I'm not asking"*: ibid.

p. 76 *"But he is"*: ibid.

p. 76 *"I believe that's"*: ibid.

p. 77 *"It was sort of"*: Jackie Burke, Jr., phone interview, June 1999.

p. 77 *"That had been brewing"*: Burke, phone interview.

p. 77 *"Due to the"*: *San Diego Union*, January 15, 1952, p. b-4.

p. 77 *"This is the"*: United Press International, in the *Philadelphia Inquirer*, January 16, 1952, n.a.

p. 78 *Among them was a baseball player*: Arnold Rampersad, *Jackie Robinson: A Biography* (New York: Ballantine Books, 1997), p. 122.

p. 78 *"That Horton Smith"*: Barkow, p. 232.

p. 79 *"I just don't think"*: Burke, phone interview.

p. 79 *"Yeah, we've got"*: Barkow, p. 233.

p. 80 *"Sure, but if"*: Barkow, p. 233.

p. 80 *"I've heard all this"*: *The Compass*, January 18, 1952, n.a.

p. 80 *As Louis stood by*: Associated Press, January 17, 1952, n.a.

p. 81 *"I'm opposed to"*: Associated Press, in the *(Philadelphia) Evening Bulletin*, January 16, 1952, n.a.

p. 81 *As it was*: Jack Murphy column, *San Diego Union*, January 18, 1952, p. b-3.

p. 81 *"Mr. Smith"*: *Sport* magazine, July 1952, p. 39.

p. 82 *"I sure enjoyed"*: Jack Murphy column, *San Diego Union*, January 18, 1952, p. b-3.

p. 82 *For his part*: *San Diego Union*, January 19, 1952, p. b-3.

p. 82 *"I play for money"*: *New York Times*, January 18, 1952, n.a.

p. 82 *"Because in those days"*: Al Barkow, phone interview, January 12, 1999.

p. 82 *To his credit*: *Chicago Defender*, February 2, 1952, p. 16.

p. 83 *A committee of five*: *San Diego Union*, January 19, 1952, p. b-5.

p. 83 *"I'll go along"*: *San Diego Union*, January 20, 1952, p. b-2.

p. 84 *On Sunday night*: Winchell radio scripts.

p. 85 *"What a crude"*: Charlie Sifford, *Just Let Me Play* (Latham, N.Y.: British-American, 1992), p. 66.

p. 85   *"He suggested that":* ibid.

p. 86   *Spiller argued:* Barkow, p. 234.

p. 86   *As if: Sports Illustrated,* March 24, 1980, pp. 30–31.

p. 86   *Clark dropped out: Golf World,* February 1, 1952, p. 4.

p. 86   *"Never have I": Golf World,* February 8, 1952, p. 4.

p. 87   *That same year: Current Biography,* July 1952, n.a.

p. 88   *"Not only": Chicago Defender,* February 16, 1952, p. 15.

9. Running to the 1st Tee

p. 90   *Dr. Holmes had made:* Charles Bell, phone interview, May 31, 1999.

p. 91   *Tup and Oliver's sister: Black Enterprise,* September 1996, n.a.

p. 91   *A prominent black:* Bell, phone interview.

p. 91   *"We have": Time* magazine, January 2, 1956, pp. 14–15.

p. 92   *"chosen to throw in the towel": Atlanta Journal,* December 23, 1955, n.a.

p. 92   *"We decided to put": Atlanta Journal,* December 24, 1955, p. 2.

p. 93   *"Many times":* Bell, phone interview.

p. 93   *Those limitations: Atlanta History,* vol. 14, no. 1, p. 25.

p. 93   *"As soon as we":* Bell, phone interview.

p. 94   *"He looked around":* Bell, phone interview.

p. 94   *"They seemed to hit a good ball":* Associated Press in the *New York Times,* December 25, 1955, n.a.

p. 94   *The Holmes brothers: Atlanta Journal,* December 24, 1955, p. 1.

p. 94   *"I thought it looked":* Bell, phone interview.

p. 94   *"Five Negroes played": Atlanta Journal,* December 24, 1955, p. 2.

p. 94   *"That was a fact":* Bell, phone interview.

p. 95   *Those others included: Atlanta Constitution,* May 12, 1990, p. F-1.

p. 96   *"This is but a foretaste": Atlanta Journal,* December 24, 1955, p. 2.

p. 96   *As for the Holmes brothers:* Bell, phone interview.

10. Just Another Golfer

p. 98   *"Give me a year":* Bill Wright, phone interview, June 26, 1999.

p. 98   *"I didn't take it": Denver Post,* July 19, 1959, p. 1-B.

p. 99   *"An entry":* Minutes of the USGA Executive Committee, May 7, 1930, stored at Golf House, Short Hills, New Jersey.

p. 100   *In 1952, the Miami: Golf, the Greatest Game: The USGA Celebrates Golf in America* (New York: HarperCollins, 1994), p. 49.

p. 101   *"I made it":* Wright, phone interview.

p. 102   *"Bill, you're gonna":* Wright, phone interview.

p. 102   *Palacio also gave Wright:* Wright, phone interview.

p. 103   *"Look here":* Cliff Brown, interview, Nashville, September 1998.

p. 104   *"I caddied for him":* Wright, phone interview.

p. 104   *"I was thinking": Denver Post,* July 19, 1959, p. 1-B.

p. 104   *Campbell shook:* Wright, phone interview.

p. 104   *"Some of you folks": USGA Journal,* August 1959, p. 13.

p. 105   *"another fine champion":* Denver Post, July 19, 1959, p. 1-B.

p. 105   *"How does it feel":* Wright, phone interview.

11. "I Am Somebody"

p. 106   *Up to then:* New York Times, March 31, 1961, p. 1.

p. 106   *"I could win":* ibid.

p. 107   *Caddies who carried:* ibid., p. 3.

p. 107   *"They were protecting":* Bob Rickey, phone interview, January 29, 1999.

p. 108   *He had won, by rough estimates:* Golf Digest, April 1998, n.a.

p. 109   *"We colored pros":* Golf magazine, February 1961, p. 47.

p. 109   *"Teddy told me":* Sports Illustrated, May 31, 1993, p. 105.

p. 110   *He was admired:* Joe Hampton, phone interview, May 21, 1999.

p. 110   *"A sucker couldn't":* Joe Roach, interview, Nashville, September 1998.

p. 110   *"He always walked":* Harold Dunovant, interview, Winston-Salem, North Carolina, March 27, 1999.

p. 111   *"Look, old buddy":* Dunovant, interview.

p. 111   *"You would think":* Dunovant, interview.

p. 111   Golf *magazine:* Golf magazine, February 1961, p. 53.

p. 112   *"We may yet see":* ibid.

12. "We Just Don't Want Them Near Us"

p. 113   *"I thought this was":* Al Barkow, Getting to the Dance Floor: An Oral History of American Golf (New York: Atheneum, 1986), p. 234.

p. 113   *"The PGA told me":* Pete Brown, interview, Dayton, Ohio, June 5, 1998.

p. 114   *"There's your goddamn":* Bob Rickey, phone interview, January 29, 1999.

p. 115   *"When Dad was home":* Pamela Spiller Stewart, phone interview, 1999.

p. 115   *"He was from":* Bill Spiller, Jr., interview, Los Angeles, June 1998.

p. 116   *"I grew up with that":* Spiller, interview.

p. 116   *"I played with":* Spiller, interview.

p. 118   *For years, blacks had to:* Joe Black, phone interview, 1998.

p. 119   *"Mr. Rickey":* Ebony, December 1972, p. 194.

p. 120   *"C'mon":* Eural Clark, phone interview, February 23, 1999.

p. 120   *Black sports historian:* Ebony, August 1992, pp. 38–40.

p. 121   *Doc Young:* A. S. "Doc" Young, Negro Firsts in Sports (Chicago: Johnson Publishing Company, 1963), p. 165.

p. 121   *"He went into":* Frank Snow, interview, Los Angeles, June 1998.

p. 121   *"I think it's that old":* Sam Lacy, interview, Baltimore, August 24, 1998.

p. 122   *When he was made:* Baltimore Afro-American, January 11, 1964, p. 9.

p. 122   *"Regardless of race":* Joe Hampton, phone interview, May 21, 1999.

p. 123   *And in Chicago:* Robert Horton, phone interview, July 1999.

p. 123   *"If kids who don't":* Golf Digest, January 1965, p. 40.

p. 124   *In fact, the same week:* Oakland Tribune, January 21, 1948, n.a.

p. 124   *"His passion":* Dick Lotz, phone interview, January 1999.

p. 124   *"Some of the":* Dick Lotz, phone interview.

p. 124   *"Colored boys don't think"*: *Golf Digest,* January 1965, p. 40.

p. 125   *"He was like"*: Dick Lotz, phone interview.

p. 126   *Miss Horne:* Maggie Hathaway, interview, Los Angeles, June 1998.

p. 127   *"I lost his friendship"*: Hathaway, interview.

p. 127   *"Maggie, I'm"*: Hathaway, interview.

p. 127   *"She was"*: Jackie Burke, Jr., phone interview, June 15, 1999.

p. 128   *"You're causing all"*: Bill Wright, phone interview, June 1999.

p. 128   *Sifford may have been:* Stanley Mosk, written answers to questions, April 29, 1999.

p. 128   *If so, Sifford:* Charlie Sifford, *Just Let Me Play* (Latham, N.Y.: British-American, 1992), p. 98.

p. 129   *The PGA wasn't:* ibid., p. 99.

p. 129   *In 1957, after:* New York Post, November 13, 1957, n.a.

p. 129   *And beginning in 1960:* Sifford, p. 117.

p. 130   *"We know Charlie"*: *Pittsburgh Courier,* April 15, 1961, n.a.

p. 130   *Sifford said:* Sifford, pp. 118–19.

p. 130   *"Charlie Sifford?"*: ibid., p. 121.

p. 131   *"Nice shot, Smokey"*: ibid.

p. 131   *"My job's tougher"*: New York Post, April 21, 1961, n.a.

p. 132   *A group of Negroes:* Associated Press, April 22, 1961, n.a.

p. 132   *This time, he didn't:* Sifford, p. 130.

13. Four Fewer Words

p. 133   *In the 1950s:* Stanley Mosk, written answers to questions, April 29, 1999.

p. 134   *"I have advised"*: New York Post, May 10, 1961, n.a.

p. 134   *"I believed then"*: Mosk, written answers.

p. 134   *"I advised the PGA"*: *Goin' Deep,* Fox Sports, 1998.

p. 134   *"Under present"*: United Press International, in the *New York Times,* May 18, 1961, n.a.

p. 135   *"In the meantime"*: New York Post, May 10, 1961, n.a.

p. 135   *"The PGA is"*: *Sports Illustrated,* May 22, 1961, p. 9.

p. 135   *"But somehow"*: *Goin' Deep,* Fox Sports, 1998.

p. 136   *"We are extremely unhappy"*: *Philadelphia Inquirer,* June 21, 1961, n.a.

p. 136   *"It does shock me"*: *Goin' Deep,* Fox Sports, 1998.

p. 137   *"It is unfortunate"*: United Press International, in the *(Philadelphia) Evening Bulletin,* June 22, 1961, p. 34.

p. 138   *"in keeping with the realization"*: New York Times, November 10, 1961, p. 44.

p. 139   *"Lou"*: *Professional Golfer,* January 1962, p. 59.

p. 141   *"Laddie"*: Gary Player, phone interview, June 15, 1999.

14. "Laugh at 'Em and Keep Going"

p. 143   *"I dreamed you shot"*: Pete and Margaret Brown, interview, Dayton, Ohio, June 1998.

p. 143   *"Hey, nigger":* Pete and Margaret Brown, interview. Brown's opponent, Tom Talkington, said he had no recollection of such an incident.

p. 144   *"Guys in the South":* Pete and Margaret Brown, interview.

p. 144   *"If they say something":* Pete and Margaret Brown, interview.

p. 144   *"He didn't":* Bob Goalby, phone interview, 1998.

p. 145   *"I'm the Jackie Robinson": Wall Street Journal,* March 21, 1974, p. 1.

p. 145   *"Charlie was mean":* Pete and Margaret Brown, interview.

p. 145   *On occasion:* Maggie Hathaway, interview, Los Angeles, June 1998.

p. 146   *"I decided to":* Pete Brown, phone interview, summer 1997.

p. 146   *"I was exposed to":* Brown, phone interview.

p. 147   *"Some of the guys":* Brown, phone interview.

p. 149   *"What are you":* Pete and Margaret Brown, interview.

p. 150   *Waco (after the Waco Indians): Sports Illustrated,* May 28, 1964, p. 28.

p. 150   *"When you woke":* Jack Tuthill, phone interview, May 24, 1999.

p. 151   *A few years earlier:* Tuthill, phone interview.

p. 151   *"It's probably one":* Pete and Margaret Brown, interview.

p. 152   *"You want me":* Pete and Margaret Brown, interview.

p. 152   *"How'd you":* Pete and Margaret Brown, interview.

15. Hustling

p. 154   *"Your honor": Sports Illustrated,* October 9, 1972, p. 97.

p. 154   *He had married:* Carlton Stowers, *The Unsinkable Titanic Thompson* (Burnet, Tex.: Eakin Press, 1982), pp. 73–74.

p. 155   *"A year or so": Sports Illustrated,* October 9, 1972, p. 97.

p. 155   *As Thompson told it:* ibid.

p. 156   *And Elder said: (Detroit) Sunday News Magazine,* April 6, 1975, pp. 18–21.

p. 156   *"I bet even": Current Biography,* 1976, p. 130.

p. 156   *"I didn't care": Sports Illustrated,* October 9, 1972, p. 111.

p. 157   *"I felt bad": Potomac* magazine, October 7, 1973, n.a.

p. 158   *"And he could hit":* Pete and Margaret Brown, interview, Dayton, Ohio, June 1998.

p. 159   *As the story goes: Sports Illustrated,* n.a.

p. 159   *"That ball":* Felton Mason, interview, Washington, D.C., June 1998.

p. 161   *"You take him": (Detroit) Sunday News Magazine,* April 6, 1975, pp. 18–21.

p. 161   *While in Los Angeles:* Pete and Margaret Brown, interview.

p. 163   *"Okay?":* James Black, interview, Charlotte, North Carolina, March 28, 1999.

p. 163   *"They got": New York Post,* May 27, 1964, p. 80.

p. 163   *Some of his friends:* James Walker, interview, Los Angeles, June 1998.

p. 164   *"James Black":* Jim Dent, interview, Philadelphia, May 1998.

p. 165   *"They are doing": Los Angeles Times,* December 31, 1963, sect. 4, p. 1.

p. 167   *At the L.A. Open:* Black, phone interview.

p. 168   *"To me, they were": Los Angeles Times,* January 4, 1964, sect. 2, p. 3.

p. 168   *In fact, Black's name: Norfolk Journal and Guide,* January 1964, n.a.

p. 169 *"Ginsberg, Black":* Los Angeles Times, January 4, 1964, sect. 2, p. 3.
p. 169 *"The handsome Negro":* ibid.
p. 169 *"Jim Black":* Los Angeles Times, January 5, 1964, p. D-2.
p. 170 *"is off to a runaway":* Los Angeles Times, January 7, 1964, sect. 4, p. 3.
p. 170 *"Why don't you":* Black, interview.
p. 171 *"You got a great pair":* Black, interview.
p. 172 *"Most white people":* Harold Dunovant, interview, Winston-Salem, North Carolina, March 1999.
p. 172 *"I was playing five":* Black, interview.
p. 173 *"A lot of inconvenience":* Black, interview.
p. 174 *"Charlie, Ted":* Dunovant, interview.
p. 174 *Black came to a friend:* Bobby Mays, interview, Trenton, New Jersey, June 1998.
p. 174 *"This is what":* Mays, interview.
p. 175 *"Best gambler":* Mays, interview.
p. 175 *"No, I was letting":* Black, interview.
p. 176 *"Just about all":* Dunovant, interview.
p. 176 *"I was living":* Black, interview.
p. 178 *"Seldom have spectators":* New York Times, August 12, 1968, n.a.
p. 179 *"Oh, how sweet it could":* Michigan Chronicle, August 24, 1968, p. D-2.
p. 179 *"It seemed like everyone":* ibid.
p. 179 *"I want Jack":* Wall Street Journal, March 21, 1974, p. 27.
p. 179 *"Elder did more for Negro golf":* Golf Digest, December 1968, p. 30.

16. "You Know, a Shank'll Jump on You"

p. 182 *"Wherever we went":* Bud Garnier, phone interview, June 25, 1999.
p. 182 *So in October 1967:* Palm Beach Post-Times, October 8, 1967, p. D-1.
p. 183 *"He never showed":* Garnier, phone interview.
p. 183 *"I'm not gonna":* Garnier, phone interview.
p. 183 *"Nobody would want":* Curtis Sifford, phone interview, July 1999.
p. 184 *"He was up in age":* James Walker, interview, Los Angeles, July 1998.
p. 184 *Pete Brown remembered:* Pete and Margaret Brown, interview, Dayton, Ohio, June 1998.

17. The Masters? "I Hope You're Right"

p. 185 *Sports columnist:* Jim Murray column, Los Angeles Times, January 9, 1969, sect. 3, p. 1.
p. 186 *"On the whole":* ibid., sect. 3. p. 4.
p. 186 *Growing up in Rocky Mount:* James Walker, interview, Los Angeles, June 1998.
p. 187 *Sifford hit a one-iron:* New York Times, January 10, 1969, p. 56.
p. 187 *It was Charlie's lowest:* Ebony, April 1969, n.a.
p. 187 *"Give that old":* Los Angeles Times, January 10, 1969, sect. 3, p. 1.
p. 187 *"I feel better":* New York Times, January 11, 1969, n.a.

p. 188   *"Whatever is going"*: *New York Times,* January 12, 1969, sports sect., p. 1.

p. 188   *"His swing"*: Jim Murray column, *Los Angeles Times,* January 9, 1969, sect. 3, p. 1.

p. 190   *"There were so many"*: Walker, interview.

p. 190   *"He should not be here"*: *Los Angeles Sentinel,* January 16, 1969, p. 1.

p. 191   *"Everybody asked except"*: Maggie Hathaway column, *Los Angeles Sentinel,* January 23, 1969, n.a.

p. 192   *"I got one real"*: *Sports Illustrated,* January 20, 1969, p. 17.

p. 192   *"I am not a politician"*: Maggie Hathaway column, *Los Angeles Sentinel,* January 16, 1969, p. D-3.

p. 193   *"Sifford's great sudden-death"*: *Los Angeles Sentinel,* January 16, 1969, p. D-4.

p. 193   *"It's just so wonderful"*: *Sports Illustrated,* March 31 1969, p. 58.

p. 194   *As Charlie rode: Los Angeles Sentinel,* February 13, 1969, n.a.

p. 196   *When an old friend:* Steve Eubanks, *Augusta: Home of the Masters Tournament* (Nashville, Tenn.: Rutledge Hill Press, 1997), p. 158.

p. 196   *"The Augusta National"*: *Golf* magazine, April 1993, pp. 25–26.

p. 197   *For example, Sifford said:* Charlie Sifford, *Just Let Me Play* (Latham, N.Y.: British-American, 1992), p. 175.

p. 197   *"Certainly the barrier"*: Frank Lett, Sr., column, *Michigan Chronicle,* p. B-2.

p. 198   *"I didn't want"*: Pete Brown, phone interview, July 1998.

p. 198   *Those rules the Masters: Sports Illustrated,* March 10, 1975, p. 26.

p. 198   *"I was so close"*: Pete and Margaret Brown, interview, Dayton, Ohio, June 1998.

p. 198   *"They would have played"*: Pete and Margaret Brown, interview.

p. 199   *"It's not my business"*: Art Wall, phone interview, 1998.

p. 199   *Sifford's last chance:* Jim Murray column, *Los Angeles Times,* April 6, 1969, pp. D-1, D-6.

p. 199   *"I don't know"*: Wall, phone interview.

p. 200   *"It was like sending money"*: Jim Murray column, *Los Angeles Times,* April 15, 1969, sect. 3, p. 6.

p. 200   *Perhaps if they had taken: Golf Digest,* March 1988, pp. 41–44.

p. 201   *"You jes' don't"*: ibid.

p. 201   *"No-saa. Ah's"*: ibid.

p. 201   *"If he knew this"*: ibid.

p. 202   *"Charlie lived in"*: ibid.

p. 202   *"America's greatest Negro golfer"*: *Los Angeles Times,* January 4, 1947, p. 6.

p. 203   *And his irons:* Joe Hampton, phone interview, May 21, 1999.

p. 203   *"Young guys like me"*: "Leaders of Afro-American Nashville," a pamphlet published by the 1988 Nashville Conference on Afro-American History and Culture, n.a.

p. 203   *"But Ted's love"*: John Bibb column, *Nashville Tennessean,* July 9, 1969, p. 28.

p. 203   *But his short game:* Hampton, phone interview.

p. 204   *"We were going"*: Hampton, phone interview.

p. 204   *"No question, he would"*: Bob Rickey, phone interview, January 29, 1999.

p. 204   *"So long, old pro"*: Maggie Hathaway column, *Los Angeles Sentinel*, July 10, 1969, n.a.

18. "What Have I Done to You, Sir?"

p. 205   *"We were like twins"*: Pete Brown, phone interview, July 1998.

p. 206   *"What have I done"*: *New York Times*, August 18, 1969, p. 46.

p. 206   *"My hands were"*: *Sports Illustrated*, August 28, 1969, p. 26.

p. 207   *"I honestly thought"*: *Sports Illustrated*, August 28, 1969, p. 26.

p. 207   *"I think the majority"*: *New York Times*, August 17, 1969, sect. 5, p. 6.

p. 207   *"Never"*: ibid., sect. 5, p. 1.

p. 207   *"Does it look bad out?"* *New York Times*, August 18, 1969, p. 46.

p. 207   *"I will go to my grave"*: Gary Player, phone interview, June 15, 1999.

p. 208   *"I just explained"*: Player, phone interview.

p. 208   *Player's black caddie*: *Sports Illustrated*, March 23, 1970, p. 60.

p. 209   *"Here we are again"*: *Los Angeles Sentinel*, April 2, 1970, p. b-4.

p. 210   *"What's more"*: *Los Angeles Sentinel*, June 18, 1970, p. b-1.

p. 210   *"My grandchildren will look"*: Player, phone interview.

p. 211   *"Arthur Ashe"*: *New York Times*, June 18, 1971, p. 46.

p. 211   *"This is a heck"*: United Press International, in the *New York Times*, June 20, 1971, sect. 5, p. 5.

p. 211   *"We do hope"*: Maggie Hathaway column, *Los Angeles Sentinel*, 1971, n.a.

p. 212   *Even years later*: Harold Dunovant, interview, Winston-Salem, North Carolina, March 27, 1999.

p. 212   *"You couldn't ask"*: *Pittsburgh New Courier*, July 3, 1971, p. 14.

p. 212   *"If it'll help"*: ibid.

p. 212   *During the Elder's three-week trip*: *Los Angeles Sentinel*, December 9, 1971, p. b-3; *Jet* magazine, January 12, 1973.

p. 212   *"We did what"*: Player, phone interview.

p. 212   *"At this point"*: *Los Angeles Sentinel*, December 9, 1971, p. b-3.

19. The "Garbage Tour"

p. 214   *It may have come from*: Curtis Sifford, phone interview, July 1999.

p. 214   *"We play 'garbage courses'"*: *Los Angeles Sentinel*, September 2, 1971, n.a.

p. 215   *Jim Dent was another*: *Black Sports*, March 1976, p. 35.

p. 215   *"This guy makes me"*: *Black Sports*, September 1974, p. 32.

p. 215   *"They're giving away"*: *Ebony*, May 1973, p. 142.

p. 215   *A local club professional*: Jack Price, phone interview, July 25, 1999.

p. 216   *"What are you thinking"*: Price, phone interview.

p. 216   *"Nobody took"*: *Golf* magazine, October 1968, p. 37.

p. 217   *"All these guys"*: Thomas "Smitty" Smith, interview, Atlanta, Georgia, March 26, 1999.

p. 218   *The playoff lasted*: *Los Angeles Sentinel*, February 5, 1970, p. 1.

p. 219   *"I heard somebody"*: Jack Tuthill, phone interview, May 24, 1999.

p. 219   *It was his moderating:* Rose Harper Elder, interview, Washington, D.C., February 19, 1999.

p. 220   *Of course, he had:* Pete and Margaret Brown, interview, Dayton, Ohio, June 1998.

p. 220   *"When I saw people":* Michigan Chronicle, July 25, 1970, p. B-5.

20. Black Orchid

p. 221   *"Baby, we did it":* Jet magazine, May 9, 1974, p. 48.

p. 221   *Years earlier: Wall Street Journal,* March 21, 1974, p. 1.

p. 222   *Elder was quoted:* Associated Press, June 5, 1969, n.a.

p. 222   *(A few days):* Associated Press, in the *New York Times,* June 6, 1969, n.a.

p. 223   *"It's a year away":* Washington Post, April 22, 1974, p. A-1.

p. 223   *"He has automatically":* New York Times, April 22, 1974, p. 51.

p. 223   *"That's fine":* Associated Press, April 22, 1974, n.a.

p. 224   *"I appreciate":* Sports Illustrated, March 25, 1975, p. 25.

p. 225   *The commissioner of the PGA: Washington Post,* May 4, 1974, p. D-4.

p. 226   *He'd been a hustler:* Rose Harper Elder, phone interview, February 19, 1999.

p. 226   *"We don't have":* Harper Elder, phone interview.

p. 227   *But she also:* Harper Elder, phone interview.

p. 227   *"Without Rose":* People, April 7, 1975, p. 34.

p. 227   *"The Masters":* Washington Post story, reprinted in the *Philadelphia Inquirer,* February 23, 1975, n.a.

p. 228   *Augusta was: New York Times,* April 6, 1975, p. 7.

p. 228   *Asked when Elder: Washington Post,* April 8, 1975, p. D-2.

p. 229   *"All you":* Harper Elder, phone interview.

p. 229   *"I'm not talking":* Atlanta Constitution, April 8, 1975, p. 1-D.

p. 229   *"All he has":* Associated Press, in the *New York Times,* April 8, 1975, p. 44.

p. 230   *"I hope you understand":* (Philadelphia) Evening Bulletin, April 9, 1975, sports sect., p. 1.

p. 230   *"It's been a long time":* "Lee Elder's Masters Journal," *Sport* magazine, July 1975, pp. 65–74.

p. 231   *"Green has always been":* Philadelphia Daily News, April 11, 1975, n.a.

p. 231   *Elder had received: Washington Post,* April 9, 1975, p. D-1.

p. 232   *"He walked up":* Maggie Hathaway, interview, Los Angeles, June 1998.

p. 232   *"Never thought":* Los Angeles Sentinel, n.a.

p. 232   *Rose Elder never:* Harper Elder, phone interview.

p. 233   *Elder himself: Sport* magazine, July 1975, pp. 65–74.

p. 234   *The 520-yard:* Curt Sampson, *The Masters: Golf, Money and Power in Augusta, Georgia* (New York: Villard, 1998), pp. 35–36.

p. 234   *On the 16th: Sports Illustrated,* April 21, 1975, p. 21.

p. 235   *"Knock a stroke off":* Sport magazine, July 1975, p. 74.

p. 235   *"I felt":* Washington Post, April 12, 1975, p. D-1.

p. 236   *"That to me":* Rose Harper Elder, interview, Washington, D.C., February 19, 1999.

p. 236   *Yes, he saw: New York Times,* April 12, 1975, n.a.

p. 237   *The first was Rose's:* United Press International, in the *Philadelphia Evening Bulletin,* May 3, 1976, n.a.

p. 238   *"I guess": Golf World,* n.d., pp. 24–26.

p. 238   *"By now":* ibid.

p. 238   *(Meanwhile): Washington Post,* May 4, 1976, p. D-1.

p. 238   *"Go get 'em, Lee": New York Times,* May 3, 1976, p. 48.

p. 239   *"Okay":* ibid.

p. 239   *"I'm going to": Washington Post,* May 4, 1976, p. D-1.

p. 239   *"I called home":* ibid.

p. 240   *The captain:* ibid.

21. Implacable, Impeccable

p. 241   *Two a.m.:* Calvin Peete, phone interview, July 19, 1999.

p. 242   *He had to grow: People,* June 13, 1983, p. 75.

p. 242   *They picked him:* Arthur R. Ashe, Jr., *A Hard Road to Glory: A History of the African-American Athlete since 1946* (New York: Warner Books, 1988), p. 155.

p. 243   *"It was the individuality":* Peete phone interview.

p. 244   *"That's why I":* Peete, phone interview.

p. 244   *"I still get":* Peete, phone interview.

p. 245   *"It's not God": People,* June 13, 1983, p. 78.

p. 245   *"The hole kept getting": Reader's Digest,* October 1983, p. 174.

p. 246   *"Calvin has a tremendous":* ibid., p. 169.

p. 246   *"About eleven-thirty":* ibid., p. 170.

p. 246   *"Let's face it":* ibid.

p. 246   *"I became":* Peete, phone interview.

p. 247   *Otherwise:* Bill Spiller, Jr., interview, Los Angeles, June 1998.

p. 247   *"But I didn't":* Spiller, interview.

p. 248   *As Bill junior: Los Angeles Times,* February 27, 1997, p. S-1.

p. 248   *And he'd ask:* Frank Snow, phone interview, July 1998.

22. "You Are the Ones . . ."

p. 249   *"The country club is": Golf World,* August 3, 1990, p. 9.

p. 250   *Charlie Owens: People,* August 4, 1986, p. 40; New York Times Biographical Service, July 1986, p. 951.

p. 250   *But on the regular: Ebony,* May 1973, n.a.

p. 252   *The numbers: Black Enterprise,* August 1992, p. 98.

p. 253   *In fact: Fortune,* May 12, 1997, p. 84.

p. 254   *"I thank them": Washington Post,* April 14, 1997, p. C-1.

p. 254   *"What kind":* Charlie Sifford, phone interview, 1999.

p. 255   *"I told him": Washington Post,* April 14, 1997, p. C-7.

p. 255   *To Pete Brown:* Pete Brown, phone interview, July 1999.

p. 255   *"I thought he":* Maggie Hathaway, phone interview, August 1999.

p. 256   *"There's never been":* Bill Spiller, Jr., phone interview, July 1999.

p. 256   *"I didn't look":* James Black, phone interview, June 8, 1999.

Works

Ashe, Arthur R., Jr. *A Hard Road to Glory: A History of the African-American Athlete, 1919–1945.* New York: Warner Books, 1988.
———. *A Hard Road to Glory: A History of the African-American Athlete since 1946.* New York: Warner Books, 1988.

Barkow, Al. *Getting to the Dance Floor: An Oral History of American Golf.* New York: Atheneum, 1986.
———. *Golf's Golden Grind: The History of the Tour.* New York: Harcourt Brace Jovanovich, 1974.

Branch, Taylor. *Pillar of Fire: America in the King Years, 1963–65.* New York: Simon & Shuster, 1998.

Eubanks, J. Stephen. *Augusta: Home of the Masters Tournament.* Nashville, Tenn.: Rutledge Hill Press, 1997.

Feinstein, John. *A Good Walk Spoiled: Days and Nights on the PGA Tour.* Boston: Little, Brown and Company, 1995.

Goodwin, Doris Kearns. *No Ordinary Time: Franklin and Eleanor Roosevelt: The Home Front in World War II.* New York: Simon & Shuster, 1994.

Graffis, Herbert. *PGA: Official History of the PGA of America.* New York: Thomas Y. Crowell Publishers, 1975.

Green, Robert. *The Illustrated Encyclopedia of Golf.* London: CollinsWillow, 1993.

Grimsley, Will. *Golf: Its History, People and Events.* Englewood Cliffs, N.J.: Prentice Hall, 1966.

Henderson, Edwin, and the editors of *Sport* magazine. *The Black Athlete, Emergence and Arrival.* New York: Publishers Company, Inc., 1968.

Louis, Joe. *Joe Louis, My Life.* New York: Harcourt Brace, 1978.

Palmer, Arnold. *Golf, the Greatest Game: The USGA Celebrates Golf in America.* New York: HarperCollins, 1994.

Porter, David, ed. *African-American Sports Greats: A Biographical Dictionary.* Westport, Conn.: Greenwood Press, 1995.

Rampersad, Arnold. *Jackie Robinson: A Biography.* New York: Ballantine Books, 1997.

Robinson, Lenwood, Jr. *Skins and Grins: The Plight of the Black American Golfer.* Evanston, Ill.: Chicago Spectrum Press, 1997.

Salzman, Jack, ed. *Encyclopedia of African-American Culture and History.* New York: Macmillan Library Reference USA, 1996.

Sampson, Curt. *The Masters: Golf, Money and Power in Augusta, Georgia.* New York: Villard, 1998.

Sifford, Charlie. *Just Let Me Play: The Story of Charlie Sifford, the First Black PGA Golfer.* Latham, N.Y.: British-American, 1992.

Sinnette, Calvin H. *Forbidden Fairways: African Americans and the Game of Golf.* Chelsea, Mich.: Sleeping Bear Press, 1998.

Stowers, Carlton. *The Unsinkable Titanic Thompson.* Burnet, Tex.: Eakin Press, 1982.

Young, A. S. "Doc." *Negro Firsts in Sports.* Chicago: Johnson Publishing Company, Inc., 1963.